NAVAL TERMS DICTIONARY

Fourth Edition

by

John V. Noel, Jr.
Captain, U.S. Navy (Retired)

and

Edward L. Beach
Captain, U.S. Navy (Retired)

Naval Institute Press,
Annapolis, Maryland

TO MARY
AND
INGRID

CONTENTS

PREFACE TO THE FOURTH EDITION

As in the previous editions, the primary consideration in selecting terms for inclusion in *Naval Terms Dictionary* has been current usage, but a number of Old Navy expressions have been included in recognition of the fact that old sailors never die. The lore of the sea is a continuum that changes slowly even in these days of nuclear power and guided missiles. Besides, not everything old should be forgotten. Old naval terms, many dating to the days of sail, are frequently encountered today, sometimes in new guises or with new meanings or connotations. In such cases particularly, derivations as well as definitions are useful.

Five appendices also add to the book's usefulness. *Appendix A* lists all ship types in the Navy. *Appendix B* explains the enlisted rating structure, lists the various rates, and explains the paygrade and petty officer designations. Only those ratings presumed to be of greatest interest to the greatest number of persons have been defined in the body of the text. The designations and popular names of naval aircraft are given in *Appendix C*. Missiles are treated in the same manner in *Appendix D*. The electronics nomenclature system, often referred to as the AN system, is explained in *Appendix E*.

A great number of people have helped put together the information in this dictionary. We have also received the willing cooperation of official sources whose interest, obviously, is to see that accuracy is maintained. This, of course, is our overriding concern also. Our thanks, as before, to the many thoughtful and helpful people who have given their time and assistance.

The Authors

A

AAW
See *anti-air-warfare.*

aback
With the wind on the wrong side of the sail(s), tending to drive the ship astern instead of forward. A square rigger may be *taken aback* or *taken flat back* by an unexpected shift of wind or poor steering. Square-rigged ships usually wear when coming about (stern through the wind), instead of tacking (bow through the wind), because there is less danger of "landing in irons" or being damaged when the wind suddenly snaps all the sails in the reverse direction. Fore-and-aft-rigged ships, on the other hand, would for the same reason prefer to tack than wear or jibe.

abaft
To the rear of.

abandon ship
To leave the ship in an emergency such as sinking.

abeam
In approximately the same horizontal plane of the observing ship or aircraft, bearing 90 degrees away from its heading or course.

Able
Former phonetic word for the letter A. See *alfa.*

able seaman
Merchant and civil service marine rating above an ordinary seaman. It is also known as able-bodied seaman, from which the colloquial term *AB* is derived.

aboard
In a ship, on or at any activity such as a naval station. See *close aboard.*

abort
Failure to accomplish a mission for any reason other than enemy action.

about
See *come about.*

abreast
By the side of; side by side. See *abeam.*

absence indicator
Pennant flown by a ship to indicate absence of commanding officer or embarked flag or staff officer. See *absentee.*

absence without leave (AWOL)
See *unauthorized absentee.*

absentee
Man missing at a muster. Slang for *absence indicator.*

abyssalbenthic zone
Subdivision of the deep-sea system of the benthic division, including waters deeper than 1,000 meters.

accepting authority
The officer designated to accept a ship for the government, usually a naval district commandant or his representative.

access, classified material
The ability and opportunity of an individual to gain knowledge or possession of classified material.

accommodation ladder
Portable steps from a ship's gangway down to the waterline or a pier alongside, rigged from a davit or crane on board. Sometimes incorrectly referred to as the *gangway.* See *bail.*

accountability
The responsibility and obligation imposed by law on military personnel for keeping accurate records of property or funds and for submitting periodic reports thereon. See *responsibility.*

accountable officer
One detailed to duty involving personal financial responsibility for government funds.

ace
Pilot who has shot down five or more enemy aircraft.

Ace High
Tropospheric forward-scatter communications system.

acey-deucy
Nautical version of backgammon.

acknowledge
To notify originator that his message has been understood.

ACORN
Unit of administrative personnel and material needed to establish and operate an advanced naval air base.

acoustic data analysis center (ADAC)
Computerized library of data on underwater sound characteristics maintained at Naval Research and Development Center, Carderock, Maryland.

acoustic dispersion
Sound-speed changes caused by frequency changes.

acoustic mine
See *mine.*

acoustics
The science of sound dealing with its propagation, transmission, and effects.

acoustic scattering
Dispersion of sound waves caused by irregular reflection, refraction, etc.

acoustic torpedo
Torpedo guided by sound. Active versions emit sounds and home in on their echoes; passive types home in on sound emanations of target. See *torpedo.*

action data automation system (ADAS)
British version of naval tactical data system (NTDS).

action port (starboard)
Command to gun and missile crews to indicate direction of enemy attack.

action report
Detailed report of combat with the enemy.

activation
The process, work, and fitting out required to prepare a ship of the reserve fleet for transfer to the active fleet.

active acoustic torpedo
Torpedo that homes in on the reflected sound it emits. See *acoustic torpedo.*

active duty
Full-time service as distinct from inactive, retired, or reserve duty.

active sonar
Equipment that provides information on distant underwater objectives by evaluation of reflections of its own sound emissions. See *passive sonar.*

activity
Organizational unit of the Navy established under an officer-in-charge or a commanding officer.

adapter
Coupling or similar device that permits joining fittings of different size. See *reducer.*

addressee
Activity or individual to whom a naval message is directed for action or information.

adiabatic phenomena
Changes in material state (volume or pressure) occurring without a gain or loss of heat. (Note: Temperature will change. Freezing of pipelines due to adiabatic expansion of compressed air when she attempted to blow main ballast tanks is believed to have contributed to the loss of USS *Thresher* in 1963.)

administration
The management of all phases of naval operations not directly concerned with strategy or tactics.

administrative command (ADCOM)
Command without operational functions; concerned only with logistics, maintenance, etc.

administrative contracting officer
Contracting officer assigned to administer a contract at the contract administration office.

administrative lead time
Interval between start of a procurement action and the actual contracting or ordering.

admiral
The highest rank in the Navy, equivalent to general. An officer of four-star rank. Rear admirals and major generals wear two stars, vice admirals and lieutenant generals wear three. Fleet admirals and generals of the army had five stars; this was a special rank created by Congress for WWII leaders only. The four-star admiral is sometimes called *full admiral* to distinguish him from other admirals, inasmuch as the title *admiral* is loosely used for all. A commodore wears one star and is equivalent to a brigadier general, but this rank is not used in the Navy in peacetime. (Note: The rank of Commodore Admiral, a one-star officer, may be created in new legislation.) Commodores and admirals are flag officers, since they are authorized to fly flags with stars to denote their ranks. The Army, Air Force, and Marine Corps term corresponding to flag officer is general officer.

Admiral's March
Ceremonial music for flag officers and officials of equivalent ranks. The number of ruffles and flourishes preceding the ceremonial tune denotes the number of stars authorized for the individual honored.

admiralty law
Laws that deal with maritime cases.

adrift
Loose from towline or moorings; scattered about; not in proper stowage.

advance
Distance gained in the direction of the original course when turning a ship, measured from the point at which the rudder is put over to the point where the ship has changed heading 90 degrees. See *transfer*.

advanced development objective
Prepared by CNO outlining an experimental system of still untested military usefulness, technical feasibility and financial acceptability prior to preparation of a specific operational requirement.

advanced sea-based deterrent
Program to develop follow-on to the Polaris-Poseidon missile systems for use in the late 1970s and '80s. See *Trident*.

advanced surface missile system
Development effort to produce a successor to the Tartar, Talos, and Terrier missiles.

advance force
Task force preceding the attack force in an amphibious assault, conducting preparatory minesweeping, bombardment, and reconnaissance.

advance material requirements
List of materials requisitioned in advance of actual shipbuilding construction, conversion, or repair.

advancement in rating
Promotion of an enlisted man or woman to a higher rate.

advection fog
Fog formed when warm air passes over cold water.

Aeolus
Small meteorological sounding rocket.

Aegis
A modern, integrated, total combat system for combatant ships.

aerial mine
See *mine*.

AER
Alteration equivalent to a repair.

aerographer
Warrant officer advanced from aerographer's mate.

affirmative
Communications term meaning: Yes; permission granted; authorized; approved; approval recommended; etc.

afloat
Supported by the water. Also, at sea, as in *forces afloat*.

aft (after)
Pertaining to the stern or toward the stern of a ship or aircraft.

after body
The section of a ship or boat hull abaft the center. The detachable portion of a torpedo, immediately abaft the energy storage compartment (air flask or battery compartment), which contains the propulsive and guidance mechanisms.

after bow (quarter) spring
Mooring line leading aft at an angle from the bow (quarter) of a ship to the pier alongside. The combination of forward and after springs prevents the ship from moving up and down the pier, while the breast lines prevent her from drifting out or away from it. See *forward bow (quarter) spring, spring.*

afterburner
Part of a jet engine into which fuel is injected and ignited by exhaust to increase thrust for short periods.

afterburning
The process of fuel injection and combustion in the exhaust of a jet.

aftermost
Nearest the stern.

afternoon effect
Thermal gradient caused by the sun's warming of the sea's surface. The effect could mean a possible reduction in sonar effectiveness.

afternoon watch
The watch from noon to 4 PM (1200-1600).

aground
Fast to the bottom and in contact therewith. Immobile by consequence and probably damaged as well. Distinguished from deliberate grounding, as by a landing ship in amphibious warfare, or being fast to the bottom via anchor and chain. A ship *runs aground* or *goes aground.* See *touch and go.*

ahead
Forward of the bow.

ahead-thrown weapon
Missile projected by rocket power or fired from a launcher ahead of a ship; used against submarines.

ahoy
A distinctly nautical hail. Supposedly once the dreaded war cry of the Vikings.

aide
Officer assigned as administrative or personal assistant to a flag officer or senior civilian official. The aide wears aiguillettes.

aids to navigation
Buoys, markers, lights, bells, fog horns, radio and loran stations, or any similar device to assist navigators. Most aids to navigation are in fact piloting aids, as distinguished from aids to navigation offshore such as loran.

aiguillette
The badge of office of a personal aide to a high ranking officer. The aides to the President of the United States wear their aiguillettes on the right shoulder. Aides to all other senior officers and dignitaries wear them on the left shoulder. Dress aiguillettes are extremely ornate—braided loops terminating in two devices resembling pencils which, in fact, are so called. Service aiguillettes are merely simple loops pinned over the shoulder, but distinguish the rank of the officer aided, e.g., four loops for officers of four-star rank and above, otherwise a number of loops equal to the number of his stars. Presidential aides wear aiguillettes of solid gold. Aides to other officers wear blue and gold braid if Navy, red and gold if Marine Corps or Army.
One theory of the origin of aiguillettes is that the aide-de-camp of a superior officer carried the rope and pegs for tethering his superior's horse, and generally carried them around his shoulder for convenience. Thus the rope and pegs became a distinguishing mark. A variant theory is that the pegs were indeed pencils with which to write the leader's orders. Slang: loafer's loops, chicken guts.

aileron
Movable control surface of an aircraft wing, used to impart rolling motion to the aircraft.

Air and Naval Gunfire Liaison Company (ANGLICO)
An organization of Marine and Navy personnel specially qualified for shore control of naval gunfire and close air support.

air bedding
Aboard ship, to bring bedding topside for exposure to the sun and fresh air.

airborne early warning (AEW)
The extension of radar detection range by means of airborne search radar and relay equipment to provide early warning.

airborne radiation thermometer
A device used to measure ocean surface temperature by radiation.

air bunting
To hoist signal flags for drying.

air cock
Valve placed at the highest point of a boiler to release trapped air.

air-control center
A space set aside for control of aircraft, ashore or afloat.

air controller
One who directs aircraft by radar, radio, electronic pilot, etc.

air-control ship
A ship capable of controlling aircraft in air defense. Also used operationally to designate ship performing that function.

air corridors
Restricted air routes specified for aircraft.

aircraft accident report (AAR)
Required after any kind of aircraft accident.

aircraft antisubmarine attack
Classified by submarine position when ordnance is launched: blind, submarine fully submerged, not visible; early, submarine surfaced or diving with part exposed; late, submarine submerged 10 to 20 minutes; tardy, submarine in dive less than 10 seconds; visible, submarine submerged or snorkeling, but visible.

aircraft carrier
Major offensive ship of the fleet. Its chief weapon is its aircraft. See *Appendix A.*

aircraft designation system
See *Appendix C.*

aircraft division
Two sections of aircraft of same type.

aircraft maintenance delayed for parts (AMDP)
Code to indicate why an aircraft is not operational (parts unavailable).

aircraft not fully equipped (ANFE)
Code used to indicate that restrictions are placed on aircraft for lack of equipment.

aircraft out-of-commission for parts (AOCP)
Code used to indicate why aircraft is not operational. Implies a longer delay than AMDP.

aircraft section
Basic tactical unit of two aircraft of the same type.

aircraft squadron
Two or more divisions of aircraft.

aircraft system
Any aircraft, including its airframe, propulsion machinery, armament, electrical, electronic, and mechanical equipment.

airdale
Jocular term for naval aviation personnel. See *brown shoe.*

air defense
All measures designed to nullify or reduce effectiveness of hostile aircraft or guided missiles after they are airborne.

air defense identification zone (ADIZ)
Airspace above specified area in which ready recognition and control of aircraft are required.

air defense warning conditions
Degree of air raid probability: air defense warning yellow—attack probable; air defense warning red—attack imminent or is taking place; air defense warning white—attack is improbable.

air ejector
Device using the suction created by steam flowing through a nozzle to remove air and other noncondensable gases from a condenser or other part of the return-feed system. The purpose is to enable the condenser to maintain a better vacuum, thus promoting efficiency of the steam cycle, and to reduce corrosion by reducing oxygen content.

airfoil
Surface designed to produce lift from the air through which it passes.

airframe
Generic term including all parts of an airplane except power plant, armament, and electronic gear.

air group
The aircraft of an escort or antisubmarine warfare carrier, made up of squadrons. The more numerous aircraft of an attack (first line) carrier are organized into an *air wing*, and may consist of two or more air groups.

air intelligence
Activity formerly known as air combat intelligence. Deals with intelligence aspects of naval air operations.

air lock
A double door giving access to and preserving air pressure in a fireroom or similar space under pressure.

airman (AN)
An enlisted man in paygrade E-3 who performs aviation duties. See *Appendix B.*

air officer
Officer responsible for aviation matters in an aircraft carrier. Heads the air department.

air operations (air plot)
Air operations control center aboard a carrier.

Air Pilot
Printed guides similar to *Coast Pilot* but of interest mainly to aviators, published by the U.S. Navy.

air port
A round window in a ship's side, fitted with a lens frame and a metal cover called *battle port*. Air scoops, screens, and ventilating deadlights are an air port's removable fixtures. Commonly called *porthole*. See *port*.

air register
A device in the casing of a boiler for regulating the amount of air for combustion.

air scoop
A sheet metal device fitted into an air port for catching a breeze.

air search attack team
Aircraft ASW team consisting of a search aircraft and one or more attack aircraft.

air search attack unit
Tactical designation given one or more ASW aircraft assigned to locate and destroy submarines.

airspeed
Speed of aircraft through and relative to the air and distinct from groundspeed. *Indicated airspeed* is an uncorrected reading of the airspeed indicator. *Calibrated airspeed* is the indicated airspeed corrected for instrument errors. *True airspeed* is corrected for altitude and temperature.

air stabilizer
A parachute-type tail stabilizer for aerial torpedoes designed to slow them down before impact with the water.

air strike
Fighter attack aircraft assigned an offensive mission against specific objectives. It may consist of several tactical organizations under a single command in the air.

air support
See *close air support*.

air surface zone
Restricted ocean area for antisubmarine operations.

Air Systems Command
Functional command replacing Bureau of Naval Weapons in 1966 Navy Department reorganization. A component of the Naval Material Command.

air-to-surface missile (ASM)
Former designation of missile launched from an aircraft against a surface target. See *Appendix D* for new designations.

air-to-underwater missile
Former designation of missile launched from aircraft against underwater targets. See *Appendix D* for new designations.

air traffic control radar beacon system
Chief of Naval Material project in cooperation with civilian agencies to permit positive identification of every plane airborne over the United States at any time.

air transportable sonar
Sonar equipment designed for aircraft use.

air transport group
A task organization of transport aircraft units organized to transport amphibious troops to the objective area, or for logistic support.

air wing
The aircraft of an attack aircraft carrier, made up of squadrons. See *air group*.

Aldis lamp
A portable signal light used in ships and aircraft.

alert, dusk or **dawn**
Special precautions, normally all hands to battle stations, at time when attack is most likely prior to first light and at sunset.

Alfa
Phonetic word for letter *A*, formerly *able*.

alidade
A telescopic device used with a gyro repeater for taking visual bearings. Same as a pelorus. An azimuth circle is an older device having sighting vanes instead of a telescope. See *bearing circle*.

align
Electronics: to adjust two or more resonant circuits. Gunnery: to adjust guns and the fire-control equipment that controls them to the same plane of reference, and to line up all aiming devices and bearing transmitters.

all hands
All those aboard ship (except, under certain circumstances, those on watch). Name of a call on boatswain's pipe. *All Hands* magazine is a monthly publication produced for free distribution to naval personnel.

all hands parade
A designated assembly place for all hands on board ship. Used for such events as change-of-command ceremony.

all night in
A full night's sleep with no watch.

allotment
Portion of a man's pay or of an appropriation or fund, regularly assigned to a specific account.

allowance
Authorized personnel on a peacetime level, reduced from the wartime complement. Based on peacetime operations, habitability, budgetary considerations, and upkeep requirements. See *complement* and *manning level.*

allowance list
A listing of repair parts, equipage, and consumable supplies authorized and required to be on board a ship or in a naval activity.

all-weather air stations
Designated air station to which single pilot aircraft may be cleared under instrument flight rules (IFR).

Almanac, air* and *nautical
Naval Observatory publications providing astronomical data needed for navigation.

ALNAV
Message intended for general distribution to all naval personnel.

aloft
Up high, as on a mast, or *strong winds aloft.*

alongside
Near the side of the ship, pier, dock, etc.

altars
Steps in the side of a graving dock extending virtually all of the way around the dock. Used to support shores.

alteration
Any change in equipment or machinery that involves a change in design, materials, number, location, or relationship of the component parts of an assembly.

alternating light
Navigational light showing color variations. May be flashing, group flashing, occulting, or fixed.

altimeter
An aneroid barometer that measures in feet, yards, or meters an aircraft's elevation above a given reference plane, such as sea level. Must be corrected constantly for barometric pressure at ground level. Radio, electronic, and radar altimeters are now common as well.

altitude
The height of an aircraft above a reference point. *True altitude* is height above sea level, corrected for temperature. *Absolute altitude* is height above ground.

ALUSNA
United States Naval Attache, normally followed by name of city, or nation in which stationed, e.g. ALUSNA, Rome. Letters AL are added to distinguish from U.S. Naval Academy. See *naval attache.*

ambient noise
Sound produced in water by sources external to the measuring equipment.

amidships
In or toward the middle of a ship.

ammo
Slang for ammunition.

amphibian
An airplane designed to operate from land or water.

amphibious
Capable of operating on land and sea.

amphibious assault ship (LPH)
Ship designed to transport and land troops, equipment, and supplies by helicopters.

amphibious construction battalion (ACB)
Naval unit organized to provide and operate ship-to-shore fuel systems, pontoon causeways, transfer barges and tugs, and to provide salvage and beach improvement capability to a naval beach group.

amphibious control group
Personnel, ships, and aircraft designated to control the water-borne ship-to-shore movement in an amphibious operation.

amphibious force
Naval force and landing force, together with supporting forces, who are trained, organized, and equipped for amphibious operations.

amphibious group
Command within the amphibious force, designed to execute all phases of a division-size amphibious operation.

amphibious lift
See *lift.*

amphibious operation
Attack launched from the sea by naval and landing forces embarked in ships or craft.

amphibious squadron
Organization of amphibious assault shipping used to transport troops and equipment for an amphibious assault.

amphibious transport dock (LPD)
Ship designed to transport and land troops, equipment, and supplies by means of embarked landing craft, amphibious vehicles, and helicopters.

amphibious troops
Troop components, ground and airborne, assigned to land in an amphibious operation. Synonymous with *landing forces* as defined in the National Security Act of 1947.

amphibious vessel
A ship designed to participate in amphibious operations. See *Appendix A.*

analytical studies of surface effects of submerged submarines
A system for detecting of submarines independent of acoustic phenomena.

anchor (n)
A device used to hold a ship or boat fast to the bottom. Old-fashioned anchors were in the form of the traditional hook. Weight for weight, such anchors still have the best holding power. They are, however, so difficult to rig for sea that, as ships became bigger and required heavier anchors, the currently familiar stockless type was developed. Such anchors can very simply be hoisted snugly into their hawsepipes when the ship gets underway, in contrast to the old-fashioned ones that required fishing, catting, and stowing and then had to be strongly secured—all very hazardous in a seaway.

Anchors may be: *bower, stream, stern, kedge, boat,* and *sheet.* Naval stockless anchors may be *Dunn, Baldt* or *Norfolk,* but such distinctions are of little interest to operating personnel. See *patent anchor.*

anchor (v)
The process of dropping the anchor, of veering chain to the prescribed scope, ar.d of securing, so the ship can ride to the anchor in its designated berth. In nautical terms the maneuver was traditionally called *bringing a ship to an anchor.*

anchorage
Area assigned for anchoring ships. Also any stationary object that acts as a stop or anchor for bracing or shoring.

anchorage buoy
Buoy marking limit of an anchorage area; not to be confused with mooring buoy or an anchor buoy.

anchor at short stay
Anchor chain at minimum length with anchor still down. Anchor is *hove short.*

anchor ball
A black, circular shape hoisted to indicate that the ship is anchored.

anchor buoy
Small float attached to the anchor to facilitate location and recovery if the chain is slipped or parted.

anchor cable
Wire or line running between anchor and small vessel.

anchor chain
Heavy stud-linked chain used for anchoring large ships.

anchor detail
Men on forecastle assigned to handle the ground tackle.

anchor engine
The driving mechanism for the windlass or capstan by which the anchor may be raised. Located under the forecastle.

anchor ice
Ice that is attached to sea bottom.

anchor in sight
A report made by anchor detail on forecastle to the bridge when the anchor itself has been sighted. Followed by *"foul anchor"* or *"clear anchor"* depending on whether the anchor is clear for hoisting to the housed position.

anchor lights
Lights required by *Rules of the Road* indicating that a vessel is anchored. Also called riding lights.

anchor man
Last man of a list or of a group. The *anchor man* of a U.S. Naval Academy class is the last in academic standing and consequently ranks junior to all his classmates. He is the last man graduated and is greeted with cheers by his classmates.

anchor watch
Seamen on deck (or turned in topside on cots) available during the night when their ship is moored or anchored to assist the OOD, particularly with ground tackle.

anchor's aweigh
Expression used to report that an anchor has just been lifted clear of bottom. The ship now bears the weight of her anchor and is considered to be underway (not "underweigh"), although not necessarily with *way on.*

anemometer
Instrument for measuring wind velocity.

aneroid barometer
Instrument using a bellows device to measure atmospheric pressure, thereby indicating changes in weather. See *barometer.*

ANFE
Aircraft not fully equipped.

angle, drift
Horizontal angle between the fore and aft axis of an aircraft and its path relative to the ground.

angle of attack
Angle between a fixed airframe reference line and the apparent relative flow line of the air.

angle on the bow
Angle between fore and aft axis of target and the line of sight, measured from target's bow to port or to starboard through 180 degrees. Estimated angle on the bow is one of the critical observations made through a submarine periscope during an approach to a torpedo firing position. See *target angle.*

annunciator
Signal device on a ship's bridge for delivering orders to engine-room. See *engine-order telegraph.*

antiaircraft projectile
General term applied to projectiles for antiaircraft ammunition.

antiair warfare (AAW)
Warfare directed against airborne vehicles.

antiair warfare area
An area to be kept under surveillance and where protective measures are to be started. Associated terms are: anti-air warfare axis, cross-over point, destruction area, surveillance area, and vital area.

antiair warfare axis
The true bearing from the center of the area to be protected, or the task group position, in the most probable direction of attack.

antiblackout suit
Pilot's suit which, when inflated, helps a pilot resist centrifugal force. Also called a G-suit and pressure suit.

anticorrosive paint
A composition applied to prevent rust.

antifouling paint
A composition applied over the anticorrosive paint on a ship's bottom to prevent attachment of marine growth.

antirecovery device
Device incorporated into mine to explode if disturbed.

antisubmarine warfare (ASW)
All-inclusive term embracing all techniques employed against enemy submarines.

antisubmarine warfare (ASW) screen
Formation of ships and aircraft in advance of a Navy force designed to protect against submarine attack.

Antisubmarine Warfare Systems Analysis Group (ASWAG)
Staff of the Undersea Warfare Research and Development Planning Council established at the Naval Ordnance Laboratory (NOL), White Oak, Maryland, to continually review R&D programs.

apogee
The point at which a missile trajectory or a satellite orbit is farthest from the center of the gravitational field of the controlling body or bodies. See *perigee*.

applied research
Research conducted in support of some fleet need.

apprehension
Taking a person into custody. See *arrest*.

appropriation
Government funds provided by Congress for specific purposes. May be continuing or annual. Not the same as *authorization*. Most defense legislation requires both *authorization* and *appropriation*.

appropriation, annual
An appropriation available only during the fiscal year specified in the appropriation act.

appropriation, continuing
An appropriation available until exhausted for the purpose made without any time limit.

appropriation title
The descriptive name assigned to an appropriation account. It does not specify a fiscal year; hence it could include money available from several fiscal years' accounts.

approved circuit
A communication channel or frequency approved for transmission of classified traffic in the clear.

approved program
Individual program element or component of the Five-Year Defense Program approved by the Secretary of Defense.

apron
Area of a pier or wharf on which cargo is unloaded. Also the edge of an airfield, just short of the runway.

arbor, depth charge
Device holding a depth charge on its projector. See *K-gun, Y-gun*.

archibenthic zone
Subdivision of the deep-sea system of the benthic division, including waters of 200 to 1,000 meters in deep.

arc of visibility
Portion of the horizon, expressed in degrees, through which a navigational light is visible from seaward.

Arctic Research Laboratory
Located at Point Barrow, Alaska, operated by the University of Alaska for the Office of Naval Research (ONR).

ardent
Said of a sailing vessel if her head tends to come up into the wind when sailing close hauled. See *lee helm, weathercocks.*

area, forward
Geographical: combat zone.

area, mounting
Where forces are assembled prior to an amphibious operation.

area, objective
Definite geographical area containing a military objective.

Argus Island
Oceanographic Research Laboratory located on Plantagenet Bank near Bermuda.

arm
To make a weapon ready to fire or explode. To equip a ship or aircraft with weapons. To fill a cavity at the bottom of a sounding lead with soap or tallow to obtain a bottom sample.

armament
Weapon of a ship or aircraft.

armed forces of the U.S.
Collective term for all the components of the Army, Navy, Marine Corps, and Air Force. Includes Coast Guard, when part of the U.S. Navy during time of war. See *United States Armed Forces.*

armed guard
Naval gun crews on merchant ships during wartime.

armed services procurement planning officer
Staff member of a military field office assigned to coordinate all production planning for DOD in specified plants.

armed services procurement regulations (ASPR)
Regulations governing the writing of all contracts for supplies or services to DOD.

armed services vocational aptitude battery (ASVAB)
A test for scoring basic capabilities for enlisted men and women. Replaces General Classification Test (GCT).

arming crew
Men who provide weapons and ammunition to carrier aircraft.

armor
Steel or other protection against projectiles, in ships, aircraft, or special uniform.

armored cruiser
In the early days of steel warship design, battleships (ships of the line of battle) were the most powerful ships that technology permitted. Big guns and heavy armor were their forte. Speed was secondary. Cruisers were smaller, faster, and lightly armored. Gunboats were tiny, slow, and lightly gunned, and torpedo boats were small high-speed vessels armed with one or two torpedoes. The torpedo boat destroyer (henceforth called simply destroyer) replaced both gunboats and torpedo boats as viable types; everything between destroyer and battleship was a cruiser. These were subdivided into many short-lived classes: protected cruiser, belted cruiser, armored cruiser (armor); heavy and light cruisers (size and armament); scout cruiser, training cruiser (mission); battle cruiser (armament and speed); and "treaty" cruiser (displacement not over 10,000 tons, resulting from London Naval Treaty). Until the advent of the battle cruiser, the largest and heaviest of the cruisers was the armored cruiser type: heavily armored (but less so than a battleship), heavily gunned (though not so heavily as a battleship) and, of course, several knots faster than a battleship. HMS *Dreadnought*, built quickly and secretly by Great Britain in 1906 (henceforth all battleships were known either as dreadnoughts or pre-dreadnoughts) increased battleship speed by several knots and thus ended the speed advantage of most cruisers. The battle cruiser, mounting battleship guns on a large, lightly aromored but very fast hull, made the armored cruiser obsolete. The Battle of Falkland Islands (Dec. 8, 1914) proved the point. The battle cruisers, in turn, became obsolete when battleship speeds began to approach 30 knots— although many thought this was already the case after the Battle of Jutland (May 31, 1916) when they suffered unacceptable damage as part of the British battle line. In World War II the battleship was displaced as the capital ship of large navies by the aircraft carrier, which quickly demonstrated more total gunfire, far greater offensive range, and the mobility to arrive at the scene of action quickly. Destroyers, in the meantime, have grown so big and have so many capabilities that the largest have been re-designated as cruisers; at the same time, their principal function has been re-defined as antiair and antisubmarine escorts for carriers.

armored rope
Rope with hemp core and a flat wire wound around outside of each strand; used chiefly in salvage or similar work.

armor piercing (AP)
Ammunition specially designed to penetrate armor.

armor-piercing incendiary (API)
Armor-piercing projectiles specially designed to set fires after piercing armor.

armor-piercing tracer (APT)
An armor-piercing projectile fitted with a tracer for spotting.

armory
Compartment aboard ship where small arms and light machine guns are stowed and serviced.

array
Two or more hydrophones feeding into a common receiver. There may also be antenna arrays for radio or radar in air.

arrest
Restraint of a person by competent authority. Involves relief from military duties. See *apprehension, restriction.*

arresting gear
Arrangement of wires on a carrier flight deck that stops an aircraft after the plane's tailhook has engaged it.

Articles for the Government of the Navy
No longer effective, replaced by the Uniform Code of Military Justice. See *"Rocks and Shoals".*

artificial horizon
An instrument indicating the attitude of an aircraft by simulating the appearance of a natural horizon with reference to a miniature airplane. Also a simulated horizon in a navigating instrument. A pool of mercury used for a mirror. Since the mercury will lie absolutely horizontally, a sight may be taken using the heavenly body's own reflection in place of a horizon, and dividing the observed angle by two.

asbestos kit
Fire-resistant clothing for firefighting. Also called *hot suit,* worn by a *hot suitman.*

A-scope
Cathode-ray indicator used to measure target ranges and size through vertical deflections on a horizontal scale.

ASDIC
Echo-ranging equipment; the British equivalent of sonar equipment.

ashcan
Slang for *depth charge.*

ashore
On the beach or shore. A man may go ashore on *liberty,* but if a ship goes ashore, she is *aground.*

Aspect
Short-pulse ASW classification device designed for destroyer use but now used in the *Sea King* helicopter.

aspect ratio
For an aircraft wing: its span divided by its width. For a rudder: its depth divided by its width. Thus: the length of any moving surface, measured across the direction of motion, divided by its length in the direction of motion. A long thin wing therefore has a higher aspect ratio than a short stubby one.

ASROC (antisubmarine rocket)
Model designation: RUR-5. Fired from a trainable mount in a surface ship, functions as a depth charge after entering the water. See *Appendix D.*

assault craft
Landing craft used in amphibious operations.

assault group
Subordinate task organization of Navy forces of an attack force, e.g., an amphibious attack group is composed of assault shipping and supporting naval units designed to transport, protect, land, and initially support a landing group.

assault shipping
Amphibious vessels carrying assault troops and equipment for a landing operation.

assault waves
Scheduled leading waves of boats and amphibious vehicles of an amphibious landing.

astern
Toward the back or after end of a ship or formation. Generally used in the sense of *behind*, or out of the ship. Thus, a fast ship leaves a slower one *astern*. A man who falls overboard would be left *astern*. One would *go aft* in one's own ship, not *astern*.

astro compass
Optical device for solving the astronomical triangle mechanically. Used by aircraft for determining true heading.

ASVAB
See *armed services vocational aptitude battery.*

ASW
See *antisubmarine warfare.*

asymmetry factor
Ratio of length to width of a sea target.

as you were
Command meaning: *Resume former activity or formation.*

athwart, athwartships
At right angles to the fore and aft centerline of a ship or boat. Sometimes pronounced "thwartships." *Thwarts* are always athwartships.

Atlantic Ridge
Undersea ridge which runs from Iceland to Bouvet Island and separates the Atlantic Ocean into two large basins. Also called "Mid-Atlantic Ridge."

Atlantic Undersea Test and Evaluation Center (AUTEC)
Located in Tongue of the Ocean, in the Bahamas. Environmental laboratory for calibration of sonar, measurement of sounds emanating from a ship and testing of weapons undersea, on the surface, or in the air. Instrumentation area is five miles wide by approximately 50 miles in length.

Atlantis
Long-range study of feasibility of large ocean surveillance systems.

atoll
A ring-shaped coral reef usually found in the Pacific and Indian Oceans, often with low sand islands. The body of water enclosed by the reef is a lagoon.

atomizer
Device feeding fuel oil into a boiler as a fine spray. Together with the air register it forms the burner.

attack aircraft carrier (CV, CVN)
Warship designed to support and operate aircraft in attacks on targets afloat or ashore, and engage in sustained operations in support of other forces. See *Appendix A.*

attack director
Computing element of a fire-control system.

attack force
All ships, troops, and aircraft used in the attack phase of an amphibious assault.

attack group
Subordinate task organization of an attack force, e.g., an amphibious attack group is composed of assault shipping and supporting naval units designed to transport, protect, land, and initially support a landing group.

attack plane
Multiweapon carrier aircraft that can carry bombs, torpedoes, and rockets.

attack plotter
Device displaying movement of ship and target, part of a fire-control system.

attack teacher
Training device for simulation of actual tactics involved in submarine or antisubmarine combat. Originally devised to train submarine commanders in attacking ships. Subsequently a modification was developed for ASW attacks on submarines.

attend the side
To be on the quarterdeck to meet important persons. Same as *tend the side*

attention to port, starboard
Command given to topside personnel when ship is rendering passing honors. Personnel in view of the honored ship are required to come to attention, facing the designated side, and salute if ordered.

augmentor
Device for increasing the efficiency of an air pump in a steam power plant.

Aurora
Concept for a submarine-launched satellite interceptor.

authentication
Communication security measure designed to prevent fraudulent transmissions.

authorization
Congressional permission to carry out a program (generally procurement of ships, aircraft, or weapons), involving expenditure of funds. Actual *appropriation* of the funds is necessary before they can be spent (or obligated).

authorized data list
Master list of technical data and information from which data requirements must be selected.

auto cat
Airplane used to relay radio messages automatically.

automatic carrier landing system
Designated project of the Chief of Naval Operations (CNO) for development of a system to automatically control planes landing on carrier decks.

automatic merchant vessel report
The U.S. Coast Guard's computerized worldwide merchant ship plotting system that provides search and rescue information.

auxiliary machinery
All machinery other than the main engines aboard ship. Examples are condensers, feed pumps, anchor engine, evaporators, ice machines, etc.

auxiliary power plant
Applied to aircraft, usually refers to the model of afterburner used in jets.

auxiliary tanks
In submarines, variable (ballast) tanks equidistant from bow and stern, built to take full sea pressure and connected into the trimming system. See *trim, trim tanks, ballast tanks.*

availability
Period assigned a ship for accomplishing work at a repair activity. May be restricted, technical, regular overhaul, voyage repairs, or upkeep period availability

availability factor
Percentage of aircraft that is operational or *on the line.*

avast
Order to stop or cease.

awaiting aircraft availability
Term applied to indicate that an aircraft is due for overhaul.

awash
So low that water washes over.

away
Term used in passing the word aboard ship, e.g.: *"Call away the gig."* Refers to prospective departure from the ship on a mission or errand, e.g.: *"Away rescue and assistance party, away!"*

aweigh
Said of an anchor when clear of the bottom. See *anchor's aweigh.*

AWOL
Absent without leave. See *unauthorized absentee.*

axis
Reference line for stationing ships, originating at the formation center.

aye aye
A seamanlike response to an order or instruction signifying that the order is heard, is understood, and will be carried out. *Aye* is Old English for "yes." Pronounced "eye."

azimuth
Angle measured clockwise between north and the object being sighted. Almost always refers to the bearing of a celestial body.

azimuth circle
Fitting used on a compass or gyro repeater for measuring bearings or azimuths, usually of celestial objects. Has an adjustable mirror so that the azimuth of an elevated line of sight may be taken, thus differing from a simple bearing circle or alidade (which has a small telescope). See *alidade, bearing circle, pelorus.*

B

Babbitt metal
Soft, white antifriction alloy of copper, tin, and antimony used for bearing surfaces.

back
To reverse engines so that a ship may be stopped or made to go astern.

background noise
Noise that limits echo detection. At sea it may interfere with sonar and can be caused by sea life, sea action, or the system itself.

back pressure
Pressure on the exhaust side of a steam or reciprocating engine.

backrush
The flow of water down the foreshore after the uprush of incoming waves. Also called backwash. See *uprush.*

back to battery
Return of a gun after recoil to firing position. Also, slang for personal recovery from shock, injury, or illness.

backs
The wind backs when it changes direction counterclockwise. See *haul.* (Note: the direction of the wind is the direction from which it is blowing.)

backstay
A stay supporting a mast from aft. See *forestay.*

backwash
Water thrown aft by turning of ship's propeller.

back water
Command given to oarsmen to reverse usual rowing motion.

bad conduct discharge (BCD)
A punitive discharge awarded to an enlisted person for severe infractions of regulations. The only type of discharge that carries greater prejudice is the dishonorable discharge (DD).

baffle
Plate used to deflect fluids, gases, or sound waves.

baffle area
An area roughly 30 degrees either side of the stern of a ship in which maintenance of a sonar contact is most difficult. Because of the noise from its own propellers, sonar equipment is frequently designed with a baffle area astern.

bail
To dip water out of a boat. The spreader to which the accommodation ladder topping lift is secured.

bail out
To jump or eject from aircraft. Slang: to rescue one from an administrative predicament.

bail shackle
The part of a pelican hook that holds the hook closed over the chain. Also referred to as the link or slip hook link. Sometimes spelled *bale.*

baiting
Tactic designed to lull an enemy, especially a submarine, into a false sense of security and induce it to take action, making it liable to detection or attack.

balanced rudder
Rudder in which part of the blade surface is forward of the axis to counterbalance water pressure on after part.

balance point
With reference to an old-fashioned anchor, that point on the shank where the anchor balances. Usually fitted with a pad eye for convenience of the cat-davit.

balancing
In submarines, the maintenance of depth with no way on by riding on top of a density layer. Also called hovering.

bale
See *bail shackle.*

ballast
The weight added to a ship or boat to insure stability; to pump sea water into empty fuel tanks.

ballast tanks
Tanks used to surface or submerge a submarine. They are lightly constructed with bottoms always open to the sea, fitted with quick-opening vents to release entrapped air on diving. During submergence, ballast tanks cannot have any air in them since the air bubble will be compressed or expanded as the depth changes and alter submerged trim. Usually blown dry for surface operations, although during WWII, submarines on surface patrol sometimes reduced silhouette by leaving ballast tanks partially flooded. Distinguished from variable or trim tanks, which must withstand full submergence pressure because they are carried only partly filled and closed off from the sea. A few surface ships have ballast tanks for varying trim and buoyancy (amphibious landing ships, for example) but such tanks are relatively simple, and are never deeply submerged.

ballistic correction
Correction in aiming a gun, necessary because of variation in powder temperature, gun erosion, or the motion of the target, wind, or gun itself. Also a correction in a gyro compass due to a change of course or speed.

ballistics
The science of projectile motion. Interior ballistics deals with the inside of a gun, exterior ballistics deals with action of projectiles in flight.

ballonet
Gastight fabric compartment within an airship.

bank
Relatively flat subsurface elevation that is comparatively shallow but whose depth is sufficient for surface navigation. Also, to incline an aircraft about its longitudinal axis; the shore(s) of a river, lake, or harbor.

bank effect
Lateral motion of a ship in a narrow channel where the bank tends to attract the stern (bank suction) and repel the bow (bank cushion).

bar
Shallow-water feature, an obstruction to navigation, usually at a harbor entrance, either exposed or submerged, made up of sand, gravel, and other sediment. Also, a unit of pressure equal to 10^6 dynes per square centimeter.

barbette
Nonrotating armor protecting the rotating part of a ship's turret below the gun house.

bare boat charter
Lease of a ship without equipment or crew.

barge
Boat for official use of a flag officer. A non-self-propelled cargo carrier in harbors or rivers. Also called a *lighter*, or *scow*. As a verb, "The coal was *barged* alongside." See *scow*.

bark or barque
Usually a three-masted sailing ship with the first two masts square-rigged and the third fore-and-aft rigged. If there are more than three masts all but last one are square-rigged.

barkentine
A three-masted sailing ship with the first mast square-rigged and the second and third fore-and-aft rigged.

barnacles
Marine crustaceans that attach to and grow on hard objects at or below the surface, particularly on the hulls of ships. A growth of barnacles will have a noticeable effect on a ship's speed.

barograph
Instrument that provides a continuous record of atmospheric pressure on a revolving drum. A recording aneroid barometer.

barometer
Instrument that measures atmospheric pressure either with a column of mercury (mercurial barometer) or by the reaction of a metallic chamber, or bellows, exhausted of air (aneroid barometer).

barricade
Prior to the development of the present angled-deck aircraft carriers, propeller-driven aircraft had to be parked on the flight deck forward when other planes were landing on the after portion. Once a plane's landing roll was stopped by the arresting gear, the flight deck crew would quickly detach the tail hook from the gear and roll it forward to join the other parked planes, after which the barrier or barricade protecting them would be re-erected. Generally, the barricade was a collapsible fence, made of webbing or wire, intended to catch wings or landing gear struts of a plane that failed to engage the regular arresting gear. Small or even heavy damage to a single plane was preferable to lesser damage to several, especially during wartime operations. See *bolter* for different techniques for jets using the angled deck.

barrier combat air patrol (BARCAP)
One or more divisions of fighter aircraft deployed between an objective area and an enemy force as a defensive barrier across the most probable direction of attack.

barrier ice
Edge of shelf ice.

barrier line
See *barrier patrol.*

barrier patrol
Ship or aircraft patrol designated to detect passage of enemy ships or aircraft, especially submarines, through a particular ocean area or across a designated barrier line.

barrier reef
Name given to offshore reefs separated from land by channels or lagoons as distinct from fringing reefs.

basegram
A message delivered by radio to delivery authorities, such as port directors, who give them, by hand, on request, to forces afloat. Used for general messages.

base line, base line extension
The arc of a great circle passing through two loran stations. A ship on or near this line cannot use readings from these two stations to obtain a position.

base loading
Loading of a ship intended for delivery to a base or a replenishment group. Distinguished from combat loading.

base, naval
A shore command providing administrative logistic support to the operating forces.

base speed
Resultant speed along a base course when evasive steering, such as zigzagging, is being carried out.

basic naval establishment plan (BNEP)
Outline of the naval establishment for the current year including force level, deployment of forces, personnel strengths, state of training and degree of readiness, etc., to be maintained during peacetime, prepared in OPNAV for SECNAV approval.

basic test battery
Series of tests designed to measure intelligence, aptitudes, and potential skills of recruits. Has been replaced by a similar series of tests known as the armed services vocational aptitude battery (ASVAB).

basin
Ocean bottom feature of large size and roughly circular shape where the average depth is greater than depths on its perimeter.

bathyconductograph
Device to measure the conductivity of sea water at various depths while a ship is underway.

bathymetric chart
One showing depths of water by use of contour lines and color shading. See *bottom contour chart.*

bathymetry
Measurement of water depths, temperature, salinity, etc.

bathythermograph (BT)
Temperature- and depth-sensing device used to obtain water temperatures at various depths while a ship is at anchor or underway.

battalion landing team (BLT)
Battalion of troops specially organized for an amphibious landing.

batten
Strip of wood or steel used in securing tarpaulins in place over a hatch; locking device for aircraft control surfaces. A strip of wood or plastic used to stiffen the leech of a sail.

batten down
To cover and fasten down; to close off a hatch or watertight door. To make secure, as in *"Batten down for heavy weather."*

battery
Ship's guns of the same caliber or used for the same purpose, e.g., main, secondary, and antiaircraft batteries. In submarines, the main (electrical) storage battery.

battery control
Fire control of all mounts or turrets of a similar caliber or purpose. Types of control—collective, dispersed, divided, and sector—determine how battery command is exercised.

battery record book
Charge and discharge data and data on capacity of a submarine's main storage battery.

battle bill
List of battle assignments based on ship's armament and ship's complement. See *watch, quarter, and station bill.*

battle cruiser
A lightly armored, high-speed cruiser with the offensive power of a battleship, developed by the British navy before WWI. Although it was designed for cruiser employment, British naval authorities placed the battle cruiser in the battle line at the Battle of Jutland, with disastrous results. When the fast battleship was developed, a matter only of adequate horsepower, the battle cruiser was finished. See *armored cruiser, cruiser, battle line.*

battle dress
Flash and splinter protective clothing worn in battle by Navy men on surface ships.

battle efficiency award
An award to ships and aircraft squadrons of the active fleet. See *prize money* and *E award.*

battle efficiency pennant
Red pennant with a black ball flown by a ship winning that award. Slang: meat ball.

battle lantern
Electric lantern, battery powered, for emergency use.

battle lights
Dim red lights below decks for necessary illumination during *darken ship* periods. The red spectrum has less of the temporary blinding effect on the retina of the eye than any other color; hence, red lighting permits the quickest possible dark adaptation and has the least deleterious effect on night vision. The blue "battle lanterns" previously used had a devastating effect on the ability to see in the dark.

battle line
Two or more battleships formed into a line of battle for the purpose of engaging the enemy in surface gun action. In WWI, battle cruisers were considered marginally capable of standing in the battle line, but the Battle of Jutland, 31 May 1916, proved otherwise, at least as far as the British battle cruisers were concerned. German battle cruisers, more heavily armored, fared better. In WWII, a battle line was employed by U.S. forces at the Battle of Surigao Strait, but this is considered an anachronism of that war. At present, battle line is a figure of speech that might be used to refer to almost any assembly of fighting ships.

battle pin
Marine Corps term for collar pin.

battle port
Hinged metal cover for an air port, or porthole.

battle problem
Simulated battle exercise.

battleship (BB)
Derived from "line of battle ship" or "ship of the battle line." The battleship, whether of wood or steel, was originally the largest and most powerful man-of-war that could be built. Development of the airplane produced the aircraft carrier, which in World War II decisively replaced the battleship as the primary capital ship of navies. The biggest battleships ever built were the 80,000-ton *Yamatos* of Japan. The only ones now in existence and potentially usable are the four 65,000-ton *Iowa* class (nine 16-inch guns, 30 knots speed) of the United States. USS *New Jersey* of this class was put in commission for shore bombardment in the Vietnam War but is now back in the reserve fleet. USS *Missouri* was the site of the surrender of Japan in World War II; the others are the USS *Iowa* and USS *Wisconsin*. Note: a number of WWII battleships, and other ships as well, have been preserved in state memorial parks.

battle stations
See *watch, quarter, and station bill.*

battle wagon
Slang for battleship.

Baxter bolt
Fitting that screws flush into deck, used to fasten down aircraft.

beach
As used in amphibious operations, portion of shoreline required for landing one battalion landing team. To run a ship or boat ashore is to beach it. Slang for shore. In oceanography, area extending from shoreline inland to a marked change in physiographic form, or to line of permanent vegetation.

beach capacity
An estimate, in tons, of the amount of cargo it is possible to unload daily on a strip of beach during and amphibious operation.

beachcomber
A person who haunts the waterfront in seacoast towns, occasionally begging a handout or working for a short time. Most frequently encountered in ports in the warm seas, such as the Caribbean or Central Pacific.

beach dump
Temporary storage for supplies landed in an amphibious operation.

beach exit
Route for movement of material and personnel inland from the beach.

beach gear
Generic term for all equipment meant to be used on the beach during an amphibious landing. Includes all material intended to remain under the command and disposition of the beachmaster, as distinct from that intended for the troops who have been or are to be landed.

beach group, naval
Naval unit that provides personnel, boats, and equipment to supplement the shore party of the landing force in an amphibious operation.

beachhead
The initial objective of an assault landing. A section of enemy coast, which, after capture, will be used for continuous landing of men and equipment in an amphibious operation. After consolidation of the beachhead, the next move is to break out of same, and at this point the operation takes on the characteristics of regular land warfare, except that until capture of a suitable harbor or port, the beachhead remains the support base, under the charge of a beachmaster.

beaching gear
Cradles on wheels used for hauling boats and seaplanes out of the water and onto a ramp or beach.

beach marker
Colored panel or other device marking limit of specific landing beaches for assault craft in an amphibious landing.

beachmaster
In amphibious operations, the officer designated to take charge of logistic activities on the beach once the assault phase of the landing has been concluded.

beachmaster unit
Personnel assigned to the beachmaster.

beach matting
Steel netting or mesh laid on soft sand to improve traction of vehicles.

beach party (amphibious)
Naval shore party to control boats, survey channels, salvage landing craft, etc

beach patrol
A patrol along the beach that warns vessels of danger and, in time of war, prevents sabotage and landing of contraband.

beach wagon
A cart used to carry a surfboat along the beach.

beacon
A navigational aid for establishing position of ship or aircraft. May be lighted, aerial, radar, radio, radio-marker, radio-range, two-marker, or infrared.

beacon, fan marker
Aircraft radio marker beacon transmitting signals in a vertical, fanshaped pattern.

beam
Extreme width of a ship or boat. In wooden ship construction, the heavy horizontal athwartships timbers on which the deck planking was laid were called beams. The longest beam spanned the maximum width of a ship, external planking excepted, giving rise to the term *beam* to denote this measurement. A ship heeled over 90 degrees was said to be *on her beam ends.* Any other ship or object reasonably nearby in the direction that the beams normally pointed was said to be *abeam,* or *on the beam.*

beam rider
Guided missile that follows a radar beam to the target.

beam width
Critical characteristic of a radar transmission governing accuracy of the bearings measured by radar.

bean rag
Slang for flag flown in port to indicate that the crew is at mess and that other than routine honors should not be expected.

bear
To be in a certain direction from the speaker, or the ship, e.g., the target *bears* 170 degrees.

bear a hand
Hurry up; expedite.

bearing
The direction of an object from the observer, expressed in three figures from 000 clockwise through 360 degrees. True bearing is measured from true north. Magnetic bearing is measured from the magnetic north and is now rarely used except internally for boats or aircraft equipped only with magnetic compasses. Relative bearing is measured from the bow of a ship or aircraft.

bearing circle
A ring fitted over a compass bowl or compass repeater with which bearings can be taken by sighting through vanes. If a reflecting device is fitted to facilitate bearings of celestial bodies it is called an azimuth circle. If a telescope is fitted instead of vanes it is an alidade or a pelorus.

Beaufort scale
Standard, graduated table of wind velocities. Devised by Admiral Sir Francis Beaufort, R.N.

becket
An eye for securing one end of a line to a block. A rope eye as on a cargo net.

beef boat
Slang for a supply ship or cargo ship.

beep
To control a drone or pilotless plane. The man who controls is a *beeper.*

beer muster
Slang for beer party ashore.

belay
To make fast or secure, as in *"Belay the line."* To cancel, as in *"Belay the last word."*

belaying pin
A long, round metal rod used for securing lines. Most common use today is in the pin rail of a flag bag for securing signal halyards. In the hands of an angry sailor of the old school, a large belaying pin was a lethal instrument.

bell book, engineer's
Official record of the engine orders received in the engineroom from the bridge.

bell, ship's
Used for sounding fog or distress signals, as fire signal, and to denote time. See *ship's bell.*

below
Downward; below decks; downstairs.

bench mark
A permanently fixed point of known position used for reference in survey or alignment, as in aligning a gun.

bend on
To secure one thing to another, as to *bend* a flag *on* to a halyard. To *bend on 10 turns* means to increase propeller speed by 10 rpm.

bends
Affliction caused by formation of nitrogen bubbles in the blood, resulting in paralysis, vertigo, cerebral shock, blindness, etc. Experienced by divers after excessive exposure to pressure or too rapid decompression. Pilots also sometimes experience too rapid a change in pressure and resulting discomfort. The experience is popularly known as the bends, but because the pressure change is so much less, it cannot compare in severity with the bends experienced by divers.

bent
Attached. To *bend on* means to attach. Also, slang for a victim of the bends.

benthic division
Primary division of the sea, including its floor. Subdivisions are: littoral system, including waters between high water and depths of 200 meters or the continental shelf edge; and deep-sea system, including all other waters. Other divisions are: eulittoral, sublittoral, archibenthic, and abyssalbenthic zones.

benhos
Collective term used to describe all plants and animals living on the ocean bottom.

berg
See *iceberg.*

bergy-bit
Medium-size piece of glacial ice floating in the sea. Smaller pieces are growlers.

berm
Nearly horizontal position of a beach or backshore having an abrupt fall, formed by materials deposited by wave action.

Berne List
Volume listing international call signs, radio stations, etc., published by International Union of Telecommunications, Geneva, Switzerland.

berth
Anchorage or mooring space assigned a vessel. Sleeping place assigned a man on board ship. A margin in passing something, as a wide berth. To inhabit, as *"He is berthing in the forward compartment."*

between wind and water or betwixt wind and water
Refers to that part of a ship just at the waterline which is alternately exposed and underwater as the ship heels and rolls. To receive a shot between wind and water is to be hit in a very vulnerable place. Hence the reference has come to mean the vulerable part of anything.

bight
Loop of rope, line, or chain. An indentation in the coast; a small cove. Slang: *caught in a bight* is to be entangled in some sort of difficulty.

bilge(s)
The inside bottom of a ship or boat. The *turn of the bilge* refers to the curved plating where a ship's side joins the bottom. A ship is said to be *bilged* if her bottom has been damaged sufficiently to take on water, as when running aground, but the expression is almost never used to refer to battle damage, even though torpedo damage could technically be so described. To *bilge* an examination is slang for receiving an unsatisfactory grade. To *bilge* someone is to fail that person, if one is an instructor or superior, or to get a higher grade if a peer. To refer to something (e.g., the opinion of another) as *bilge* or *bilge-water* is to be contemptuous.

bilge blocks
Wooden supports under a vessel's bilge in drydock.

bilge keels (chocks)
Fins at the turn of the bilge that reduce rolling of a ship. Also called *anti-rolling chocks*, or simply *rolling chocks*.

bilge pump
Pump used to clear the bilge of water.

bill
Assignments, with names, for training, administrative, or emergency activities, e.g., rescue and assistance bill. Also, the end of the arm of an old-fashioned anchor.

billboard
The inclined platform near the bows of a ship on which the old-fashioned anchor is stowed, ready to be dropped. See *cat, cat and fish, cathead.*

billet
Duties, tasks, and responsibilities performed by one person. Also, a specific assignment in a ship or station organization.

billet slip
Printed form, giving a man his duty and living assignments aboard ship.

bill of lading (blading)
Shipping document showing the name and address of the shipper and consignee and a list of cargo with weights and dimensions.

bill of material
Descriptive and quantitative list of materials, supplies, parts, and components needed for specific end-items or assemblies, for overhaul and repair of items, or for construction or repair of structures or facilities. May include cost estimates.

binnacle
The stand or support for a magnetic compass. Originally spelled "bittacle." In the old navy, this was a wooden structure mounted in a location convenient to the helmsman. In later years it took on a characteristic shape and was made of brass because ot the nonmagnetic properties of that metal. Wooden binnacles of various designs were frequently fitted with small cupboard-like compartments for stowage of accoutrements for the watch on deck, such as the log book, candles, or any nonmagnetic gear. Because of the effect on the compass, placing magnetic material in the binnacle was of course an offense. See *binnacle list*.

binnacle list
A list of men excused from duty because of illness or injury, customarily placed in the binnacle for the information of the officer of the watch. Although the binnacle list survives with the same meaning, it is no longer placed in the binnacle.

binoculars
Telescopic instrument used for distant seeing. Actually a pair of telescopes, attached in such a way that a single view is presented to both eyes in a manner as near as possible to normal vision.

bioluminescence
The emission of visible light by living organisms.

bird cage
Air-control officer's station in the island of an aircraft carrier.

birdfarm
Slang for aircraft carrier.

bitter end
The absolute end of a piece of line or cable.

bitts
Pair of short steel posts or horns on board ship used to secure lines. See *bollard*.

black gang
Slang for personnel of the engineering department of a ship. Now obsolete because the reference was to coal and the coal dust with which all old-time engineers had to contend.

black oil
Navy standard fuel oil (NSFO). More highly refined than *bunker crude*.

black shoe
Slang for an officer who is not in the aviation or submarine communities. See *brown shoe*.

blading
See *bill of lading*.

blast
Signal on a ship's whistle: short (1 second), prolonged (4-6 seconds), long (over 6 seconds), as defined by the *International Rules of the Road.*

blind bombing zones
Areas restricted to air operations. Bombing permitted without restrictions.

blind zone
Electronic countermeasures term meaning an area where echoes cannot be received.

blinker tube (gun)
Directional, low-powered, visual-signaling device used aboard ship.

blinker, yardarm
Signal lights at end of yardarms keyed from signal bridge.

blinking
Distinctive loran signal used to indicate unusable impulses.

blip
Echo as recorded on a radar or sonar screen. Also pip.

blister
Bulge in fuselage or wing of airplane enclosing equipment such as machine guns. Also, a built-in bulge in the hull of a man-of-war to protect against mines, bombs, and torpedoes.

block
Device consisting of a pulley encased in a shell, over which a line or wire rope can run freely. A *snatch block* is one in which the shell opens to take the bight of a line or wire. See *dead-eye.*

blockade
Naval operation barring ships from certain ports or ocean areas. Although many different types of blockades have been proclaimed, including "paper" blockades, international law has generally held that to be meaningful, a blockade must be physically enforced at the spot (i.e., a neutral nation blockade runner is not subject to capture merely because she had, sometime previously, run a blockade).

block coefficient
The ratio of a ship's immersed volume divided by the product of the ship's length, beam, and draft. Serves as a measure of the vessel's fullness. The block coefficient of a cube is, of course, unity.

blocking
Arrangement of keel and bilge blocks in a drydock in accordance with the docking plan.

blockship
Ship sunk to block off a channel or harbor entrance.

bloomer
See *buckler*. Also loosely used for any canvas cover topside.

blow
To expel water from a tank by using compressed air. Also, a gale or storm.

blower
Motor-driven fan in ventilating and exhaust systems.

blowerman
Man in fireroom who controls blowers that force air through boilers.

blow tubes
To inject steam into fireside of boilers for purposes of removing soot from tubes.

Blue Angels
A team of Navy aviators that specializes in precision-formation aerobatics.

bluejacket
Navy enlisted man below the rank of CPO (E-7). Slang: white hat, tar, swabbie.

Bluejackets' Manual, The
The Navy's bastic-training book since 1902.

bluenose
One who has been north of the Arctic Circle by ship or boat.

blues
Blue uniform worn by naval personnel.

boarders
Also called *boarding party*. Men and officers detailed to go aboard an enemy ship in order to capture or destroy it. The term *boarders* is more generally applied to those who spontaneously board an enemy vessel when the opportunity presents itself, as when antagonists foul each other. This occurred in the battles between the *Constitution* and the *Guerriere* and between the *Chesapeake* and the *Shannon*, in 1812-13. A boarding party, having been detailed and organized, may board the enemy ship directly but is more frequently sent by boat or other secondary means. One of the most famous boarding parties in history was Stephen Decatur's in the *Intrepid* when he boarded and burned the *Philadelphia* in 1804. See *boarding party* for use in a social sense.

boarding call
Official visit by a naval boarding officer to another ship of war or public vessel of importance. Generally made to foreign ships when they call in U.S. ports, but may be made in foreign ports also, and in such cases may be made to U.S. ships as well. The visit is initiated by the senior officer in port to ships arriving, with the purpose of exchanging courtesies and information leading to mutual beneficial cooperation. The boarding

officer should be as senior as possible, but always junior in rank to the senior officer of the ships on which the call is made. The call is always returned in kind as soon as possible, again by an officer junior to both seniors. Such calls do not take the place of official calls between the seniors themselves, to which they are preliminaries.

boarding party

See *boarders*. Also, a group of men that makes a boarding call or other official visit afloat. Sometimes, following an official call and exchange of calls between the commanders of ships, organized visits, known as *boarding parties*, will be exchanged between wardrooms and even between enlisted groups. Occasionally, during time of war, incoming merchant ships of a belligerent nation will be visited by a boarding officer and a party of men to determine nationality, destination, cargo, and other facts relating to the war. Such a visiting group can also be termed a *boarding party*.

Board of Inspection and Survey

Legally constituted group of experienced officers representing Office of the Chief of Naval Operations (OPNAV) who make periodic inspections of naval ships to evaluate their material and operational readiness.

boat

A small craft usually capable of being hoisted aboard a ship. Submarines have traditionally been called boats, but this term of affection is clearly no longer appropriate.

boat ahoy

Used to hail a boat; one of the boat hails.

boat anchor

A very light anchor with extra large flukes for use in small boats. Generally small and light enough to be handled by hand and stowed in the bottom of the boat or in a locker. Part of the necessary equipment of every boat.

boat boom

A spar swung out from a ship's side from which boats can be hauled out or made fast. Also called a boat spar or riding boom. Permits boats to ride safely alongside a ship while at anchor.

boat box

First-aid kit for use in a boat.

boat call

Flag signal used to establish communication with a boat. *Recall* is a signal used to direct boats to return.

boat chock

A strong deck fitting that supports one end of a boat that is resting on deck. See *saddle*.

boat cloak

Officer's cloak; now an optional article of uniform

boat deck
Partial deck above the main deck, usually fitted with boat davits or cranes. See *deck.*

boat falls
The lines used in hoisting or lowering a boat.

boat gong
Signal used to indicate departure of officer's boats and the arrival or departure of various officers.

boat hails
Ships at anchor hail approaching boats at night with *"Boat ahoy."* Responses depend on passengers; e.g., if commanding officer, response is the name of his ship; if a commissioned officer, response is *"Aye, aye;"* if an enlisted man, it is *"Hello,"* etc.

boat hook
Wooden staff with combined hook and pushing surface usually made of brass to reduce danger of sparks, employed to engage rings, lines, or buoys from the deck of a small craft, or to push away from any object on the surface.

boat oars
Command given to the crew of a pulling boat, directing them to lay oars inside the boat alongside the gunwales, blades pointed forward. See *oars, point oars, toss oars, in bows.*

boat painter
Line attached to the bow or stern of a boat, used to tow it or to secure it. Not to be confused with the sea-painter, which is a much longer line used exclusively for towing alongside; hence, must be on the near bow but never on the stem.

boat plug
Threaded drain plug fitting in the bilge of a boat.

boat pool
Group of boats available for general use at a harbor, port, or base.

boat skids
Deck fittings designed to hold and support a boat.

boat sling
Rope or chain for hoisting or lowering large size boats with a single davit or crane.

boat station
Allotted place of each person when a boat is being lowered.

boatswain
Pronounced "BO-sun." A warrant officer whose major duties are related to deck and boat seamanship.

boatswain's call
A rudimentary tune played on a boatswain's pipe announcing or calling for some standard evolution such as meals for the crew, piping the side, lower away, etc. It can refer to the boatswain's pipe. See *pipe down.*

boatswain's chair
Seat sent aloft or over the side on a line to facilitate repairs or painting.

boatswain's locker
Compartment where deck gear is stowed.

boatswain's mate (BM)
Petty officer or seaman identified as a striker who supervises the deck force in seamanship duties. See *Appendix B.*

boatswain's pipe
Whistle used to call attention before passing the word, to render honors, piping the side, and to give orders to winchmen, crane operators, etc. A call is the notes played on the pipe, but sometimes the pipe itself is referred to as a boatswain's call.

Boehme equipment
An automatic code-sending and code-receiving device.

bogey
Unidentified aircraft. Also used to describe image on a radarscope.

Bogie wire (cable)
Wire that pulls a bogie car, holding mine, along a track of minelayers.

boiler
Metal chamber in which steam is generated. Consists of components such as a firebox or furnace, tubes, steam drum, etc. according to type and design.

boiler central control station
Centrally located station in a multi-fireroom ship for directing the control of all boilers and boiler operating stations.

boiler emergency station
Station for a chief water tender from which he can quickly reach any fireroom, boiler room, or boiler operating station.

boiler full-power capacity
Total quantity of steam in pounds per hour at the contract-specified pressure and temperature that the boiler can produce.

boiler operating station
Location from which boilers are operated.

boiler pick
See *chipping hammer.*

boiler room
Compartment containing boilers.

boiler technician (BT)
A petty officer who operates and maintains boilers and fireroom equipment. Combines two older rates, boilermaker and boilerman. See *Appendix B*.

bollard
Steel or iron post on a dock, pier, or wharf, used in securing a ship's lines. See *bitts, cleat, dolphin*.

bolo line
A nylon line with a padded lead weight or a weighted *monkey fist*, thrown from ship to ship or from ship to pier in underway replenishments and mooring.

bolt rope
Line sewn around the edge to strengthen a sail, tarpaulin, or awning.

bolter
A jet aircraft attempting to land on a carrier which misses the arresting gear and takes off again for another try. With jets, power is applied just before touch-down and is not cut until the tailhook has engaged the arresting gear. With the clear angle deck ahead, missing the gear no longer means hitting a barrier which, at jet speeds, might as well be called a crash. An automatic dividend of the angled deck is practice landings with the arresting gear secured, also called *bolters*. See *barricade* for comparison with earlier landing procedure for propeller-driven planes.

bomb
Explosive dropped from an aircraft other than a guided missile, torpedo, or mine.

bomb farm
Slang for topside stockpile of bombs used for rearming carrier aircraft.

bombing, types of
Glide bombing: attack at angles of 30-55 degrees without brakes or flaps. *Dive bombing*: high angle attack (60-70 degrees) using dive brakes. *Masthead* or *ski bombing*: level flight or shallow glide (under 30 degrees). *Horizontal bombing*: attack from steady, level flight at high or medium altitude.

Booklet of General Plans
Set of ship's plans including the list of a ship's dimensions.

boom
A horizontal spar, hinged at the forward end to a mast a few feet above the deck, to which the foot of a fore-and-aft sail would be *bent*. With the sail removed and a suitable topping lift attached, the boom could be used as a lifting device, or derrick, and from this has developed the cargo booms seen commonly on cargo ships. *Boat booms* are hinged to a ship's side and are rigged out for securing a ship's boats when the ship is moored or anchored.

boondocks
The "sticks"; a long way from the center of action. *Boondockers*: slang for field boots or work shoes.

boost
To supply an aircraft engine with more air or a mixture of fuel and air. As a noun, it refers to manifold pressure.

boot
Slang for recruit. A newly enlisted Marine or sailor.

boot-topping (paint)
Special paint applied to waterline area; both anticorrosive and antifouling. Generally also applied on hatch coamings where foot scuff marks are likely as well. Usually black.

bore
The abrupt front of churning water, waves, or series of waves produced as a rising tide proceeds upstream. Also, the interior of a gun barrel, from the after end of the rifling to muzzle.

bore sight
To align the axis of a gun with its sights. In slang use, to *bore-sight* an object or to *bore-sight* on it is to prepare to give it a quick, accurate attack.

bottom blow (valve)
Valve at the bottom of the boiler (water drum) for blowing out the sediment.

bottom bounce
Technique that employs sonar impulses reflected off the ocean bottom for the location of targets.

bottom contour chart
See *bathymetric chart.*

bottom reverberation
Reverberation of sound from the sea bottom.

bottom sediments
Materials of varying size and origin that remain unconsolidated on the sea bottom.

bounce field
Slang for simulated carrier deck ashore.

bouncer line
In night underwater demolition team (UDT) operations, the point off the enemy beach at which rubber boats are launched.

boundary layer
Any object moving in water drags along adjacent to its surface a relatively thin layer of water called a boundary layer. Movement in other liquids results in the same phenomenon with the thickness of the boundary layer being dependent on the viscosity of the fluid.

bourrelet
The forward bearing surface of a projectile, machined in a band around its body to provide support for the projectile in the bore. See *rotating band.*

bow
The front or forward part of a ship. Sometimes referred to as *bows,* since every ship has a starboard and a port bow.

bow door
See *ramp.*

bower anchor
Generally, an anchor carried on a ship's bows. When ships began to be built of steel and became much greater in size, it became customary to carry the sheet anchor on the bow instead of in the waist. The steel construction made the bow strong enough to hold this additional weight. In the new position, the sheet anchor came to be called the "best bower" or simply "the bower," to distinguish it from the port or starboard anchors. Some U.S. battleships and aircraft carriers built between the two world wars had a pronounced clipper bow with an anchor right in the stem which, though the same size as the others, became known as the bower.

bow hook
Member of a boat's crew who mans the boathook forward and who handles lines. See also *stern hook.*

bow insignia
Stars, pennants, or arrows displayed on bow of boat assigned to an officer for his regular use.

bowline
A classic knot that forms a loop that will not slip nor become tighter under tension.

bow number
Hull number of a ship, painted on the bow (or on the sail of a submarine). Since the type of ship is generally evident, the number gives positive identification.

bow painter
A line attached to the stem of a boat. See *stern fast, sea painter, boat painter.*

bowsprit
A built-in spar projecting forward and slightly up from the bow of a sailing vessel. It extends the head sails and helps support the mast(s) through headstays.

bowser boat
Boat used to refuel boats, aircraft, or vehicles.

box
In convoy operations, the three rear stations in the commodore's column and in the columns adjacent on either side are left vacant for air operations when a carrier is stationed in the convoy. This vacant space is known as the box.

box the compass
To name all points of a compass in succession.

BPA
Blanket purchase agreement

brace
See *main brace.*

bracket
A succession of two salvos: one over and one short or one left and one right of the target. Thus the target has been bracketed, and a correction approximately half the previous one, in the opposite direction, should produce a straddle.

brackish water
Slightly salty water; specifically, water with a salinity roughly between 0.5 and 17 parts per thousand.

brash ice
Small fragments of sea or river ice with a diameter of less than six feet.

brassard
Arm band, e.g., shore patrol brassard.

brass hat
Slang for an officer in rank of commander or above. Refers to gold cap visor. Originally this was a term of mild disrespect, but this inference is now obsolete.

Bravo
Phonetic word for the letter *B.*

bravo pattern:
The sound-range pattern obtained by bathythermograph reading in water less than 100 fathoms deep. The term means bottom effect.

bread and water
Reduced rations authorized with confinement as punishment. Slang: cake and wine.

break
To unfurl a flag with a quick motion. In ship construction, an abrupt change in the fore and aft contour of a ship's main deck, e.g., the *break of the deck.* See *broken deck.*

breakbulk cargo
General cargo handled item by item as distinct from containerized cargo

breakdown lights
Two vertical red lights on foremast that denote *"Not under command."* Also, if pulsating, they denote *"Man overboard."*

breaker
A small container for stowing drinking water carried by boats or rafts. A wave that breaks into foam against the shore.

breaker height
Vertical distance from crest of a breaker to preceding trough.

breaker, plunging
A surf wave that builds up rapidly and then crashes forward violently, indicating a rapidly shoaling bottom.

breaker, spilling
A surf wave that breaks gradually with the top spilling over forward with little violence, indicating a gradually shoaling bottom.

break ground
Come loose from the bottom, as an anchor does when it is hoisted.

break-off position
Position at which a unit or units of a convoy break off in order to proceed to a terminal port different from that of the main convoy.

break out
Take out of stock or storage. To prepare for use.

breakwater
Structure that shelters a port or anchorage from the sea. Also, a low bulkhead forward that prevents solid water from sweeping the deck of a ship.

breasting float
See *camel.*

breast line
A mooring line from ship to pier, perpendicular to the fore-and-aft axis of the ship. See *forward bow (quarter) spring* and *after bow (quarter) spring.*

breast out
To maneuver a ship or boat broadside away from another ship or pier of which she has previously been alongside. A variant, *breast off,* is sometimes used to mean fend off.

breech
Opposite end from the muzzle of a gun; where rounds are inserted for firing. Generally refers to large guns.

breech block
Device that closes the firing chamber of a large gun after loading. In small arms, the same device is called the bolt.

breeches buoy
A device for transferring personnel between ships via highline, or from a stranded ship to the shore. Derived from the early design: a life buoy fitted with a strong canvas bottom with leg holes. Thus, if the buoy fell into the water, the passenger would be automatically provided with flotation gear.

breech mechanism
Device for closing the breech of a gun; the moving parts which insert the breech block (or plug) and lock or unlock it.

breeze
General term for winds: 22-27 knots (strong); 17-21 knots (fresh); 11-16 knots (moderate); 7-10 knots (gentle); 4-6 knots (light).

BRICK-BAT
Urgency designator established by JCS to show the relative priority between end-products destined for DOD. BRICK-BAT has higher priority than CUE-CAP.

bridge
Ship's structure, topside and usually forward, which contains control and visual communication stations. Sailing ships were conned from the main deck aft, abaft the after-most mast. The huge paddle wheel boxes of early steamers so interfered with vision that underway OODs stood their watches on the cross-over bridge built between them. The bridge has been the underway conning station ever since, except in submerged submarines.

bridge deck
On merchant-type ships, a partial deck above main deck, usually amidships.

bridge gauge
A machinery tool or instrument used to determine the drop of a journal in any type of sleeve bearing which is made in halves. It bridges between the two sides of the lower bearing half, thus the term.

bridle
A span of rope, chain, or wire with both ends secured and the strain taken on the midpart, as in towing a ship or pulling an aircraft on a catapult.

brief
To instruct people for a specific mission or operation. *Debriefing* means a verbal report after the operation has been completed.

briefing
Conference or meeting held to give instruction or provide details on a specific operation.

brig
A place of confinement. A prison. A type of small, fast, sailing vessel popular 150 years ago. A two-masted, square-rigged sailing ship.

brigantine
Sailing vessel with two masts, the foremast square-rigged and the mainmast fore-and-aft rigged. Same as a hermaphrodite brig, except that a square topsail might be carried on the mainmast, well above the normal position for a topsail.

brightwork
Unpainted and uncovered metal, generally brass or chromium, which is kept bright by polishing.

bring home
To move a piece of gear to its proper or stowed position, as, a boom being rigged in is *brought home.*

broach
To be thrown broadside to a surf or heavy sea. To break surface partially, either deliberately or accidentally, as with a submarine, but not come fully to the surface.

broadcast
Originally a naval term meaning to transmit radio messages to the fleet.

broad command pennant
Blue and white pennant flown by an officer—not a flag officer—who commands a major unit of ships or aircraft. See *burgee command pennant.*

broad on the port (starboard) bow
Said of something having a relative bearing midway between the beam and dead ahead, on the port (starboard) side.

broad on the port (starboard) quarter
Bearing midway between the beam and the stern, on the port (starboard) side.

broadside
Simultaneous firing of all main battery guns on one side of a warship. In the British navy, half the guns are fired in alternate salvos at half the interval.

broken deck
A weather deck of a ship that is not continuous from bow to stern. Thus a ship with a raised forecastle would have a broken deck. Different classes of destroyers are frequently referred to as *broken deckers* or *flush deckers.* See *break.*

broken stowage
Wasted space in a ship's hold. Small packages are used to fill such hold space.

broken water
An area of small waves and eddies in otherwise calm water.

brow
Portable wooden bridge or ramp between the ship and a wharf, pier, or dock. Usually fitted with wheels at the shore end. Also, gangplank.

brown bagger
Slang for a married man; one who carries his lunch to work.

brown shoe
Slang for aviation or submarine officers. The brown shoe officer is entitled to extra hazardous duty pay for flight or submarine duty. The term originally referred to uniforms; before WWII, only aviators and submariners wore khakis and "greens" and the brown shoes that went with them. See *black shoe*.

bryozoans
Minute animals that usually form into plantlike colonies and attach themselves to submerged objects.

B-scope
Cathode ray indicator that presents a plot of target range versus bearing.

bubble pulse
Echo caused by collapse of the bubble following an underwater explosion.

bubble sextant (octant)
Sextant (octant) that determines the horizontal plane by a bubble instead of the horizon. Less accurate than a regular sextant; hence, it is used only in aircraft or when the horizon is otherwise not usable.

buccaneer
A pirate. The term was first given to early Frenchmen in Haiti. The word *boucan* was of Caribbean origin, meaning a dealer in smoked or dried meats. In the Caribbean area, hunters placed meat to dry on wooden lattice work known as boucans. Some *boucanners* took to privateering and general lawlessness, and ultimately buccaneer became a synonym for pirate.

buck
Small object placed on the wardroom table to mark the place of the officer who is to be served first.

bucket of steam
Nonexistent item, often requested of new men aboard ship.

buckled
Bent or distorted; misshapen.

buckler
Flexible cover attached externally to a turret's front armor plate so that the guns are free to train or elevate, yet water cannot enter the gunport. Slang: bloomer. Also, the metal plate over a hawse hole to keep water from squirting on deck through it when the ship plunges into a sea. In general, any device used for a similar purpose anywhere

bug
Synonymous with speed key in transmitting by Morse code.

bugle
A horn with limited notes, all controlled by the player's lips, used for military purposes to broadcast a general order to all hands within hearing range, such as Taps, Reveille, Retreat, Liberty Call, Torpedo Defense, General Quarters. The first bugle calls were supposedly written by Joseph Hayden, the celebrated musician, in about 1793, but of course the bugle has been used for military purposes since antiquity. The first bugles were made from the horns of wild oxen. The Horn of Roland was one of these.

builder's trials
Trials conducted at sea or at a dock by the builder to prove the readiness of a ship for preliminary acceptance trials.

build-up
The reinforcement and maintenance of an expeditionary force or of a base.

bulkhead
Walls or partitions within a ship, generally referring to those with structural functions such as strength or water-tightness. Light partitions are sometimes called partition bulkheads.

bulkheading
Slang for complaining or grumbling with the intention of being overheard by seniors.

bull gear
Part of a main engine reduction gear. Specifically, the largest, slowest-turning gear in the gear train.

bull horn
High-powered, directional, electric megaphone.

bullnose
Closed chock at the bow of a vessel. Has the appearance of a large flared nostril.

bull rope (line)
The line taking the greatest weight in cargo handling or supporting a topping lift. *Bull chain* if chain is used. In general, the biggest rope or device in a group with a similar purpose is referred to as the *bull* device or thing.

BULLSEYE
Tactical communications system.

bulwark
Section of ship's side continued above the main deck as a protection against heavy weather.

bumblebee
Noise-making device for sweeping acoustic mines. See *foxer gear*.

bumboat
A civilian boat selling supplies, provisions, and other articles to the crews of ships. Supposedly derived from "boomboat" signifying a boat permitted to lie at the ships' booms. Bumboats and bumboatsmen had a bad reputation because they frequently were the source of a great deal of trouble among a ship's crew.

bumwad
Slang for a newspaper or magazine. Also, toilet paper.

bungee
Securing line for the control stick of an airplane; part of the parking harness used when the airplane is on deck.

bunk
Bed.

bunk bottom
Canvas laced to bunk frame, used instead of springs to support a mattress.

bunk covers
Flamepoof covers for bedding aboard ship.

bunker
Compartment or tank used for stowing fuel.

bunting
Cloth from which signal flags are made. Also, the flags themselves, as in the order *air bunting*.

buoy
Floating object, anchored to the bottom, indicating a position on the water, an obstruction or shallow area, or to provide a mooring for a ship. Buoys may be of various shapes and types, with special markings. Many are lighted, with their characteristics shown on harbor charts, and some have a whistle or bell actuated by wave action. See *can, nun, spar, mooring, dan buoys*.

buoy tender
Vessel designed for and engaged in servicing aids to navigation, especially buoys.

burdened vessel
The vessel required to take action to avoid collision under the *Rules of the Road*. The other vessel is the privileged vessel, which must maintain its course and speed. See *general prudential rule*.

bureau
Major organizational unit of the Navy Department, established by law. Most now replaced by systems commands.

Bureau of Medicine and Surgery (BUMED)
Generally responsible for medical and dental care of Navy, Marine Corps, dependents, and retired personnel; for training of medical personnel, operation of naval hospitals.

Bureau of Naval Personnel (BUPERS)
Generally concerned with the procurement, training, promotion, assignment, and discipline of officers and enlisted personnel of the Navy.

Bureau of Naval Weapons (BUWEPS)
Dissolved in May 1966. Was responsible for design, development, procurement, production, testing, fitting out, maintenance, alteration, and repair of all Navy weapons and aircraft. BUWEPS was replaced by the Naval Air Systems Command and the Naval Ordnance Systems Command.

Bureau of Navigation (BUNAV)
Name changed to Bureau of Naval Personnel (BUPERS) in 1942.

Bureau of Ships (BUSHIPS)
Was responsible for design, procurement, and maintenance of all types of ships for the Navy and other military services. It was replaced in May 1966 by the Naval Electronics Systems Command and the Naval Ships Systems Command.

Bureau of Supplies and Accounts (BUSANDA)
Dissolved in May 1966. Was responsible for supervision of procurement, warehousing, transportation, and issuance of Navy supplies and materials (except ammunition) and for the supervision of food-service installations ashore and afloat. It was replaced by the Naval Supply Systems Command.

Bureau of Yards and Docks (BUDOCKS)
Was responsible for design, construction, and maintenance of shore facilities of the Navy, real estate management; and procurement and maintenance of railroad equipment, heavy lifting gear, automotive equipment. Duties in general were assumed in May 1966 by the Naval Facilities Engineering Command.

Bureau Planned Procurement Guide
Publication by the former BuWeps listing planned procurements.

burgee
A swallow-tailed pennant. See *broad command pennant.*

burgee command pennant
Red and white or blue and white burgee flown by an officer who commands a division or squadron of ships, such as submarines or destroyers. Such an officer has the courtesy title of commodore while so serving. If he held the rank of commodore, he would be a flag officer and would fly a blue flag with a single white star.

burn bag or basket
Receptacle for classified matter that is to be destroyed.

burnout
Point in time or in the missile trajectory when combustion of fuels in the rocket engine is terminated by other than programmed cutoff.

burton
Small tackle formed by two single-sheave blocks with a hook block in the bight of the running part. Generally used for setting up or tightening rigging, for shifting weights on board, etc. For transferring supplies during replenishment at sea, a burton rig might be set up between ships, in which case the gear used might be quite heavy.

bury
To hide or conceal certain words or phrases in the text of a message.

bushing
Metal liners serving as a bearing for a shaft.

bust
Slang meaning to reduce in rate. Also, to fail or make a mistake.

butt bucket, butt kit
Slang for ash tray.

butts
That part of a rifle range where targets are tended.

butterworth
Method of cleaning and gas-freeing oil tanks by use of seawater under pressure.

by-pass
To divert the flow of gas or liquid. Also, the line that diverts the flow.

by the board
Overboard, as to go by the board.

by the head
Ship's attitude with a greater draft forward than aft. *Down by the head.*

by the stern
Opposite of *by the head.*

by the wind
See *full and bye.*

C

cabin
Quarters aboard ship for the captain or an admiral.

cable
Any heavy wire or rope such as towing cable or degaussing cable. A unit of length, 120 fathoms or 720 feet. (100 fathoms in the British navy: 600 feet, approximately one tenth of a nautical mile.) See *mariners' measurements*.

cable jack
Device for lifting an anchor chain off the deck to insert a slip hook. Sometimes shortened to jack.

cable-laid rope
Three or four plain-laid, three-stranded ropes twisted in a direction opposite to the twists in each rope; used for ropes much exposed to water.

cable markings
Turns of wire and stripes of paint on anchor-chain links to show scope of chain out.

caduceus
Symbol of Medical Corps, a staff entwined by two snakes, topped by a pair of wings.

caisson
Any temporary structure of wood or metal built to hold back water for repairs or construction. Also, the floating gate of a drydock.

cake and wine
Slang for bread and water (as punishment).

caliber
Diameter of a gun's bore measured in inches: 3-in./50 gun is 3 inches in bore diameter. The barrel length is three times 50 or 150 inches long. A .50-caliber machine gun is one whose bore is half an inch or 0.50 caliber.

call
Formal social visit by an officer and his wife to the home of another. It involves leaving calling cards and was once rigidly prescribed and carefully followed, including return calls. Now a call is largely passé as a custom, although large stations may have an annual party with the understanding that it also constitutes "all calls made and returned." An informal visit of courtesy to another ship just arrived. Made by an officer junior to the commander of the arriving unit and the visiting unit, and requires no special ceremonies, other than piping the side. See *official visit, boarding call*. If made by a principal, the call is termed an official call or official visit. Also, a tune played on a boatswain's pipe, calling for certain prescribed evolutions.

call away
To order a ship's boat or vehicle manned and made ready for a trip.

call book
See *morning callbook*.

call sign (communications)
A group of letters and/or numerals that identifies a station, command, or activity.

calving
The breaking away of ice from a berg, a glacier, or from shelf ice.

camber
Convex curvature athwartships of the deck of a ship.

camel
Float used as a fender between two ships or a ship and a pier. Also called breasting float.

Canada balsam
Optical cement, used in binoculars, periscopes, etc.

can buoy
Cylindrical, flat-topped metal buoy.

can-do
Slang for efficient, capable and willing, e.g., a repair ship might be praised as a can-do ship.

canister
A large number of bullets, or balls, similar to grape, made up in a can of the proper diameter to fit the bore of the gun for which it is designed. The can would burst when the gun was fired, resulting in a shotgun effect. An antipersonnel weapon. The same as grape, except that the canister was more easily loaded, gave a more uniform load and, because it fit the bore of the gun better, gave more accuracy. In historical accounts of 17th, 18th, and early 19th century action, the phrase *grape and canister* is frequently encountered. See also *langrage, dismantling shot*, and *double-shot*.

cannibalize
To remove serviceable parts from one item of equipment for use in another.

canopy
Canvas or metal cover fitted over part of a boat. Also a plexiglass covering over an aircraft cockpit.

canopy, parachute
Main supporting surface of a parachute.

cant
The inclination of an object from the perpendicular.

cap
The proper term for the top of a mast except for the highest mast where it is called a truck.

capillary waves
Small waves, less than about 0.5 centimeters in length, with rounded crests and v-shaped troughs whose characteristics are a function of surface tension.

capsize
To turn over; to upset.

capstan
The rotating mechanism that actually raises the anchor or other heavy weight. In sailing days it was turned by wooden bars inserted into the capstan head itself, thus giving it a characteristic look. Small ships built in the 1920s still used capstan bars as a standby in case of failure of the anchor engine. Development of engines to do this heavy work resulted in various other power take-offs for lesser jobs involving heaving in lines, called gipsy or warping heads. The term *niggerhead,* once also used in this context, has been abandoned by general consent. If the mechanism has no connection with the anchor it is called a winch. See *windlass.*

captain
Commanding officer of any naval unit or activity. The next rank above commander. Equivalent to colonel.

captain of the head
Man responsible for cleaning washrooms and toilets. Known to Marines as the head orderly.

captain of the port
The Coast Guard officer responsible for port security.

Captor
Deep water mine involving an encapsulated torpedo. The torpedo homes in on the source that activates the release mechanism.

cardinal point
One of the four principal points of the compass—north, east, south, and west.

caretaker status
Condition in which a non-operational activity, such as an air station, is preserved and guarded.

cargo
Material carried in ships or aircraft. Classified as dry, bulk, general, heavy lift, deck, dangerous, liquid, refrigerated, etc. May be palletized, breakbulk, or containerized.

CARGO
Consolidated Afloat Requisitioning Guide Overseas.

cargo classification
The division of military cargo for combat loading.

cargo cluster
Cluster of lamps used for lighting when working cargo at night.

cargo documentation
Papers required for a ship to enter or leave a port, including manifest, crew list, stores list, bills of lading, tonnage certificates, and other marine certificates as required.

cargo net
Square net of heavy line used to lift cargo in loading or unloading operations. Also used for quick embarkation and debarkation of personnel in amphibious operations. See *debarkation net*.

cargo papers
Documents to assist in cargo handling, including bills of lading, manifests, stowage plans, and hatch lists.

cargo plan
Plan showing the capacity of each of a ship's holds.

cargo port
Opening in a vessel's side through which cargo can be loaded.

cargo whip
Rope or chain used with a derrick and winch for handling cargo. One end has a heavy hook; the other end is rove through the derrick and taken to the winch. Also called cargo hoist, cargo rope.

carling
Short fore-and-aft timber or girder placed under a deck to stiffen it; for example, under mooring bitts, winches, masts, etc.

carpenter stopper
Holding and quick-release device for wire rope.

carriage
That part of a gun mount which supports the gun itself.

carrick bend
Most usually seen as a double carrick bend, a much-used knot for bending two lines or hawsers together.

carrier
Aircraft carrier. Also any unit of men and equipment that operates ships for ocean transport. By general use the term is now extended to include transporters of freight on land as well.

carrier controlled approach (CCA)
Landing approach to an aircraft carrier during which the pilot is guided in speed, heading, and altitude by a controller aboard the carrier.

carrier onboard delivery (COD)
System of delivering support items and mail from shore to aircraft carrier underway.

carrier qualification (CARQUAL)
Qualified to land aboard aircraft carriers.

carrier task force
Aircraft carriers and supporting AAW and ASW escorts.

carrier wave (CW)
Radio transmission in code, in contrast to voice. See *bug, speed key.*

carry away
Tear or break loose; break; part; wash away. To break a spar or part a piece of rigging.

carry on
An order to resume or continue previous activity, usually after men have come to attention.

carry rudder
To require constant right or left rudder in order to maintain course.

case depth
The vertical distance from the surface of the water to a planted mine case.

CASREP (casualty report)
A routine report of any material breakdown, in standard format. Necessary to permit accumulation of service experience leading to redesign, or improved operating procedures.

cast
Act of heaving the lead into the sea to determine depth of water; to direct the ship's bow in one direction or another when getting underway.

castaway
A man from a wrecked ship. Generally, but not exclusively, refers to a survivor in a primitive area.

cast loose
To let go a line or lines.

cast off
Order given to let go or throw off mooring lines. See *take in.*

casualty board
A visual display of ship's compartment and systems. Used by damage control personnel.

casualty control book, engineering
Maintained by ships to assist in control of engineering damage. Contains machinery readiness bills and examples of casualties and how to correct or repair them.

casualty report (CASREP)
Report required when casualties of a specified nature occur either to personnel or material. See *CASREP.*

cat (an anchor)
To hang an old-fashioned anchor from the cathead with the catfall to its ring, either by hoisting it from the in-sight condition when weighing anchor, or by swinging it from its at-sea stowage with the cat-davit. In preparation for anchoring, the catfall was replaced by an expendable line which was cut on the order, *"let go!"* See *cat and fish, cockbill.*

cat and fish (an anchor)
To cat the anchor, first, and then to fish for the pad eye at the balance point, hook on the cat-davit tackle, and swing the anchor into its stowed position. In iron ships, the anchors were stowed on billboards from which they could be dropped directly without first being catted, and the cathead was eliminated entirely. In hoisting it was then necessary to fish directly for the balance point pad eye without first catting the anchor, made possible by greater strength of the iron bow structure, which permitted hoisting the anchor clear of the water without catting it.

catapult
A device for launching aircraft from a ship's deck at flying speed.

cat-davit
A specially designed small davit on the forecastle used for swinging an old-fashioned anchor to its stowed position. In wooden sailing ships it was also used for swinging the anchor from the at-sea stowage to the cathead in preparation for dropping. Usually in pairs, one on each bow. In iron and steel ships, in which the catheads were eliminated, the cat-davits had to have an extremely long overhanging reach, leading to unusual but effective tripod designs. See *cat and fish.*

catenary
The dip in a length of chain or cable because of its own weight. The catenary provides spring or elastic effect in towing, anchoring, or in securing to a buoy.

catfall
Part of the anchor gear. A small tackle used to hoist an old-fashioned anchor from the water to the cathead on weighing anchor.

cathead
A strong piece of oak projecting over the bows (one on either side) of a vessel, usually with the face of a cat carved on its end. (The reason for this is unknown; perhaps it came after the term, instead of being its genesis). Preparing an anchor for sea, or for dropping, involved hanging it a-cockbill to the cathead. The anchor could be let go from this position, or fished and stowed for sea. The cat-davit was used to swing the anchor

between the at-sea stowage and the cathead. When the billboard was introduced, with iron ships, catting and the cathead became unnecessary, but the cat-davit was retained to fish the anchor and lay it on the billboard. "Cat and fish" might at this point have given way to "fish and cat," but old sailors being what they were, this did not happen.

cat-o'-nine-tails
A short piece of rope fashioned into an instrument for flogging. Traditionally the victim who was to be punished was required to make his own "cat" by unlaying a portion of a three-strand line, separating each of the strands into three parts, then tarring and braiding the parts into nine "tails." Through tradition and pride the cat was often made as fearsome as the maker could, by knotting the tails and even including small nails or other metal objects in the knots. A poorly made or soft cat was considered a mark of the craven, and in any case, if it did not pass muster, it would be replaced by one that did. See *room to swing a cat*.

cat's paw
A light puff of wind. See *flaw*.

catwalk
A walkway constructed over or around obstructions on a ship for convenience of the crew.

caulking, calking
Burring or driving up the edges of iron or steel plates along riveted seams to make them watertight; forcing a quantity of oakum (caulking material) into the wooden seams of a ship's deck or sides to make them watertight. Pronounced "kawking."

caulk-off
Slang meaning to take a nap; to doze. Also to "cork off."

cavitation
Disturbance around revolving propeller blades, struts, etc., caused by collapse of transient-pressure disturbances resulting from flow of water over their surfaces.

CBR defense
Chemical, biological, and radiological defense.

ceiling
The minimum height above the ground at which all clouds, at and below that height, cover more than half the sky. Also, a lining inside the hull of a ship to keep cargo off the side plating.

ceilometer
Instrument for measuring cloud ceiling.

celestial equator
A great circle on the celestial sphere everywhere 90 degrees from the celestial poles. The plane of the equator extended to the celestial sphere.

celestial meridian
A great circle on the celestial sphere passing through the north and south celestial poles.

celestial navigation
Determining position by observation of celestial bodies.

celestial sphere
An imaginary sphere of infinite radius concentric with the earth on which all celestial bodies, except the earth, are imagined to be projected.

centerline
An imaginary line down the middle of the ship from bow to stern.

center of buoyancy
The geometric center of gravity of the volume of a ship's displacement taken so that in computations for metacentric height the entire buoyant effect of the sea on the hull floating in it may be considered as being applied at this single point. Used in combination with center of gravity to calculate location of metacenter.

center of gravity
Point in a ship where the sum of all moments of weight is zero. With the ship at rest the center of gravity and the center of buoyancy are always in a direct vertical line. For surface ships center of buoyancy is usually below center of gravity, and the ship is prevented from capsizing by the additional displacement on the low side during a roll. Thus the point at which the deck edge enters the water is critical because from here onward increased roll will not produce corresponding increased righting force. In a submerged submarine, center of buoyancy of the submerged hull is always above the center of gravity and the ship remains upright because of the pendulum effect, which is equally important fore and aft as it is athwartships.

certificate of registry
See *registry*.

chad tape
A five-unit code tape used in teletypewriter operation with perforations not completely severed.

chaff
General name for radar confusion reflectors. Includes rope, a long roll of magnetic foil or wire for broad, low-frequency response; and rope-chaff which contains one or more rope elements.

chafing gear
Material used to prevent chafing or wearing of sails, line, etc.

chain grab
See *windlass*.

chain hook
Hand tool for handling anchor chain.

chain locker
Compartment where anchor chain is stowed.

chain of command
The succession of people through which command is exercised.

chain pipe
Heavy steel pipe to lead the anchor chain through the deck to the chain locker.

chains
The platform or position in the bows from which the leadsman heaves the lead. In the sailing navy, the masts were braced by standing rigging, much of which was secured to platforms jutting out from the sides of the ship, outboard of her bulwarks. To prevent the pull of the rigging from snapping off the platforms, short sections of chain were led from their outboard edges to points lower on the side of the ship. Leadsmen customarily used these platforms to stand upon when heaving the lead, and hence their nautical designation, *the chains*, has persisted.

chain stopper
Short length of chain fitted with a pelican hook secured to an eyebolt on the forecastle; used for quickly releasing anchor and chain upon anchoring and for securing anchor and chain, in the hoisted (housed) position. Also secures the chain after anchoring when the proper scope is out. See *stopper*.

chalk test
A test of the tightness of a watertight fitting by rubbing chalk on the knife edge. The resultant imprint on the gasket indicates whether or not the knife edge is bearing against the gasket.

challenge
A demand for identification or authentification. Can be as simple as the flashing light *AA* signal which internationally requires the recipient to respond with name and destination (warships need only identify themselves). May be a coded signal, transmitted by any of a number of means which must be properly replied to, such as in *IFF*.

chamber
The enlarged rear interior of a gun which holds the explosive charge.

chandelle
An abrupt climbing turn to nearly a stall in which the momentum of the airplane is used to obtain a steeper climb than its power plant can normally deliver.

change order
Written order directing a contractor to make changes in a contract.

channel
The frequencies within which a radio transmitter must maintain its modulated carrier signal. Also, the deeper or marked portion of a harbor or waterway through which ship traffic is directed.

channel conditioning
Surveying of areas normally traveled by shipping to detect and locate minelike objects. The purpose is to locate, avoid, and clear enemy minefields and other explosive weapons.

chantey, chanty
A sailor's song of simple lyrics and tune. Pronounced "shanty." Traditionally sung by men walking the capstan around, and became something of a ceremony if they were heaving in the anchor to get underway. If the ship was lucky enough to have a fiddler on board he might perch on top of the capstan, sawing away on his violin as his shipmates did their best to make him dizzy.

chaplain
Minister, rabbi, or priest of a recognized religious order, commissioned in the Navy. Slang: sky pilot.

Charlie
Phonetic word for letter *C*.

Charlie Noble
Sailors' nautical name for the galley smokepipe. Derived from the British merchant service captain, Charlie Noble, who required a high polish on the galley funnel of his ship. His funnel was of copper and its brightness became known in all ports his ship visited.

chart
Map. Hydrographic chart shows depths of water, nature of bottom, and aids to navigation. Aeronautical chart shows terrain features and other information for air operations.

chart, bathymetric
Chart showing depth of water by labeled contour lines.

chart correction card
Record of *Notice to Mariners* changes for a particular chart.

chart datum
The plane to which soundings on a chart are referred, in the U.S. usually *mean low water* or *mean lower low water*. Navigators in shallow water must always check their charts for this. Datum is always specified on harbor charts.

charter party
The formal, written agreement under which a vessel is leased (chartered).

charthouse or chartroom
Compartment on or near the bridge for handling and stowage of navigational equipment. Usually contains a chart table and stowage for charts.

chart, sonar
Chart containing oceanographic data useful in echo ranging under water.

chase
The sloping part of the outside of a gun between the muzzle and the slide.

chaser
In sailing days of broadside fire, a gun so placed that it could fire ahead (bow chaser) or astern (stern chaser), and thus used for pursuit or when pursued. Also modern slang for sentry or guard, i.e., *brig chaser*.

check
To keep a strain on a line but to ease it out to prevent parting. See *snub*, *hold*.

checkman
Man in fireroom who controls water level in boilers. See *watertender*.

check valve
One that emits a flow of liquid in one direction only.

chemical alarm
Distinctive signal used only on board ship to warn of impending gas or atomic attack.

cherry picker
Wheeled crane to handle crashed planes on aircraft carrier flight deck (slang). See *crash dolly, Karry Krane*.

chevron
V-shaped mark that denotes rate, located beneath the specialty mark or a rating badge.

chicken guts
Slang for aiguilettes. Also called loafer's loops.

Chief of Naval Operations (CNO)
The senior active duty officer in the Navy.

chief of staff
The captain or admiral who assists an admiral, as his second in command, especially in supervising his staff. The senior assistant to a commodore or below is a chief staff officer.

chief of the boat or **chief of the ship**

Senior chief petty officer in a submarine; the executive officer's righthand man in the administration of the crew.

chief petty officer (CPO)

An enlisted man in paygrade E-7. Until 1958, this was the highest rank attainable by an enlisted man while still in the enlisted category. For further promotion he had to look to the warrant grade. Now, however, two superior grades have been established: senior chief petty officer, paygrade E-8, and master chief petty officer, paygrade E-9.

chief staff officer

See *chief of staff.*

Chinese landing

Bringing a boat or ship alongside another bow to stern. Bringing a ship alongside down-current or landing an aircraft down-wind.

chipping hammer

Small hammer with a sharp peen and face set at right angles to each other; used for chipping and scaling metal surfaces. Also called scaling hammer or boiler pick.

chips

Slang for ship's carpenter.

chit

Letter, note, voucher, or receipt probably derived from the old East India Company, and the Hindu word *chitti.* The word gained wide acceptance in the Far East and was used throughout the British army and navy, and the U.S. Navy as well.

chlorinity

Total grams of chlorine, bromine and iodine contained in one kilogram of seawater. For computation the assumption is made that the bromine and iodine have been replaced by chlorine.

chock

Metal fitting through which hawsers and lines are passed. May be open or closed. Blocks used to prevent aircraft or vehicles from rolling. Also, blocks used to support a boat under repair. See *roller chock.*

chock-a-block

Two-blocked; full, close up.

chockmen

Men who handle chocks under wheels of aircraft on carrier.

chop

Change of operational control. The date and time at which the responsibility for operational control of a ship or convoy passes from one operational control authority to another. Also used as a verb: *"To chop to---."*

chopline

A boundary expressed in longitude and latitude, at which ships change operational control.

chopper
Slang for helicopter.

chow
Slang for food. Chow line is the mess line. *Chow down* means *mess call* or *Dinner is served.*

Christmas tree
Any control panel featuring red and green indicator lights, such as those used in submarines and magnetic minesweepers. Now falling into disuse because of conflict with requirements of night vision.

chronometer
An accurate navigational clock.

chuffing
The characteristic of some rockets to burn intermittently and with an irregular noise.

church pennant
A blue and white pennant flown during church service. By tradition, the only flag or pennant flown on the same hoist above the national colors, and then only during services aboard ship. Now being flown ashore at naval facilities as well.

cigar mess
A cooperative within the wardroom mess that sells cigars, cigarettes, candy, etc., for the convenience of all officers.

cigarette deck
Open deck abaft the bridge of a submarine. Now obsolete because of streamlining. The term developed because it was the only place where personnel were permitted to smoke in the early submarines.

cipher
Any system in which arbitrary symbols represent units of plain text of regular length (usually single letters).

cipher device
Hand-operated enciphering and deciphering apparatus.

cipher machine
A mechanical or electrical cipher apparatus.

ciphony
Term applied to equipment or transmission pertaining to enciphered messages.

circuit
Communication link between two or more points capable of providing one or more communication channels.

circuit discipline
Proper use of equipment, radio communications, adherence to prescribed frequencies and operating procedures, remedial action, net control, monitoring, and training.

circular error probable (CEP)
Estimate of the accuracy of a weapon used to determine the probable damage to a target. Developed during advent of electronically or inertially guided missiles, now applied also to bombing, esp. area bombing. Seldom used for gunfire, except shore bombardment.

clamp down
To sprinkle with water and dry with a moist or dry mop. Distinguished from swabbing, which utilizes a wet mop frequently doused and wrung out in buckets of water.

clap on
To clap on a rope means to catch hold in order to haul on it; to clap on a stopper or tackle means to put on a stopper or tackle; to clap on canvas means to put on more sail.

clapoits
Standing waves produced by the reflection of a wave train from a breakwater, bulkhead, or steep beach.

Class I property
Real property in lands, buildings, structures, and various appurtenances.

Class II property
Plant equipment of a capital nature such as machinery, equipment, furniture, vehicles, machine tools, excluding special tooling.

Class III property
Minor plant equipment items having a unit value of less than $200, and other equipment of higher value specifically designated as Class III.

Class IV property
Material or items that may be incorporated into an end-item through the manufacturing process, consumable tools, and supplies required in the production.

Class V property
Special toolings; special jigs, dies, molds, etc., of such specialized nature that they are useable only on production of specific items unless they are substantially modified.

classification (personnel)
Collection of information regarding education, abilities, pre-Navy training, performance, and experience of men and officers.

classified information
Any information whose revelation must be controlled in the interest of national security.

classified matter
Information or material which must be safeguarded in the manner and to the extent required by its importance. See *top secret, secret, confidential.*

class improvement plan (CIP)
Plan for similar improvements to any ship class for improvement of military characteristics.

clean nonmilitary vessel category
With respect to merchant ships in time of war a vessel of the United States, her allies or neutral nation for which movement information for the past six months is available and about which there is no question, or close examination raises no question.

clean vessel
One of nonmilitary vessel categories.

clear
To remove stoppages or fouled gear. To remove ammunition from a gun. To pass a point, cape, or other landmark or object. Not enciphered or coded. To approve or obtain approval for. Free for running, not fouled. A mooring line is reported clear of the water, a ship clears her berth, an anchor is reported clear when being hoisted if it is not fouled.

clearance
Determination that an individual is eligible to have access to classified information of a specific category. Also, an aspect of mine counter-measures. Permission for a ship to enter or leave harbor; clearance through quarantine, etc.

clear anchor
Report made to commanding officer that the anchor is in sight and is free of any entanglement, particularly its own chain. Opposite of foul anchor.

clear for running
Ready to run without fouling.

clear (open) hawse
No turns in chains with two anchors down. Clear for hoisting anchor with no problems. See *foul hawse.*

clear ship
Prepare a ship for action by removing items such as jackstaffs, stowing paint and other inflammables below, opening ready service ammunition boxes, etc. See *strip ship.*

cleat
An anvil-shaped deck fitting for securing or belaying lines. Wedge cleats are used in yachting to hold sheets ready for instant release. All sailors of small boats are enjoined to *never belay a sheet* because it cannot be quickly released in event of a sudden squall.

clew (of a sail)
In a fore-and-aft sail, the lower corner aft. In a square sail, the two lower corners.

clipper
General name for a fast sailing ship. The original Baltimore clippers were heavily canvassed, sharp-ended boats built on Chesapeake Bay, which developed a reputation for speed, and date from about the beginning of the 19th century. The term "clipper" had its heyday in the mid-19th century with the development of the long, rakish, heavily sparred and canvassed clipper designed for the California trade. Driven by bold speed-demon skippers, these ships set records for the lengthy voyage. This, combined with the sheer beauty of the ships (e.g., *Lightning, Flying Cloud, Sea Witch*), has earned them a place in the romantic history of the days of sail.

clinker
Noncombustible matter blocking passage of air through the grate of a coal-fired boiler.

Clinker
ASW system for sensing heat from submarine water trails.

clinometer
Device for measuring amount of roll aboard ship. Same as inclinometer.

close
To close means for a ship to go near to, take position on.

close aboard
Near; within 600 yards for ship, 400 yards for boat.

close air support
Aircraft action in support of troops so close to own forces as to require detailed integration and coordination.

close covering group
Naval vessels formed to protect ships or shore facilities against enemy surface attack.

close up
Hoisted all the way up, as signal flags; two-blocked.

clothes stop
Small cotton lanyard used for fastening clothes to a line after washing them, or for securing clothes that are rolled up.

clothing
Insulating material wrapped around pipes; covered by lagging.

clothing and small stores
A government operated shop on a base or large ship which stocks standard articles of uniforms for officers and enlisted men with such related articles as buttons, brushes, etc.

clove hitch
A knot much used for fastening a line to a spar or stanchion.

clump
Fitting welded to ship's stem for *paravane* chain.

clutter
Interference on radar scope tending to obscure targets. May be due to waves, rain, snow, or other extraneous signals.

CNO
Chief of Naval Operations.

CO
Commanding officer.

coaling bag
Large (4-by-4-foot) canvas bag used in transporting material between ships during underway replenishment. Originally designed for use when coaling ship.

coaming
Raised framework around deck or bulkhead openings and cockpits of open boats to prevent entry of water.

Coast Pilot
Directions for piloting in inland and coastal waters of the U.S. and possessions. Issued by the National Ocean Survey.

cockbill
With reference to the old-fashioned anchor, it is *a-cockbill* when hung from the cathead preparatory to being either dropped or fished and secured for sea (archaic). More recently, such anchors have been dropped directly from the billboard. Yards are *a-cockbill* when topped up at an angle to the deck, thus slanted, uneven in appearance. Yards of a square-rigged man-of-war were traditionally *cockbilled* as a sign of mourning analogous to soldiers with rifles reversed, or a horse with boots reversed in the stirrups. Also, cockeyed; drunk.

cockpit
The pilot's compartment in an aircraft; a well, or sunken place in the deck of a boat, almost always protected with a coaming, for use of the crew or passengers. In the days of fighting sail, the cockpit was a compartment below the waterline where the ship's surgeons would try to cope with battle injuries.

code word
Word that conveys a special prearranged meaning.

coding delay
Time interval between transmissions of the loran master and slave stations.

coding room
Compartment aboard ship in which coding and ciphering are done.

codress
Message having the address buried in the encrypted text.

cofferdam
Void space between compartments of a ship; waterproof wall built around a damaged area of a ship's hull.

coil down
To lay out a line in a circle with coils loosely on top of one another. See *fake down, flemish (down)*.

cold-iron watch
Security patrol in the engineering spaces of a ship whose machinery is not in use nor tended.

cold ship
One without fires lighted, thus having no source of power. Also called dead ship.

collier
Vessel specially designed to carry coal.

collision bulkhead
Watertight athwartships bulkhead of a ship, usually near the bow.

collision mat
A mat of canvas and fiber designed to be hauled down over the hole in a ship's hull caused by a collision, grounding, or battle damage. See *thrums, thrumming, hogging line*.

colors
The national flag. The ceremony of raising the flag at 0800 and lowering it at sunset aboard a ship not underway, or at a shore station.

column
Formation of ships, aircraft, or people in single file, one astern of or behind the other.

column, open order
Line of ships in a column having alternate ships staggered a few degrees to the right and to the left of the guide, even-numbered ships to the left.

COM
Prefix used with the short title of a command indicating reference to the commander rather than the command—e.g., COMCRUDESLANT indicates Commander, Cruiser-Destroyer Force, Atlantic Fleet, not the force CRUDESLANT.

combat aircrewmen
Aviation enlisted men, wearing winged insignia, who comprise the crews of combat aircraft.

combat air patrol (CAP)
Fighter aircraft over task force or objective area to provide protection against hostile aircraft.

combatant vessel or ship
One whose primary mission is combat with the enemy. See *ship*.

combat distinguishing device
A small metal V worn on the Legion of Merit, Bronze Star, and Commendation Ribbon to indicate the medal was awarded for actual combat operations.

combat information center (CIC)
The section of a ship or aircraft manned and equipped to collect and collate tactical information.

combat loading
Loading assault troops and equipment for rapid debarkation in predetermined priority during amphibious assault. See *base loading* and *commercial loading.*

combination lantern
Light divided into red and green sections, used on a small craft instead of side lights.

combined acceptance trials (CAT)
A single trial combining preliminary and final acceptance trials.

combined operations
Operation conducted by forces of two or more allied nations or services. See *joint.*

combined publications
Those designed for used with allied forces. Compare with *joint.*

combustion chamber
In a steam torpedo, the chamber in which air, fuel, and water are mixed and ignited to produce steam to power the torpedo turbine.

comealong
A fitting, flush with the deck, covering a pad eye or cleat used for securing vehicles, aircraft, cargo, etc. Also a seaplane anchor cable clamp.

come about
Tack, or wear ship. To change direction so that the wind is coming over the other side (so that the ship is on the other tack).

come home
Said of an anchor when it drags toward the ship while heaving in, or of anything as it approaches its normal stowed position.

command
Authority vested in an individual for the direction, coordination, and control of military forces. Order directing a particular action in a specific way. Unit, activity, or area under the command of one individual. See *order.*

command active sonobuoy system
Airborne ASW detection and classification device.

commander
An officer who commands. Also the rank below captain and above that of lieutenant commander. Equivalent to lieutenant colonel.

commanding officer (CO)
Officer in command of a ship, squadron or aircraft, or naval activity with duties and responsibilities as specified in U.S. Navy Regulations. May be a staff officer in special cases, as the doctor who commands a hospital.

commendatory mast
Ceremony at which the commanding officer commends, congratulates, or decorates members of his command.

commercial loading
Loading of troop and equipment for maximum utilization of space, rather than for military purposes. See *combat loading.*

commissaryman (CS)
Petty officer who performs cooking, baking, and butcher duties. Slang: bellyrobber, stewburner. In 1975, rate was changed to mess management specialist (MS). See *Appendix B.*

commissary store
Food store for military personnel. The lower prices at such stores are among the fringe benefits taken into account when military pay scales are established.

commission
To put a ship in active service under a commissioned commanding officer, who breaks his pennant and sets the watch.

commissioned officer
One who derives his authority from a commission under authority of the President confirmed by the Congress.

commission pennant
Narrow red, white, and blue pennant with seven stars, flown at the main truck of ship in commmission, under command of commissioned officer. See *distinctive mark.*

commodore
A naval rank, not used in peacetime, below rear admiral and above captain. Corresponds to brigadier general. A captain commanding two or more small ships, such as destroyers, is addressed as commodore. A convoy commodore, assisted by a rear and vice commodore, is the merchant marine or naval officer in command of the convoy. A new rank, commodore admiral, a one-star officer equivalent to brigadier general, is proposed in new legislation.

communication countermeasures
Any measures, generally highly classified as to technique, intent, and results, designed to detect, locate, interfere with, confuse, or misinform enemy communications or communications equipment. Includes intercept, search, jamming, or any other ingenious techniques which may be useful.

communications satellite
An orbiting vehicle, either active or passive, which relays signals between communications stations.

commutation of quarters
Rental allowance

commuted rations (COMRATS)
Credit for rations an enlisted man does not receive in a general mess. See *subsistence allowance.*

companionway
Set of steps leading from one deck to another. Also called a ladder.

company, ship's
Everyone assigned to a ship or station; all hands.

compartment
Room or space on board ship. Usually lettered and numbered according to location and utilization.

compartment check-off list
A list of fittings, their location, and function in a compartment for a specific purpose, such as damage control.

compass
Instrument for determining direction: magnetic, depending on the earth's magnetic field for its force; gyroscopic, depending on the tendency of a free-spinning body to seek to align its axis with that of the earth.

compass card
A circular card in a compass that is marked with the cardinal points, intercardinal points, and the others in between. The compass card appears to rotate, but it is the ship that rotates around the card. The lubber's line is marked on the fixed portion of the compass, and thus the heading of the ship can be ascertained by reading the direction marked on the compass card which lies at the lubber's line. In the days of sail, of course, a proud helmsman would steer by the wind and would only refer to the lubber's line to check that the wind had not shifted.

compass error
Total difference between compass heading and true heading. Is composed of variation and deviation.

compass rose
An outer and two inner graduated circles printed in several places on a nautical chart to assist in recording bearings and laying courses. Outer circle, in degrees, indicates true direction, the inner ones indicate magnetic and show amount of local variation plus annual change.

compensate
To adjust water in trim tanks to attain desired buoyancy in a submarine. Also, to correct the magnetic compass.

competitive year
That on which battle efficiency competition is based; the fiscal year.

complement
Authorized personnel for full combatant manning, designed for full operational effectiveness considering the inherent capabilities of the unit and the possible requirements of war. See *allowance* and *manning level*.

comply
In any naval message means *you are to comply*.

composite squadron
Two or more divisions of ships or aircraft of different types.

compound
Area set aside for temporary storage at an advanced base.

compound formation
An arrangement of two or more simple formations of ships.

compressor
Device or brake, operated by hand, in a chain pipe that governs the movement of the anchor chain.

compromise
Loss of security resulting from revelation of classified information to an unauthorized individual. May include possible compromise, as when a classified document is lost.

concentrate
Join up, as ships or aircraft concentrate to make an attack.

condenser
Low-pressure, heat-transfer device in which steam is condensed to water for further use in a closed cycle system.

condition watch
Watch stood under a particular condition of readiness.

cone of silence
Space directly over radio range station in which signals are not heard or are greatly reduced in volume. Also, space directly below a sonar transmitter or receiver where detection of a submarine is not possible.

confidential
Classification of information and material whose disclosure would be prejudicial to the national interests or prestige. A lower classification than secret or top secret.

confusion reflectors
General term for nonelectronic mechanical devices and materials used in countermeasures against radar. Examples are chaff, gull, kite and corner reflector.

conn
Control of ship's movements; the officer in control has the conn. To guide or pilot a ship is spoken of as conning.

conning tower
Control station in any armored ship. The captain's station in battle. Also submerged control station in a submarine, if separate from the control room. U.S. WWII submarines were built with conning towers to permit greater periscope-height extension. Most post-WWII submarines have been built without conning towers, and the conning station is an area set aside in the control room.

consolidated pack ice
Large area of drift ice driven closely together to produce total coverage.

consolidation (of oilers, ammunition ships, supply ships)
Transfer of cargo among designated ships to enable some to return to base to reload. Most commonly done among oilers.

constant helm plan
An evasive maneuver used by a ship which suspects the presence of a submarine in the vicinity. Although the ship appears to be changing course constantly, it will not get very far off its base track. Similar to *sinuating.*

construction battalion, naval
Specially qualified men and officers organized to do military construction work. The battalion is the basic unit of the Navy's construction force and it is from the name—construction battalion—that they draw their name: CBs—SeaBees. Construction battalions may be amphibious (ACB), mobile (MCB) or maintenance unit (CBMU).

consul
An official in the diplomatic service representing the U.S. government in foreign places. The consul is concerned with all U.S. shipping at the port in which he resides. He assists sailors in distress and undertakes the repatriation of shipwrecked or stranded American citizens.

consular shipping advisor
Naval officer appointed to the staff of a consular authority in a neutral country for naval control of shipping duties.

consumables
Materials intended to be expended or used.

contact
Indications of the presence of a target made by sight, sound, or electronic means.

contact mine
See *mine.*

contact report
Report of first sighting or knowledge of enemy forces.

containerization
The shipping of general cargo in sealed van-type boxes, which are carried aboard ships, trains, and trucks.

continental shelf
The sea bottom from shore to a depth of 200 meters. Width varies from nearly zero to 800 miles. Generally speaking, the depth increases very gradually to about 100 fathoms (200 meters), at which point it increases more rapidly at a steeper slope.

continental slope
The sea-bottom slope from the 200 meter line to great depths; varies between 3.5 and 6 percent.

contract clause book
Publication containing a variety of standard clauses required in government contracts. These clauses may be incorporated into a contract by referencing the clause book and do not need to be written out in each contract.

contractor data requirements list
Listing (on DOD form 1423) of all technical data and information required to be delivered to the government by a contractor.

contractor independent technical effort
Program for contractors for independent research and development efforts performed in connection with contracts.

contractor performance evaluation
Reports detailing the manner in which major contractors are meeting commitments.

contractor support
An interim arrangement during initial development or production requiring a contractor to furnish hardware support items before this responsibility is assumed by the government.

contractor weighted average share
Program to give contractors who take high-risk contracts special consideration in judging allowable costs on contracts.

controlled mine
See *mine*

controlled net
A communications circuit on which activity is governed by one station.

controlled port
Harbor or anchorage in which entry, departure, berthing, and traffic are controlled by military authorities.

control, operational (OPCON)
Authority over combat, service, or training operations, as opposed to administrative control.

control room
Control center of a submarine containing most of the valves, switches, gauges, and other instruments for surfacing and submerging, steering, and general operational control. May include conning station and torpedo fire-control station, but does not include torpedo tubes, torpedo-firing apparatus, engineering plant or engineering-control equipment. The control room is, however, the central station from which emanates the basic direction of all these outlying activities. See *conning tower*.

control ship
One that controls and directs the boats in an amphibious assault, usually stationed on the line of departure.

convening authority
The command legally empowered to organize courts-martial, courts of inquire, and boards of investigation.

conversion, ship
Changing a ship's design or characteristics so that there is a major change in its mission or assignment to a different class. See *fram*.

convoy
A number of merchant ships or naval auxiliaries, or both, usually escorted by warships and aircraft. A single merchant ship or naval auxiliary under surface escort.

convoy commodore
Officer (naval or merchant) designated to command convoy. He is subordinate to the escort commander.

convoy escort
Naval ships or aircraft in company with a convoy and responsible for its protection.

convoy routing
The assignment of specific ocean paths for convoys to follow.

cook-off
Explosion of a projectile due to heat in the firing chamber alone.

coppers
Large cooking kettles in the galley.

copy
To maintain a continuous radio receiver watch, recording all transmissions. See *guard, cover, listen.*

corange lines
Lines on a map or chart passing through all points having the same tidal range. See *cotidal lines.*

cordage
General term for rope and line of all kinds.

CORE
Project to use waste products of reactor cores for conversion of gamma rays directly into electrical energy and for the direct conversion of nuclear energy to electricity.

Coriolis force
Effect of the earth's rotation on all moving bodies, including air and water masses.

corner reflector
Reflector formed of mutually perpendicular surfaces or planes. It increases the radar reflection from any object to which it is attached.

correction for datum
Conversion factor in tidal prediction to resolve chart datum of the reference and secondary station.

COSAL
Coordinated ships' allowance list.

cost and economic information system (CEIS)
System administered by DOD for collecting data from contractors on post-production experience and its use in establishing costs of future weapons systems.

cotidal lines
Lines on a map or chart passing through all points where high waters occur at the same time. See *corange lines.*

counter
Overhang at the stern of a ship. A ship with a *cruiser stern* has no counter.

counterbattery fire
Fire delivered against active enemy weapons and/or fire control stations.

counter countermeasures
Warfare or equipment designed to impair or reduce the effectiveness of enemy countermeasures.

counter current
A secondary ocean current adjacent to and setting in a direction opposite to the main, current as on both sides of the Gulf Stream

counter flood
To take water into a ship's tanks or compartments to reduce list or inclination by bow or stern. Must be done with care, for total buoyancy is also reduced.

countermeasures
A form of warfare carried on to eliminate or reduce the threat from or effectiveness of enemy equipment.

countermining
The explosion, either accidental or deliberate, of ammunition or weapons by nearby external explosions.

countermining distance
The limiting distance between mines that will avoid chain-countermining. Recommended mimimum spacing for each type of mine is prescribed from statistical results of experiments. Also called countermining radius.

country
Definite area of a ship, such as admirals' country, officers' country, CPO country. Never used without modifier.

coupling
Metal fitting at the ends of a fire hose or fuel hose to permit attachment to another length, or to a fitting.

course
A rhumb line direction. The intended direction of travel. Often designated as true, magnetic, compass, or grid, e.g., *Steer course 000 degrees pgc* (per gyro compass). In aviation, because of high winds aloft, the course to steer may be quite different from the intended course of travel, referred to as *course made good* by navigators everywhere.

course recorder
Device that graphically records ship's path.

courses
The lowest sails on the masts of a square-rigger, excluding the mizzenmast with a spanker. Called foresail, mainsail, according to the mast concerned. See *sail nomenclature*.

court of inquiry
A body of three or more officers convened by any person authorized to convene a general court-martial to investigate something.

courts-martial
Courts of law for military personnel.

cover
To maintain a continuous radio receiver watch with the transmitter calibrated and available. Also a term used to describe a hat or a command to don hats. See *guard, copy, listen*.

covert
In intelligence work: secret, clandestine. Opposite of overt.

cowl
Bell-shaped air funnel or scoop, projecting above the deck or deckhouse of a vessel, used for ventilation.

cowling
Removable covering on aircraft, as over a cockpit or around an engine.

cow's tail
Frayed end of a rope; also called a fag or fag end.

coxcombing
Fancy knot work consisting of coils of line worked around a tiller handle, stanchion, etc. See *sennet, square knotting, MacNamara lace.*

coxswain
Man in charge of a small boat, pronounced "COX-un."

crab
To move sidewise through the water. To *catch a crab* in rowing is to strike the water on the recovery stroke.

crack
Unnavigable break in sea ice caused by tide, temperature changes, current or wind.

cradle
A stowage rest for a ship's boat, or any large object secured on deck. Also called a *saddle.*

crane
Mechanical device for lifting weights.

crash dolly
Slang: wheeled device for moving crashed aircraft on a carrier flight deck. With increased size and weight of aircraft, a wheeled crane is now generally used. Flight deck personnel have any number of names for it, such as "Tilly the Toiler," "cherry picker," etc.

creeping attack
Coordinated ASW attack using noiseless approach with all target information furnished by an assisting ship. The attacking ship does not echo range. The submarine can hear the assisting ship echo ranging at a distance and is unaware of the quiet approach of the other until the carefully placed depth charges go off.

crest of berm
The seaward margin of the berm.

crew
The men who operate a ship, boat, aircraft, turret, gun, missile, etc. Also, as noun or adjective, may refer to the sport of competitive rowing

crib
Rigid structure of timber, rock, concrete, and heavy wire used to close a harbor entrance, serve as a bridge support or temporary breakwater, etc.

critical
Said of a reactor when the number of neutrons produced by fission is just enough to continue the reaction. Associated terms are *criticality* and *critical position* of control rods. See *self-sustaining*.

critical velocity
The speed at which a current can scour the bottom enough to maintain required channel depth.

critique
Critical review of an operation or exercise held in the form of a conference.

Cromwell current
Sub-surface current of the Pacific which flows west to east under the north equatorial current.

crossing the line
Crossing the equator.

crossing the T
Classic tactic in surface engagement wherein one battle line crosses and concentrates its fire upon the van or leading units of the other. The British crossed the German T three times at Jutland, but the Germans had drilled in a course-reversal maneuver (ripple movement from the rear), which extricated their forces.

crosspointing
Line or strips of canvas or leather braided about a rail or stanchion as decoration and protection. Also tapering a rope's end by cutting away the inner yarns and braiding the outer yarns.

cross signal
Illegal practice of answering a ship's whistle signal of two blasts with one blast, or vice versa.

crosstree
Wooden or steel spreader with a slot at each end at right angles to the mast over which the masthead shrouds are passed in fore-and-aft-rigged sailing craft.

crow
Slang for the eagle on a petty officer's rating badge.

crow's nest
Lookout station aloft generally on the foremast.

crud
In nuclear reactor operations, an old slang term that has been legitimatized to a degree. Refers to the black radioactive coating that

precipitates from the pure water of the primary loop during the production of power. An acronym was created to go with the letters of the old word: Corrosive, Radioactive, Undetermined Deposit, proving that the most demanding of technical matters can have their light-hearted moments.

crud burst

See *crud*. Occasional temporary peaks of radioactivity in the primary loop have been theoretically ascribed to a piece of crud which, breaking loose from the inner surface on which it was originally deposited, then lodges on or near one of the radioactivity sensors. According to reactor operating instructions, a rise in radioactivity beyond a specific point requires shutdown of the reactor, regardless of its suspected cause. Thus a crud burst can give rise to an erroneous suspicion of a serious reactor casualty.

cruise

Tour of sea duty. A period of enlistment. Also, a voyage to several ports, such as a shakedown cruise, or to a specific ocean area. See *deployment.*

cruiser

A type of warship, less armored and armed than a battleship, usually smaller and faster, thus cheaper to build and operate, suitable for any naval duty except combat against battleships. Currently, cruisers are almost exclusively employed as large AAW escorts for aircraft carriers, and those with main battery guns have had at least some of them replaced with surface-to-air missiles. Cruisers have been traditionally named after cities, battleships after states, and destroyers, destroyer leaders, and frigates after naval heros. For a time, frigates were considered the equivalent of cruisers as large AAW escorts, the quality of their missiles being the determinant, of course. Most recently, the designation *frigate* has been brought in line with foreign use: an ocean going escort smaller than a destroyer. The large destroyers and former frigates are now given the names of states and, exceeding many cruisers in displacement, are called cruisers. The present confusion in names and types will undoubtedly continue some years. See *heavy cruiser, armored cruiser,* and *Appendix A.*

cruiser stern

A stern so shaped that it does not overhang the water, usually with a nearly perpendicular drop to the waterline, after which it is cut away radically to provide for rudder and screw(s). Differs from a *counter* stern, which is cut away before it enters the water. The rudder post, or operating shaft, cannot be seen in a ship with a cruiser stern whereas it can be seen under a counter. The cruiser stern is so named because it resembles the stern of a man-of-war. See *counter.*

cruising range

The endurance of a ship in nautical miles at moderate or cruising speed.

cryptanalysis

Solving encrypted messages without access to the decryption system.

cryptoboard
Group of personnel specifically designated for encrypting and decrypting messages.

cryptocenter
Compartment used by the cryptoboard.

cryptochannel
Crypto aids, indicators, and instructions that comprise a basic unit in cryptographic communications.

cryptogram
A communication in visible, secret writing.

cryptographer
One who encrypts or decrypts messages.

cryptography
The science of rendering plain text into unintelligible text and vice versa.

CUE-CAP
An urgency designator of the JCS to show relative priority among programs; CUE-CAP is subordinate to BRICK BAT.

cumshaw
Something procured without official payment. Free; a gift. Comes from the beggars of Amoy, China, who said *kam sia*, meaning "grateful thanks." The historic reference is to graft for personal gain. In the U.S. Navy the term now relates to unauthorized work done for or equipment given to a ship or station, and usually no connotation of personal gain exists. A *cumshaw artist* is a man who is adept at getting cumshaw work done, usually by liberal handouts of food and coffee to shipyard workers. Thus, a good ship's cook can be important.

current direction
The compass heading toward which water moves. It differs from wind direction, which is the compass heading from which it comes.

current, ocean
Continuous movement of the sea, sometimes caused by prevailing winds, as well as large constant forces, such as the rotation of the earth, or the apparent rotation of the sun and moon. Examples are the Gulf Stream, the Cromwell Current, and the Kurishiro (Japanese Current). See *inshore currents, offshore currents, rip current (tide)*

current pattern secondary
Water movement which varies from the prevailing current pattern.

current ship's maintenance project (CSMP)
Card record of repairs, alterations, etc.

Current Tables
National Ocean Survery (former Coast and Geodetic Survey) publications giving data on tidal currents for various localities throughout the world. See *tide tables.*

current, tidal
Currents along the coast caused by the rise and fall of the tides. Water movement associated with the rising tide is the *flood current*; that associated with the falling tide is the *ebb current.* Between flood and ebb currents is a period of no current, slack water, which corresponds to the stand between flood and ebb tides.

cusp
Sand deposited, by wave action, in the form of points or bars projecting seaward along a beach.

custodian
Officer responsible to his commanding officer for custody, handling, and safeguarding of classified publications.

customs of the service
Unwritten naval practice having the force of usage and tradition. An example is the removal of caps or hats by officers entering a compartment where the crew is eating.

cut
Landing signal officer's (LSO's) signal to a pilot to close the throttle, allowing the aircraft to settle aboard the carrier. Also, a bearing line or a set of bearing lines that result in a ship's position or visual fix.

cut of the jib
General appearance of a vessel or of a person. Derivation dates back to sailing days when ships of different nationalities shaped their jib sails somewhat differently. Thus a ship would be identified by the *cut of her jib.*

cutter
A type of rig used on sailing yachts, having a single mast located further aft than that of a sloop. The original revenue vessels used this rig and hence were called cutters. Today the term is applied to all Coast Guard ships above a certain size. Also a type of square-sterned pulling boat.

cutwater
The stem of a ship, the forward-most portion of the bow, which cuts the water as she moves.

D

daily estimated position summary (DEPSUM)
Daily broadcast summary by the operational control authority of the estimated positions of ocean shipping within a specific area. It includes courses, speeds, and expected alterations within the next 24 hours.

daily movement summary (MOVSUM)
Confidential tabulation of departures and arrivals of all merchant ships (including neutrals) from ports during a 24-hour period.

damage control
Measures necessary to preserve and re-establish shipboard watertight integrity, stability, maneuverability, and offensive power; to control list and trim; to make rapid repairs of materiel; to limit the spread of and provide adequate protection from fire; to limit the spread of, remove the contamination by, and provide adequate protection from toxic agents; and to care for wounded personnel.

damage-control bills
Written procedures for operating the various systems of a ship (such as ship's drainage system) to further efficient damage control.

damage control book
Contains material information in the form of texts, tables, and plates concerning facilities and characteristics of those ships that are highly subdivided with complicated piping and wiring systems.

damage control central
Compartment behind a ship's armor, if any—otherwise located in as protected a position as practical—from which measures for control of damage and preservation of the ship's fighting capability are directed.

damping
The reduction of oscillation of a system by friction or other means.

dan buoy
Temporary marker buoy used during minesweeping operations to indicate boundaries of swept path, swept area, known hazards, etc.

danger bearing (angle)
Limited bearing (angle) of fixed object(s) on shore which may be used to insure safe passage clear of an outlying shoal or other danger.

danger signal
Five or more rapid short blasts of a whistle to indicate a possible collision or other emergency.

dan layers
Vessels assigned the duty of laying dan buoys during mine-warfare operations.

dark adaptation
Becoming accustomed to darkness in order to achieve good night vision.

darken ship
Blackening out all lights visible from outside the ship.

Dark Fence
Alternate name for Space Surveillance System (SPASUR).

data communications
Electronic or electrical transfer of data from one place to another and the translation necessary to make it acceptable at its destination.

date-time-group (DTG)
Six numerals and a letter indicating date (first two digits), time (four digits), and time zone description (letter) of origin of a message.

datum and datum time
The last known position of a submarine is the datum; its time at that point is the datum time. If a ship is torpedoed and no additional information is available, the position and time of torpedoing are used as datum and datum time.

datum plane
Same as chart datum.

davit(s)
A fixed or movable crane that projects over the side of a ship or over a hatchway for hoisting heavy objects. Used in pairs to handle boats, one at each end. Some of the tragic losses of life during nautical disasters such as the *Titanic* and *Lusitania* sinkings were traceable to lifeboat davits that could not be handled properly under the existing circumstances (heavy list, overloaded boats, panicky passengers, inexperienced and nervous crew), with the result that many improved styles have been developed by which a boat can be readily swung inboard or outboat, and even launched automatically using only the force of gravity. Pronounced "day-vit."

Davy Jones' Locker
The bottom of the sea.

dawn alert
See *alert, dusk* or *dawn.*

dawn and dusk combat air patrol (DADCAP)
Special applications of night combat air patrol that fill the gap during dawn or dusk between the use of combat air patrol and night combat air patrol; an extension of the use of night fighters *(ZIPPERS)* over a target area.

day and night distress signal
Hand-held smoke and flare projector.

day beacon
Unlighted structure that serves as a daytime aid to navigation. See *daymark*.

daymark
The daytime identifying characteristics of any aid to navigation. Also the shape or signals displayed by a vessel to indicate her special status, such as fishing, laying cable, etc.

day's duty
A tour of duty or a watch lasting 24 hours.

day's work
Twenty-four hours of navigating a ship; a periodic requirement for junior officers.

D-day
Term used to designate unnamed day on which an operation commences. D+7 means seven days after D-day.

dead ahead
Directly ahead; bearing 000 degrees relative.

dead astern
Directly aft; bearing 180 degrees relative.

dead-eyes
Circular blocks of wood with three holes and no sheaves, and a groove for a rope or an iron strap around them. With pairs of dead-eyes the rigging could be set taut by lanyards. Many ship models use miniature dead-eyes to simulate blocks.

deadhead
Log floating on end and mostly submerged. Also called a sleeper. A heavy post on a pier to which lines are secured.

dead horse
Slang for an advance in pay.

dead in the water
Said of a vessel that has stopppd and has no way on, but is not moored or anchored, nor is in any way fast to the ground or a pier, etc.

deadlight
A hinged metal cover, a battle port, for an air port. A cover, fitted with light-obscuring baffles to permit ventilation without the escape of light, is a ventilating deadlight. Also, a heavy glass set flush with the deck for admitting light below.

deadman
Timber or similar object buried in ice or in the ground to secure guys, tackles, or a ship's lines. If in ice, can also be called ice anchor. Also synonym for Irish pennant.

dead reckoning (DR)
Method of navigation using direction and amount of progress from the last well-determined position to a new dead reckoning or DR, pronounced "dee-are," position.

dead-reckoning tracer (DRT)
Plotting device that records the track of a ship by continuously integrating course and speed as input from compass and log.

deadrise
Vertical distance between a vessel's keel and the turn of the bilge.

dead ship
One without power; also called a cold ship.

dead space
Area within maximum range of weapon, radar, radio, or observer which cannot be covered because of obstacles or inherent limitations.

dead water
See *internal waves.*

deadweight, deadweight tonnage
The difference between a ship's loaded and light displacement. Total deadweight refers to carrying capacity of a ship; cargo deadweight is the total deadweight minus fuel, water, stores, dunnage and other items required on voyage—expressed in long tons.

deadwood
Narrow part of a ship's hull between keel and stern post aft or between stem and keel forward. In wooden ships these were solid timbers because there was insufficient space for framing in the usual manner.

debarkation net
Large net type rope used as a ladder on ship's side for troops embarking or disembarking. Similar to cargo net.

debarkation station
Where men on a ship assemble to debark into boats.

Decca
Medium-frequency continuous-wave radio navigation system. For precise positioning within short range of transmitters. Currently used in heavily traveled coastal areas of Europe and the United States.

decipher
To convert an enciphered message into plain text by means of cipher system (not by cryptanalysis).

deck
A floor in a ship. The uppermost complete deck is the main deck. Complete decks below it are numbered from the top down: second deck, third deck, etc. Partial decks between complete decks are called half decks; those below the lowest complete deck are platform decks, or flats. Partial decks above the main deck, if they extend to the sides of the

ship are called, according to location, the forecastle deck, middle deck, or poop deck. Those which do not extend to the side are superstructure decks. Weather deck(s) are those exposed to the weather. In aircraft carriers however, the topmost deck is the flight deck, and the next one below is the hangar deck. The main deck is the one below the hangar deck, after which the numbering system proceeds normally, and partial decks above the hangar deck are called gallery decks. Decks often get their names from construction, as armored flight deck, protective deck, splinter deck, all three of which are fitted with armor, or from employment, as boat deck, gun deck, berth deck. As an added use of the word deck, the OOD's watch is called *the deck*, as in the expression, ---*has the deck*, meaning he has charge of all deck functions and, if underway, is supervising all maneuvers of the ship. See *flat(s)*.

decker
Describes the size and offensive power of a sailing man-of-war. A three-decker carried guns (as many as 120) on three gun decks as well as on the upper or weather deck. History records only one four-decker, the *Santissima Trinidad* of Spain. Ships rated as two-deckers and above were considered fit to "lie in the line of battle," thus "ships of the line," thus "battleship." HMS *Victory* is a three-decker, preserved in Portsmouth, England. USS *Constitution*, a frigate, might have been called a one-decker had such a term been in use. Since her spar deck (weather deck) carried a full battery of guns, however, she was called a double-banked frigate. USS *Independence*, razeed from a marginal two-decker, became a very successful double-banked frigate.

deck gang
All men attached to the ship's deck departments, as opposed to those attached to engineering, radio, or electronics departments. In the old days the deck gang was distinguished by wearing rating insignia on the right arm, hence the expression, "right-arm rate." All others wore their rates on the left arm and, of course, were known as "left-arm rates."

deck hand
A man who works topside, on deck, usually a seaman. Slang: swab jockey, deck ape.

deckhouse
Topside ship's structure.

deck load
Gear or cargo stowed topside on weather deck.

deck log
Official day-to-day record of a ship in commission and thus a legal document when signed. Distinct from engineering log.

deck pads
Non-skid plates or mats secured to the deck where pedestrian traffic is heavy.

deck plane
Standard fire-control reference plane of a ship.

deck seamanship
Maintenance and operation of all gear topside including boats, anchors, rigging, etc.

declassify
Remove security classification from information. Notification of holders of the information is part of the process.

declination
Angular distance north or south of the celestial equator. Used as a coordinate with Greenwich hour angle (GHA) to identify positions of celestial bodies.

decode
To translate code into plain text by means of code book. Loosely used as synonym for decipher.

decontaminate
To free from the harmful residue of nuclear or chemical attack.

decoration
A medal or ribbon awarded for exceptional courage, skill, or performance.

decrypt
To convert a cryptogram into plain text by a reversal of the encryption process (not by cryptanalysis). See *decode*.

deep
An ocean bottom depression of great depth, usually more than 6,000 meters. Also a report by a leadsman: "By the deep six." See *leadline*.

deep air support
Air action against enemy forces at such a distance from friendly forces that detailed integration of each air mission with fire and movement of friendly forces is not required. See *close air support*.

deep creep attack
Suprise depth charge attack for use against a submarine deeply submerged and using slow speeds. Effective only when surprise can be achieved. See *creeping attack*.

deep scattering layer
Ocean layers that scatter sound or echo it vertically. Thought to be of biological origin, they range in depth from 150 to 200 fathoms during the day and migrate to or near the surface at night.

deep-sea lead
A heavier lead than a hand lead, used to sound in water over 30 fathoms. Also called dipsey lead. Now largely replaced by echo sounder.

deep-sea system
Sub-system of benthic division.

deep six
Slang for throwing an object away or overboard.

deep-submergence rescue vehicle (DSRV)
Small submarine, able to be carried piggyback on a large submarine or air-transported to a disaster scene, then submerge, find a sunken submarine, and make a watertight joint with the submarine's escape trunk. The development of the deep-submergence rescue vehicle was made necessary by the far-ranging, deep-diving, high-speed nuclear submarines, for which the standard rescue chamber was inadequate.

deep tanks
Compartments strengthened to carry water or liquid cargo.

deepwater waves
Surface and wind waves having a wave length less than half the water's depth. See *intermediate waves.*

Defense Mapping Agency
Government agency that produces and sells navigational charts and publications.

deflection
Lateral angular correction applied to target bearing to obtain hits in naval gunnery.

degaussing
Reducing magnetic field of a ship by wrapping the ship fore and aft permanently with energized wire, to protect against magnetic mines and torpedoes. See *deperming, flashing.*

delivery groups
Four-letter pronounceable groups that assist in transmission and delivery of a message. Assigned to activities and commands.

delta
The alluvial sand deposit, usually roughly triangular, near the mouth of a river. The triangular shape of supersonic aircraft wing.

Delta
Phonetic word for the letter *D.*

demonstration group
Component of a force organized to conduct deceptive operations involving a feint.

demurrage
Charge made when a merchant ship is delayed while loading or discharging cargo.

densitometer
Device for measuring sea water density.

Department of Defense (DOD)
The department of the executive branch of the government including the office of the Secretary of Defense and the Departments of the Army, Navy and Air Force.

Department of the Navy
The executive part of the naval establishment; the headquarters, United States Marine Corps; the entire operating forces of the U.S. Navy, including naval aviation elements, and of the U.S. Marine Corps, including reserve components of such forces; all field activities, headquarters, forces, bases, installations, activities, and functions under the control or supervision of the Secretary of the Navy; and the U.S. Coast Guard when operating as part of the Navy pursuant to law. See *Navy Department*.

departure
The technical point at which a ship leaves an anchorage or harbor. Thus a typical entry in the ship's log might read: "With Brenton Reef Lightship bearing 070° true, distance two miles, took departure for Portsmouth, England on course 135° true and per gyro compass (p.g.c.), speed 15." See *course*.

departure report
Prepared by a repair activity on completion of a ship's overhaul, listing work undertaken, percent completed, items deferred, with reasons for the deferrals, and summary of cost.

deperming
Reduction of permanent magnetism of a ship by energizing coils temporarily placed vertically around the ship. The purpose is protection against magnetic mines and torpedoes. See *degaussing, flashing*.

deploy
Specifically, to change from a cruising or approach formation to a formation of ships for battle or amphibious assault. Generally, to send ships or squadrons abroad for duty.

deployment
A cruise in foreign waters.

deployment bag
Part of parachute gear that keeps canopy deflated until shroud lines are completely paid out.

depth charge
Antisubmarine (ASW) explosive dropped from ships. Slang: ashcan. Depth bombs are dropped from aircraft, depth charges from ships. The difference is that aircraft weapons must have a predictable trajectory in air and hence require a standard bomb shape.

depth finder (sounder)
Same as *echo sounder*.

derelict
Abandoned vessel at sea, still afloat.

derrick
A device, consisting of a boom and tackle, used for hoisting heavy objects. Named after Thomas Derrick, a well-known hangman of the time of Queen Elizabeth, who devised a portable hangman's tree which he could carry about to perform his duties wherever required.

deserter
Person absent from his command without authority whose apparent purpose is to stay away. Absence over 30 days is presumptive, but not full legal proof, of desertion. See *unauthorized absentee.*

designator
A four-digit code number that describes an officer's qualifications and specialities. For example, an 1100 officer is an unrestricted line officer with no special qualifications. See *file number* and *signal number.*

design class
Ships of a type which, at the time of issue of specifications, are intended to be identical. Change orders issued may eventually make them dissimilar in some respects.

despedida
Farewell party for a person or group of people leaving a station or command.

destroyer
Originally torpedo boat destroyer (for further derivation see *armored cruiser*). A small, high speed, lightly armed and unarmored jack-of-all-trades which deservedly has become the favorite of surface officers. There are various configurations for special employment, also illustrating the design changes necessitated by constantly developing technology, and the type has grown enormously in size while still retaining the name *destroyer.* Torpedo boats were only about 100 tons, the first destroyers twice that size. By WWI destroyers were 1,000 tons, torpedo boats had disappeared, and destroyers had taken on their functions. Since WWII, destroyers have grown to more than 10,000 tons. Large destroyers, known for many years as *destroyer leaders* and *frigates* (in U.S. Navy), took on antiair warfare (AAW) duties as escorts for carrier task forces. Most recently, large destroyers have been redesignated as *cruisers,* and the name *frigate* has been relegated to smaller, slower, escort-type ships not suited for aircraft carrier escort functions. Slang: can, tincan. See *Appendix A.*

destroyer escort (DE)
As developed during WWII, an ocean escort intended principally for convoy of merchant ships but with some destroyer characteristics. Since WWII, the type has undergone some design and mission changes and is now known as a frigate. A small, ocean-going, multipurpose ship of about 4,000 tons, single screw, moderate speed, with some antiair warfare (AAW) and antisubmarine warfare (ASW) capability. See *Appendix A.*

destroyer leader
See *destroyer, frigate, Appendix A.*

destructor
An explosive or other device for intentionally destroying classified equipment, a missile or aircraft or their components because of safety considerations or to prevent compromise.

detach
Term used when officers are ordered away from present duty; they are considered *attached* to ship or station, hence *detached* when ordered elsewhere. Enlisted men are *assigned to* and eventually *transferred*. Occasionally a large transfer of men is termed an issue, especially from training station or receiving ship.

detachment
Temporary unit formed from other naval forces.

detail
To assign men to a particular duty within their duty station; the men assigned to such duty.

detail officer
An officer in the Bureau of Naval Personnel who assigns personnel. Enlisted personnel who make such assignments are called *detailers*.

detailing, personnel
Assignment of personnel to fill exact requirements of billets.

detent
Mine release gear on a minelayer.

detonation, low order
Partial or low explosion. Not as powerful as expected.

detritus
Accumulation on the sea bottom of rocks or rock particles and of broken organic material.

deviascope
Device for demonstrating the technique of compensating a magnetic compass.

deviation
Magnetic compass error due to magnetic properties of ship. Expressed in degrees east or west.

deviation table
List of compass errors due to deviation for representative headings through 360 degrees, posted near each magnetic compass.

devil's claw
Device used to hold anchor chain. See *compressor.*

diagram (beach, boat, landing, etc.)
Graphic representation of beach limits, boat assignments, landing order, etc., in amphibious operations.

Dial-X
Internal communication system for Polaris submarine.

diaphone
Fixed fog signal with a characteristic emission used as an aid to navigation.

dicing
High-speed, low-altitude, low-oblique aircraft photo operations.

digital geoballistic computer
Computer for Polaris Mark 84 fire-control system.

Dilbert
Slang for a person who dopes off, acts stupidly. Dilbert was born during WWII as the hero of an effective series of instruction books and cartoons for naval aviators.

dinette
Slang for the mess hall in a submarine.

dinghy
Small (less than 20 feet) handy pulling boat with a transom stern. May be rigged for oars or sail.

dip
To lower the national colors part way and then raise them as a salute to a passing warship. The merchantman dips first and holds his flag *at the dip*, i.e., about one-third of the way down, until after the warship has dipped in answer and two-blocked. Warships render passing honors but do not dip to each other.
A correction of observed sextant altitude because of the curvature of the earth. The sun or moon has dipped when its lower limb (bottom of observed curvature) touches the horizon.

dip, magnetic
The inclination to the horizontal of a magnetic compass needle caused by the earth's magnetic field.

dipping sonar
Sonar equipment used by helicopters or by hydrofoils.

dip the eye
To arrange the loops (eyes) of two mooring lines on the same bollard so that either line may be removed without moving the other. Accomplished by passing the eye of one line up through that of the other and then around the bollard.

direct
To give an order in a specific manner. Positive action is expected.

direct fire
Gunfire delivered using the target itself as the point of aim for the guns or director. See *indirect fire.*

directive
Military communication in which policy is established or a specific action is ordered; plan issued with a view to placing it in effect when so directed, or in the event that a stated contingency arises; any communication that initiates or governs action, conduct, or procedure.

director (gun)
Mechanical and electronic device for control of gunfire.

disbursing officer
Officer who keeps pay records and pays salary allowances and claims.

discharge
Process of separating enlisted men from the service. May be honorable, general, undesirable, bad conduct, or dishonorable.

disciplinary barracks
An activity to receive, confine, classify, segregate, and provide work, drill, and training for courts-martial prisoners.

dismantling shot
Projectile fired from a smoothbore cannon during the 17th, 18th, and early 19th centuries, intended to destroy rigging of enemy ship. Usually consisted of heavy iron bars chained together, or of two cannon balls chained together. See *grape, cansister, double-shot, langrage.*

dispatch (despatch)
Former term for message.

dispatch money
Bonus resulting from a ship loading or discharging before expiration of lay days. Paid by shipowner to the charterer. Normally included in dry-cargo voyage charter parties.

dispensary
A medical and/or dental facility offering services less elaborate than those of a hospital.

displacement
The weight of water displaced by a vessel, expressed in long tons. See *tonnage.*

disposal, mine
Clearance procedure that eliminates mine danger individually by any means requiring close approach of personnel to the mine; includes rendering safe, recovery, removal, and destruction.

disposition
Prescribed arrangement of the stations to be occupied by the several formations and single ships of a fleet, or major subdivisions of a fleet, for any purpose, such as cruising, approach, maintaining contact, or battle; prescribed arrangement of all the tactical units composing a flight or group of aircraft.

distance line
A marked line used between ships during underway replenishment operations to assist in maintaining correct distance apart.

distance (tactical)
Distance between foremasts of adjacent ships or cockpits of adjacent aircraft.

distinctive mark
Flag or pennant flown aloft to indicate that the ship is in commission and to indicate status of senior officer aboard. It may be commission pennant, broad or burgee command pennant, personal starred flag of a flag officer, or the Red Cross flag.

district, naval
Geographical area in which all naval activities except those of the operating forces come under the control of a flag officer, the commandant.

ditching
Controlled landing of a disabled aircraft on water.

ditty bag (box)
Small canvas bag or a box used by sailors and Marines to stow odds and ends of gear.

diurnal change
See *variation*.

diurnal inequality
The difference in the height and/or time of the two high waters or the two low waters each day; also the difference in the velocity of either of the two flood, or ebb, currents each day.

diurnal range
Same as great diurnal range.

divided fire
Directing the fire of one ship's batteries against more than one target.

dividers
Instrument for measuring off distance on a chart.

diving bell
See *submarine rescue chamber*.

diving planes (bow and stern)
Surfaces used to control motion of a submarine underwater in a vertical plane. In U.S. nuclear submarines, bow planes have been replaced by *sail planes*, built into the sail

division
The basic administrative unit into which Navy men are organized aboard ship, in aircraft squadrons, or at shore activities. Also, a tactical subdivision of a squadron of ships or aircraft.

division book
Division officer's record of men's names, watch, quarter, and station assignments and other pertinent data. Same data may also be kept in the form of division personnel cards.

division officer
Junior officer assigned by the commanding officer to command a division of men.

Division Officer's Guide
Standard management handbook for junior officers.

division parade
Space on deck assigned for division to fall in for muster or inspection. See *foul-weather parade*.

division police petty officer
Petty officer detailed by division officer to assist chief master-at-arms.

DLA
Defense Logistics Agency. Formerly, Defense Supply Agency.

dock
Large basin either permanently filled with water (wet dock) or capable of being filled and drained (drydock or graving dock). The term is now used interchangeably with pier or wharf.

dockmaster
Officer or civilian in charge of drydocking (or undocking) a ship.

docking plan
Drawing showing details of a ship's bottom used for arranging supports in a dock in order to leave access for sonar domes, hull openings, etc., after docking.

docking report
One giving reason for docking, ship's condition, and work performed while docked.

dock trials
Test of ship's operating equipment including engines while alongside the pier or other docking facility prior to sea trials after construction or overhaul. A part of a builder's trials for new construction. See *fast cruise*.

DOD
Department of Defense.

dodger
Canvas windshield on exposed bridge or conning station.

dog
Small metal fitting used to close ports and hatches. Also, to split a watch with a shipmate is to *dog* it.

dog down
Tighten dogs or clamps on a port, hatch or door.

dogface
Slang for soldier.

dog fight
Aerial combat between fighter-type aircraft.

dogtag
Slang for identification disk.

dog watch
One of the two-hour watches, 4-6 PM (1600-1800) or 6-8 PM (1800-2000).

doldrums
Areas on both sides of the equator where light breezes and calms persist. A person can be said to be *in the doldrums* if his personal affairs stagnate rather than progress.

dolly
A low platform with wheels used for transporting or shifting heavy objects. A large cable jack mounted on wheels, used on aircraft carriers. Now largely replaced by mobile cranes, known usually as cherry pickers (slang). See *crash dolly.*

dolphin
A cluster or clump of piles used for mooring. A single pile or a bollard on a pier is sometimes called a dolphin. Also, a small whale, or sea-going mammal, similar to a porpoise. Inaccurately applied to a colorful food and game fish, the dorado or mahimahi.

dome
A transducer sheathing device used to reduce the noise caused by passage of the transducer through the water.

donkey engine
Small auxiliary engine used for lifting, etc.

door
The device that closes an upright opening between compartments. A light-weight partition not intended to hold water might have a simple door; a watertight bulkhead would have a watertight door of equal strength. For damage control, some watertight doors are electrically or hydraulically operated from a central control station (damage control central). A hatch is a similar device in a deck.

dope
Slange for information or news, good or bad. Also called *the word. Good dope* is accurate, even though the news may be bad. *Bad dope* or *bum dope* is untrustworthy.

doppler
Apparent change in pitch (frequency) of sound or radio wave caused by change in effective length of travel between source and point of observation; caused by speed differential between source and observer.

doppler effect
In ASW this gives some indication of target motion and thus helps to confirm (or classify) a sonar blip as a submarine. See *doppler*.

dory
Small, flat-bottomed pulling boat, used chiefly by fishermen. Easily nested in large numbers because of removable thwarts and sloping sides, dories were the work boats of the famous Grand Banks fishing schooners.

dosimeter
An instrument used to measure personal cumulative exposure to radiation. Carried by all persons working on or around nuclear machinery. Its direct reading can give the individual an immediate evaluation. Not as accurate nor as foolproof, however, as the film badge.

double
A ship is said to *double* a projecting point of land when she sails around it.

double-banked
Boat with two men on a thwart or two men on an oar.

double-banked frigate
In days of sail, a frigate was a three-masted, square-rigged man-of-war carrying guns on her gun deck and on her raised forecastle and poop. The forecastle and poop decks were connected by gangways on either side for convenience, but the gangways were not heavy enough to support guns. In the development of ship design, however, large frigates were built with especially heavy gangways, until the combination of forecastle-gangway-poop deck became a single weather deck, above the gun deck, known as the spar deck, and guns were mounted along its entire length. Such a frigate was called a double-banked frigate. HMS *Serapis*, captured by John Paul Jones, was such a ship. So was USS *Constitution*. See *decker, razee*.

double-bottoms
Watertight subdivisions of a ship, next to the keel and between outer and inner bottoms. See *bilge(s)*.

double hooking
Process of switching a boat or other load from one ship's crane to another.

double luff
See *purchase*.

double-shot
The custom of loading two cannon balls into a single cannon with a single explosive charge, during 17th, 18th, and early 19th centuries. Reduced range and accuracy resulted of course, and the procedure was employed only at short range. See *grape, canister, dismantling shot, langrage.*

double-up
To double mooring lines for added security. See *single up.*

down by the head (stern)
Lower in the water than normal at the forward (after) end of the ship.

downgrade
To lower a security classification previously assigned.

downhaul
Line or wire which pulls or leads downward. See *outhaul, inhaul.*

down time
The time equipment is out of commission because of failures of parts, power, or other factors.

down with the helm, or down helm
Order to put the *helm a-lee*, i.e., down to leeward. The rudder goes opposite to the helm or tiller, turns to the weather side, and the ship's head comes to the wind. Used as maneuver in tacking.

dowse (douse)
To put out, to lower a sail quickly, or to wet down or immerse in water.

draft
Depth of a ship beneath the waterline, measured vertically to the keel Also, a group of new men assigned to a command.

drafting machine
Mechanical parallel ruler used in navigational piloting and plotting.

draft marks
Numeral figures on either side of the stem and sternpost, used to indicate the amount of the ship's draft.

drag
Forces opposing direction of motion due to skin friction, profile, and other components. The amount that a ship is down by the stern. To pull the anchor along the bottom, as a ship drags because of high winds. Also slang at the U.S. Naval Academy for girl or date.

dragon's tail
A towed thermister chain of sea temperatures. (Thermister: an electrical resistor whose resistance varies sharply in a known manner with temperature.)

drag ring
Plywood stablizer for a torpedo launched from an airplane

drainage system
Series of pipes for draining all spaces and compartments.

drain, main
Large suction line in the engineering spaces for pumping those compartments, connected to suction of main circulating pump.

dreadnought
A class of battleship (all one caliber, big gun main battery, and high speed), which took its name from the first of the type, HMS *Dreadnought*, built in 1906 with extraordinary speed and in great secrecy. At one stroke she rendered all older battleships obsolete, relegated them to the "pre-dreadnought" class, and put England and Germany back at the starting line of a brand-new naval building race (a fact agonizingly appreciated by Great Britain). The decision to go ahead was made by Admiral Jackie Fisher, First Sea Lord, on the correct grounds that the development could not be delayed in any case, and that being first with the new ships was vital to England's security.

dredging
Dragging an anchor along the bottom at short stay to steady a ship's head in narrow channels or when going alongside a pier. To deepen a harbor or channel.

dress (right or left)
When in ranks, a command to form a straight line guiding from the directed side.

dressing lines
Lines used in dressing ship.

dressing ship
Displaying national colors at all mastheads and the flagstaff; full dressing requires a rainbow of flags from bow to stern over the mastheads.

drift
The lateral motion of a rotating projectile largely due to gyroscopic action. Displacement, because of wind, of aircraft's track from its true heading. Amount of anchor chain on decks for working purposes when mooring. Speed of current in knots. See *leeway.*

drift angle
Horizontal angle between the fore-and-aft axis of an aircraft and its path relative to the ground.

drift ice
Ice that has drifted from its point of origin.

drift lead
Lead weight dropped over the side with the line slack or leading aft Indicates whether the ship is dragging her anchor.

driftmeter (drift sight)
Device in an aircraft used to observe drift.

drill
Training exercise in which actual operation is simulated, such as a general quarters drill.

drogue
Device used to slow rate of movement, e.g., a drogue parachute on an aerial mine. See *sea anchor*.

drone
Remotely controlled aircraft for target or data gathering purposes.

drone, antisubmarine helicopter (DASH)
Small, light-weight, remotely controlled helicopter capable of operating from a destroyer and delivering an antisubmarine warfare weapon to an enemy submarine. It provided destroyers with a stand-off weapon. Discontinued because of high operational losses.

DRT
See *dead-reckoning tracer*.

drum
A capstan-head mounted with axis horizontal, usually as an adjunct to ordinary windlass or capstan, used for assistance in hauling lines.

drum, steam
Large cylindrical shell at the top of a boiler in which the steam collects.

drum, water
Cylindrical tank at the bottom of a boiler; also called mud drum.

drydock
See *dock*.

dry pipe
Perforated pipe at the highest point in a steam drum to collect the steam.

dry run
Rehearsal of any kind, as in torpedo firing, when all motions are gone through except the release of the torpedo.

DSRV
See *deep submergence rescue vehicle*.

ducts
Large sheet-metal pipes that lead air from blowers to enclosed spaces.

dud
An explosive, such as a bomb, that fails to detonate.

dulcimer
Gong-like musical device used to announce dinner in the wardroom.

Dumbo
Seaplane formerly used for search and rescue.

dummy message
Message sent for some purpose other than its content. Generally, an entirely fabricated message.

dump
Temporary stock of supplies or a storage place where military supplies are temporarily stored.

dump, floating
Supply of critical items held on landing craft for quick delivery ashore to assault troops during amphibious operations.

dungarees
Blue cotton work clothes.

dunking (dunked) sonar
Sonar gear towed submerged by a helicopter. Also called dipping sonar.

dunnage
Material used in securing or protecting supplies aboard ship such as boards, mats, straps, etc. Also, a sailor's personal gear.

duplex circuit
One that permits radio communication traffic in both directions at same time.

duplex pressure proportioner
Shipboard foam firefighting device.

Dutch courage
The courage obtained from drink. Comes from the custom initiated by the famous Dutch Admirals Tromp and deRuyter of giving their crews a libera! libation before battle with the English. The practice was naturally belittled by the English, who nevertheless were forced to admit to the effectiveness of the Dutch navy.

Dutchman
A spacer piece in piping or duct aboard ship used to replace a piece of equipment such as the heating element in a ventilation duct.

duty
   Adjective signifying status, such as duty engineer, duty section, etc. Meaning those who must remain on board ship in a work or *on watch* status instead of going ashore.

dye marker
   Brightly colored chemical that spreads when released in water

E

eager
Slang for anxious for duty, employment, combat, and operations in general, presumably to the detraction of one's peers who are not so eager.

eagle screams, the
Slang for pay day.

ear banger
Slang for one who is overanxious to please.

ease
To do something slowly, as *ease away from the pier* and *ease the strain on a line*. See *handsomely*.

ease her (the rudder)
Reduce the amount of rudder during a turn. Generally, an order given as the ship approaches the desired course. The next order will probably be "rudder amidships!" and then "meet her, steady as you go!"

ease off
To ease a line; slacken it when taut.

easing-out line
Line used to release something slowly, as an unshackled anchor chain or a fuel hose.

easy
Carefully, as in *lower away easy*. See *handsomely*.

E award
The battle efficiency E ribbon is awarded to gun and mount crews for efficiency in gunnery and to ships for excellence in communication, engineering, etc.

ebb currents
Currents caused by the decreasing height of tide, generally set seaward.

ebb tide
See *tide*.

echelon
A level of command. A subdivision, e.g., rear echelon of a head-quarters.

Echo
Phonetic word for letter E.

echo sounder
Oceanographic instrument for determining depth of water by measuring time for generated sound emission to reach bottom and return as an echo. See *fathometer*. Also called depth sounder or depth finder.

economizer
Heat transfer device on a boiler that uses the heat of the stack gases to preheat the feed water. See *feed heater*.

eddy
Circular motion caused by water passing obstructions or by action of adjacent currents flowing in opposite directions. Sometimes a synonym for countercurrent.

eductor
Pump used to empty flooded spaces.

egg
Escape capsule for multispace highspeed aircraft.

eight-o'clock reports
Reports received by the executive officer shortly before 2000 (8 PM) from the heads of departments. He, in turn, reports eight o'clock to the commanding officer. Sometimes mistakenly called the "twenty-hundred reports."

ejection seat
Device that expels the pilot safely in an emergency from a high-speed aircraft.

electrician
Warrant officer advanced from electrician's mate

electrician's mate (EM)
Petty officer who maintains and repairs power and lighting circuits. See *Appendix B*.

electromagnetic log
Ship's "speedometer," using an electromagnet to produce a voltage proportionate to the vessel's speed, using the water as a conductor.

electronic countermeasures (ECM)
The use of electronics to reduce the effectiveness of enemy equipment, or to affect his resulting tactics. Active countermeasures are detectable by the enemy, passive are not.

El Nino
A meandering, westward dislocation of the Humbolt Current off the west coast of South America. Severely damages fish and bird life.

electronic navigation
Navigation using such devices as radar, loran, shoran.

electronic requirement plan
A CNO listing, by name and nomenclature, of electronic equipment required for ships, included as an appendix to the ship's approved characteristics. Orginally known as the electronic installation plan.

Electronic Systems Command
A functional command with the Naval Material Command established in May 1966.

elevation, gun
Vertical angle of the axis of the bore of a gun above the horizontal plane.

elevator
Movable section of the tail of a plane, usually hinged to the stablizer and used to head the plane up or down in flight   A lift for passengers and freight. The largest elevators are those used to transfer aircraft between the flight deck and hanger deck of an aircraft carrier

Elokomin rig
Arrangement of tackle and hoses for fueling a ship underway from another ship alongside.

embark
To go aboard a ship or aircraft

embayed
A ship is embayed when the wind is blowing right into a bay so that she cannot weather either side of the mouth of the bay

embarkation officers
Landing force officers who advise naval unit commanders on combat loading and act in liaison with troop officers   Formerly called transport quartermasters.

emergency drill
Rehearsal of action taken by ship s crew in an emergency such as fire

empennage
Tail group or assembly of an aircraft

employment schedule
Program of ship and aircraft activities promulgated by fleet or type commanders.

encapsulated torpedo
A homing mine under development.

encipher
To convert plain text into unintelligible language by a cipher system, usually letter by letter. See *encrypt.*

encode
To convert plain text into unitelligible language, usually word by word, by means of a code book. See *encrypt.*

encrypt
To convert plain text into unintelligible form by means of a cryptosystem. *Encipher, encode,* and *encrypt* are often used synonymously.

end for end
To reverse something, as *end for end the boat falls,* which means to shift ends to spread the wear evenly throughout the falls or line.

end item
The final combination of end products, sub-assemblies, components, and materials ready for their intended use, i.e., ship, tank, aircraft, etc.

end on
Said of two vessels meeting, whose centerlines, extended, lie upon a single, straight line; or of another ship whose centerline projects through own ship. Generally refers to the bows-on or the head-to-head situations.

endorsement
A form of addendum to a letter, indicating approval, disapproval, comment, or other action, that is stamped or written on the basic letter or attached thereto.

engagement stars
Small metal stars worn on campaign ribbons to detnote the wearer's participation in specific battles or operations. Also sometimes given for a specified period within a theater of operations.

engineering duty officer (EDO)
Officer of the restricted line specializing in engineering afloat and ashore. The designation for aeronautical engineering duty officer is AEDO, for ordnance engineering duty officer is OEDO.

engineer's bell book
See *bell book, engineer's.*

engine-order telegraph
Device on the ship's bridge and duplicated in the engineroom(s) for giving and acknowledging orders to the engines. Also called annunciator.

enlisted man or woman
Navy personnel below the grade of warrant officer.

enlisted rating structure
See *Appendix B.*

ensign
The most junior commissioned officer. Also the national flag flown by a man-of-war from the gaff underway, flagstaff in port.

entrance
The part of a ship's hull from amidships forward.

entry plan
Directive containing detailed instructions to a group of ships entering a port or roadstead.

Ephemeris
A publication giving the computed positions of celestial bodies for each day of the year, or for other regular intervals.

equator
The great circle of the earth equidistant from the poles. Divides northern and southern hemispheres.

equatorial tides
Tides occuring approximately every two weeks when the moon is over the equator.

equinoctial
Celestial equator.

equinox
A point marking the intersection of the ecliptic and the celestial equator, occupied by the sun or moon when its declination is zero.

equipage
General term used to designate material of a non-consumable nature which must be aboard for a ship to perform its mission properly.

equivalent full-power hours (EFPH)
A standard for indicating the amount of nuclear energy consumed. Naval reactors are rated in terms of the number of hours of full-power energy built into them, which is a direct measure of the amount of nuclear fuel. A half hour at full power is the same as one hour at half power, although distances run and speeds attained vary as the cube law. Thus a 2,000-hour reactor which has logged 1,000 EFPH is half expended.

equivalent service rounds (ESR)
A standard for indicating gun erosion. All rounds fired, including reduced charges, are recorded in terms of service rounds.

escape hatch
In general any hatch, usually small, installed to permit men to escape from a compartment when ordinary means of egress are blocked. Developed to a high degree in modern submarines, which have excape trunks fitted to receive a rescue chamber or a deep-submergence rescue vehicle, an additional hatch for unassisted escape, and numerous specialized operating mechanisms and devices.

escape trunk
A specialized escape compartment in modern submarines. See *escape hatch*.

escort
To convoy. Aircraft assigned to protect and accompany other aircraft. Combatant ships protecting a convoy or task force. A person who accompanies a body to a burial place.

escort vessel
Old name for destroyer escort (now *frigate*). Now used to designate any warship escorting another ship or ships.

estimated position (EP)
The navigational position determined from estimates rather than from known data. Frequently an arbitrary datum from which to calculate the navigational fix.

estimate of the situation
Logical process of reasoning by which a commander considers all circumstances and arrives at a decision.

Eulerian method
Measurement of rate of flow past a given point by current meters.

eulittoral zone
Subdivision of the littoral system of the benthic division including waters from zero to 50 meters in depth.

evaporator (evaps)
Device aboard ship for making fresh water from seawater by the process of evaporation.

evasive steering
Ship tactics to confuse submarines, including zigzagging, sinuating, and weaving.

even keel
Floating evenly and level without list A ship on an even keel might, however, be out of trim (r.e., down by the head or down by the stern).

evolution
The tactical maneuver or movement of ships or aircraft. Also a synonym for exercise.

execute
To actuate, as *execute the signal*

executive officer
The second in command of a ship station, aircraft squadron, etc. Slang: exec, XO.

exercise
Naval maneuver, drill, or operation for training purposes.

exercises, joint
Exercises in which two or more of the armed services take part. See *combined operations.*

expansion joint
A joint which allows expansion, contraction, or flexing in a pipe, ship's decks or superstructure.

explosimeter
Device to test presence of explosive fumes.

exposure suit
Special clothing designed to help the wearer to resist exposure to cold water. Used by aviators, fishermen, yachtsmen. Now called survival clothing.

extender
Safety device for holding the detonator of a mine or depth charge in a safe position.

extra duty
Additional work assigned as punishment under the Uniform Code of Military Justice (UCMJ).

extremely high frequency radio (EHF)
Radio operating in the range of 30,000 to 300,000 MHz.

eyebolt
A metal bolt ending in an eye.

eyebrow
Elliptical metal ridge over an air port designed to shed water.

eyes of the ship
The forward-most portion of the weather deck, as far forward as a person can stand, where fog lookouts are customarily stationed. Most old ships had figureheads on their bows, and the term *eyes of the ship* is supposed to refer either to their eyes or to those of the fog lookouts. Interestingly, the Chinese, with an entirely different cultural history, have carved or painted eyes on the bows of their junks for centuries.

F

Facilities Engineering Command
A functional command within the Naval Material Command, established in May 1966 to replace the Bureau of Yards and Docks.

facsimile
The transmission of photographs or other material by wire or radio.

fag end
The extreme end of a rope, more specifically, when it has become fagged, or untwisted.

fairlead
A fitting, such as a block, which provides a friction-free passage for a line or cable. Also, an unhampered route for a line or cable.

fair tide
Tidal current running in the same direction as the ship.

fairway
The navigable part of a body of water, including the channel.

fair wind
A favoring wind.

fake down
To lay out a line in long flat bights, the whole being much longer than wide, in such form that when needed it will pay out freely without bights or kinks. A coiled or flemished line cannot do this unless the coil of the line is able to turn, as on a reel. Otherwise, a twist results in the line which will produce a kink and jam it. Also termed flake down. See *coil down* and *flemish (down)*.

fall
The rope and blocks that make up a tackle, e.g., a boat fall. In a tackle, specifically that portion of the rope that is between the two blocks. See *purchase*.

fall in at quarters
Command to form ranks at quarters. The command to disband or fall out is: *Leave your quarters.*

falling glass
Lowering atmospheric pressure as registered by the barometer; normally a sign of approaching bad weather.

fall off
Said of a ship or the bow of a ship when it drifts away from a desired position or direction. See *haul, haul off*.

fallout area
Area of windward of atomic explosion where rain of contaminated matter is likely.

fancy work
Decorative knots and pieces of canvas used particularly in gigs and barges. See *square knotting, MacNamara lace*.

fantail
The aftermost deck area topside in a ship.

farm
Open storage area near pier entrance.

fast
Snugly secured; said of a line when it is fastened securely.

Fast Automatic Shuttle Transfer System (FAST)
Replenishment system designed to speed transfer of ordnance and supplies between ships at sea through specialized equipment aboard the supply ship.

fast cruise
Trials of several days in length conducted while the ship is fast to a pier or at anchor, with only the ship's crew aboard. The purpose is to train personnel in all operations of the ship's equipment and to check out its proper operation in as many facets as practicable. Considerable ingenuity is commonly exercised to simulate actual conditions at sea. Originally devised to check out readiness of a nuclear ship and crew after completion of the construction period and prior to sea trials. Now extended to include post-overhaul trials, and nonnuclear ships as well.

fast deployment logistic (FDL) ship
Pre-loaded ship intended to permit fast transportation of necessary equipment to troubled areas, to meet Army combat personnel transported by air. The program for development of these ships has struck many snags and has yet to be approved by Congress.

fast ice
Sea ice which remains along coast or over shoals in the position of its growth. Same as landfast ice.

fast reaction integrated submarine control (FRISCO)
A combat data processing and display system for submarines.

fathom
Measure of length, six feet. See *mariner's measurements*.

fathometer
Another name for echo sounder.

feather
To turn the blade of an oar horizontally at the finish of a stroke to reduce resistance of air or water. To change the pitch of a variable-pitch propeller of an airplane to reduce the amount of bite into the air. Also, the bow (stern) spray of a high-speed ship. Similarly, periscope feather, the spray formed by the periscope of a submerged submarine moving through the water at moderate to high speed.

feather merchant
Slang for an uncomplimentary term of mild scorn or abuse, applied to men (especially reservists) new to the service.

feedback
The audible return of a portion of the amplified stage output to the input of that stage, resulting in squealing when transmitting over a voice radio.

feed heater
Heat transfer device used to heat feed water before it goes to the boiler. See *economizer*.

feed water
Fresh water made in evaporators for use in boilers.

feel the way
To proceed cautiously, taking soundings with the lead. A ship will literally *feel its way* along an unfamiliar or uncharted channel.

fender
A device of canvas, wood, line, cork, rubber, wicker, or plastic slung over the side of a ship in position to absorb the shock of contact between ships or between a ship and pier.

fend off
To push away; pushing away from a pier or another ship when coming alongside, to prevent damage or chafing.

fetch
The distance a wind blows over the sea surface without significant change in direction, a factor in the build-up of waves.

fiber rope
General term for cordage made of vegetable fibers, such as hemp, manila, flax, cotton, or sisal, in contrast to synthetic fibers like dacron and nylon.

fid
Sharply pointed, round wooden tool used in separating the strands of a line for splicing. See *marlinespike*.

fiddle bridge
Collapsible supports under the arresting cables on an aircraft carrier's deck.

fiddle rack (boards)
Wooden device set on a table at sea in rough weather to hold table gear in place.

fiddley, fidley
Wide opening immediately above a fireroom, through which ventilators are led; iron framework around ladder of a deck hatch leading below decks.

fidley deck
Raised platform over the engine and boiler rooms, more particularly around the stack.

fidley grating
Steel gratings fitted over boiler room hatches.

field change
Necessary parts and instructions to make an authorized post factory modification to machinery, ordnance, or electronic equipment.

field change order
Written unilateral order by a field representative. Normally the technical and financial scope of such orders is less than that which can be authorized by the cognizant office or command.

field day
Cleaning day, traditionally Friday, the day before inspection.

field ice
Ice formed by freezing of the ocean surface. Also called sea ice.

field music
U.S. Marine term for bugle call or bugler.

field scarf
Marine term for khaki uniform necktie.

field-strip
To disassemble without further breakdown the major groups of a piece of ordnance for routine cleaning and oiling; opposed to detailed stripping which may be done only by authorized technicians.

fife rail
A wooden or metal rail bored with holes to receive belaying pins; seen on Navy ships at head of flag bags.

FIFO
First in, First out. A logical method of stowing supplies so that oldest stock is issued first.

fighter direction
Control of fighter aircraft. A fighter direction ship or aircraft is one specially equipped for that purpose. A fighter director is one who does the controlling

fighter sweep
Offensive mission by fighter aircraft to destroy enemy aircraft or installations.

figure-8 fake
Method of coiling rope in which the turns form a series of overlapping figure-eights advancing about one or two diameters of the rope for each turn; usually done over the lifelines.

filbert base
A dummy air base intended to give the enemy false intelligence on positions and strength or to conceal removal or abandonment of a real base.

file
Message files. Permanent: general, radio station, or visual station file. Temporary: tickler file, one that is designed to jog the memory. Also a line of men standing in formation.

file closer
Man who stands behind the file, as the CPO or junior officer does during inspection.

file number
Record identification number for naval officers, assigned upon commissioning and retained permanently. Corresponding term for Marine Corps officers is service number. Slang: serial number. File and service numbers have been replaced by social security numbers.

fill
To adjust a vessel's sails so that the wind may force her ahead. The reverse of this is backing.

film badge
A small piece of unexposed film, arranged in a badge pinned to clothing by personnel working in a nuclear environment. Changed periodically and read, i.e. developed and evaluated, in the nucleonics laboratory of the activity. Gives a more accurate measure of cumulative radiation exposure than the dosimeter.

final acceptance trials (FAT)
Final underway sea trials conducted by Navy operating personnel to show the ship meets all contractual requirements.

final diameter
Diameter of a circle made by a ship completing a turn with constant rudder angle.

fire and rescue party
Obsolete term for rescue and assistance party.

firebox
The section of a ship's boiler where fuel oil combustion takes place.

fire, call
Gunfire delivered on a target in response to a request from the supported unit.

fire, continuous
All guns firing independently when loaded; in contrast to salvo fire.

fire control
Organized system by which the offensive power of a ship's armament is directed.

fire control, shipboard
The entire system of directing and controlling the offensive and defensive weapons of a ship.

fire control technician (FT)
A petty officer who performs major repair and overhaul of the fire-control equipment.

fire-control tower
May be either a separate structure or a part of the conning tower containing fire-control equipment in warships.

fire, counter-battery
Gunfire from a ship directed at enemy artillery ashore.

fire, covering
Gunfire delivered to protect or cover certain operations, such as minesweeping.

fire, destruction
Slow, deliberate, accurate gunfire to destroy a target ashore.

fire, direct
Gunfire in which the weapon's sights bear directly on the target.

fire, harassing
Sporadic shore bombardment gunfire to prevent enemy rest, re-grouping, or movement.

fire, illuminating
Starshell firing to silhouette the enemy and provide illumination for naval operations or troop operations ashore.

fire, interdiction
Intermittent gunfire on roads, road junctions, railroads, airfields, etc., to prevent enemy use.

firemain
The salt water line that provides firefighting and flushing water throughout the ship.

fireman (FN)
Enlisted man in paygrade E-3 who works in the engineering department spaces. See *Appendix B.*

fire mission
An assignment in shore bombardment to fire on a specific target.

fire, neutralization
Gunfire designed to immobilize enemy activity in a specific area.

fire party
Men aboard ship in the duty section organized to fight fires.

fireroom
Compartment containing boilers and the station for firing or operating them.

fire, salvo
Gunfire in which all guns of a battery fire together at regular intervals. In the British navy, half the guns fire at a time, alternately. Thus, salvos are twice as fast for a given firing interval.

fire, slow
Deliberate gunfire to permit careful adjustment.

fire support
Gunfire to aid or assist a unit ashore. May be close support, deep support, or direct support fire.

fire support area (sector)
Specific terrain assigned a ship for gunfire during an amphibious operation.

fire support ship, inshore (IFS)
Shallow-draft rocket-firing ship for fire-support duty close to the beach during amphibious assault.

Firetrac
System for measuring performance of missiles fired at target drones.

firing lock
The mechanism in the breech of a gun that contains the firing pin.

firing range
Distance between firing ship and target at instant of firing torpedo. See *torpedo run*.

firing-stop mechanism
Device that prevents a gun from firing into its own ship's structure.

first-aid kit
Emergency medical equipment in a repair-party locker or on a life raft. At a gun, material is in a first-aid pouch or gun bag. In a boat, the first-aid gear is in the boat box.

first call
A bugle call sounded five minutes before quarters, colors, or tattoo.

first dog watch
The watch from 4-6 PM (1600-1800).

first lieutenant
Officer responsible for the upkeep and cleanliness of the ship, boats, ground tackle, and deck seamanship in general.

first light
The beginning of morning nautical twilight, i.e., when the center of the morning sun is 12 degrees below the horizon.

first watch
The 8 PM to midnight (2000-2400).

fish
Streamlined weight on the end of an aircraft's trailing, suspended antenna. Also, slang for torpedo. A tapered batten of hard strong wood bound to a spar to strengthen it. To *fish a spar* is to strengthen it in this way. To fish an (old-fashioned) anchor was to engage the hook of the *catfall* in the pad-eye of the balance point, an operation resembling fishing.

fist
A radio operator's key or sending hand. A slow or rusty operator is said to have a *glass fist*. An expert has a *copperplate hand*, or *fist*.

Fita Fita guard (band)
American Samoans enlisted in the Navy for duty in Samoa. Disestablished in 1951.

fitness report
Periodic evaluation of an officer's performance of duty and worth to the service, by his commanding officer.

fitting
Generic term for any part or piece of machinery or installed equipment.

fitting out
Preparing a ship for commissioning and active service by placing on board the material authorized by the allowance list.

fix
A navigational position determined from terrestial, electronic, or astronomical data.

flag bag
Container on the bridge holding the signal flags.

flag bridge
In a ship designed for service as flagship, a separate bridge for use of a flag officer and his staff. Usually on a different level from the ship's navigating bridge and distinctly separate from it. See *signal bridge*.

flaghoist
Method of communicating between ships by using flags run up on signal halyards.

flag lieutenant
Personal aide to flag officer afloat. Acts as flag visual-signal officer underway.

flag officer
Officer in rank above captain, authorized to fly a personal flag. Equivalent to general officer. See *admiral.*

flag plot
An enclosed tactical and navigational center used by the flag officer and his staff in exercising tactical command of ships and aircraft.

flag secretary
Personal aide to a flag officer who directs the paper work of a staff.

flagship
The ship from which an admiral or other unit commander exercises command.

flags, signal
Colored flags, including international alphabet flags, used for visual communications.

flagstaff
Vertical spar at stern of ship where the ensign is displayed when anchored or moored.

flagstaff insignia
Distinguishing devices such as eagles, halberds, stars, etc., fitted at top of flagstaffs used in boats of officers or of important civil officials.

flake
Mispronunciation of "fake" in *fake down.*

flake out
Slang meaning to lie down, take a nap or "take an equal strain on all parts."

flame-out
Inflight jet aircraft casualty—the fire goes out.

flame safety lamp
Special lamp designed to test oxygen content of air in a compartment.

flank speed
Maximum speed.

flap
Slang for excitement or confusion.

flapper valve
A valve, usually large, closed by swinging a hinged plate on to its seat, seated firmly by pressure above the plate or disc. Lends itself to quick closing, remote operation, and automatic action if water instead of air comes down the pipe. Disaster to USS *Squalus* in 1939 established requirement for such valves in hull air-induction system of submarines.

flare
Pyrotechnic device used to attract attention or illuminate an area.

flare (of a ship's hull)
The outward curve, away from the centerline, of the sides of a boat or ship, above the waterline; reverse of tumble home. Flare causes the sides of a ship's bows to be concave. Thus they force water away as she plunges, and simultaneously greatly increase displacement of the bow, reducing depth to which the bow plunges. See *tumble home.*

flareback
Backfire of flame and hot gases into a ship's fireroom from the firebox. Also, an ejection of flame and hot gas from the breech of a gun.

flash burn
The burn from the flash of a bomb or projectile, countered on board ship by flashproof clothing (battle dress).

flashing
Reducing the amount of permanent magnetism in a ship by placing temporary energizing coils horizontally around the ship. See *degaussing, deperming.*

flashing light
Communication using a code transmitted by blinker or signal searchlight. A navigational aid whose period of light is less than the period of darkness. See *occulting light.*

flashless charges
Powder that reduces flash of detonation for concealing firing ship at night.

flash message
A category of precedence reserved for initial enemy contact messages or operational combat messages of extreme urgency.

flash plate
Metal plate on forecastle on which anchor chain rests. So called because of the sparks when the anchor is let go.

flashproof
Clothing worn to prevent flash burn.

flat(s)
Plating or gratings installed only to provide working or walking surfaces above bilges.

flat hat
Blue cap formerly worn by the enlisted men. Similar in shape to the officer's cap (with the old blue cap cover), but without the visor.

flathatting
Slang for low flying and stunting.

flattop
Slang for aircraft carrier.

flaw
Sudden gust of wind. A very light puff during a calm is called a cat's paw.

fleet
An organization of ships, aircraft, marine forces, and shore-based fleet activities, all under a commander or commander-in-chief who may exercise operational as well as administrative control. Also, all naval operating forces.

fleet aircraft service squadron (FASRON)
A unit that maintains and repairs fleet aircraft.

fleet air detachment (FAD)
Fleet aircraft, personnel, and units based on shore. CFAD is Commander FAD.

fleet air wing
A group of patrol squadrons, land- and carrier-based, with tenders and supporting FASRON.

fleet ballistic missile (FBM)
Shipborne ballistic missile, also known as Polaris, Poseidon, or Trident missile, designed to be carried on deterrent patrols by submarines built for the purpose.

fleet ballistic missile submarine (SSBN)
Nuclear-powered submarine designed to deliver ballistic missile attacks against assigned targets from either a submerged or surfaced condition.

Fleet Guides
Naval publications describing each major U.S. port from which the fleet operates. Also, when the fleet steams in formation, one ship, usually the flagship, is designated as Fleet Guide, upon which the others keep station. Under modern organization this term is falling into disuse.

fleet in being
A naval force that acts as a factor of strength because of its existence. A classic example is German High Seas Fleet during WWI.

Fleet Logistics Air Wing (FLOGWING or FLAW)
Fleet aircraft which maintain essential air transport for fleet operations.

Fleet Marine Force (FMF)
A balanced force of combined arms comprising land, air, and service elements of the U.S. Marine Corps. A Fleet Marine Force is an integral part of a U.S. Fleet and has the status of a type command.

fleet up
To advance in position or importance, as the gunnery officer may *fleet up* to executive officer.

flemish (down)
To coil down a line on deck in a flat, circular, tight arrangement. Useful for appearance only, since unless the twists in the line are removed it will kink when taken up or used. See *fake down* and *coil down*.

flensing
Removing the blubber from a whale chained alongside; the whale rotates as a long strip of blubber is peeled off and hoisted aboard.

Flexbee
Lightweight, flexible wing reconnaissance drone used by the Marine Corps.

flight
In naval and Marine Corps usage, a specified group of aircraft usually engaged in a common mission.

flight clearance
Permission to make a flight.

flight deck
Top deck of an aircraft carrier.

flight gear
Clothing and equipment worn by an aviator.

flight leader
Pilot in tactical command of a mission, flight, sweep, or patrol station.

flight line
Prescribed path of aircraft taking photographs or making other observations; also, relating to an airfield, a line of the field on which planes are parked prior to takeoff.

flight log
Naval aviator's record of his flight time.

flight pay
Extra pay earned by aviation personnel. Slang: flight skins.

flight plan
Specified information filed either orally or in writing with air traffic control relative to intended flight of an aircraft.

flight quarters
Manning of all stations for flight operations aboard ship.

flight skins
Slang for flight pay.

flight surgeon
Medical officer specially qualified for duty with an aviation unit.

flinders bar
Iron bar inserted in the binnacle of a magnetic compass to help compensate for deviation.

floater net
Net made up of floats connected by line. Used to supplement life rafts and life boats.

floating drydock
Movable dock floating in water; ships are floated into it when the dock is *down* (i.e., partially submerged). Then the dock is raised by pumping the ballast tanks, lifting the ship to facilitate repairs to the underwater body.

floating dump (offshore dump)
Reserve of critical supplies held afloat for quick delivery to the assault troops ashore in an amphibious assault.

float, life
Emergency equipment used by ships and aircraft in case of disaster at sea.

floating reserve
Amphibious troops kept aboard ship until needed.

floe
Fragments of ice, but not icebergs, of no specific size.

flood currents
Currents due to increase in height of tide.

flood tide
Incoming tide.

floor
Wide web beams inside a ship's bottom. Also, the inside of the ship's bottom plating. See *bilges, ceiling.*

floor plates
Removable deck plating of any machinery space.

Florida Current
Water flowing north into the Atlantic Ocean from the Caribbean Sea through the Straits of Florida and off the east coast of the U.S. from Florida to Cape Hatteras, where it becomes the Gulf Stream. Part of the Gulf Stream system.

flotation gear
Devices designed to insure floating, as in an aircraft that flies over water.

flotilla
Administrative or tactical organization consisting of two or more squadrons of ships together with a flagship and/or tender.

flotsam
Floating wreckage or trash. See *jetsam.*

flukes
Broad arms or palms of an anchor.

flushdecker or **flush-deck destroyer**
Ship whose weather deck extends unbroken the length of the ship. A WWI destroyer. See *four-piper.*

fly
The long dimension or length of a flag. Also, the outboard end of a flag, away from the halyard.

fly 1, 2, 3
Subdivisions of a carrier flight deck. Fly 1 is under the direction of the flight deck officer and catapult officer; fly 2, the taxi signal officer, and fly 3, the landing-signal officer.

flyable dud
An aircraft that can be flown but is not in shape for combat.

flycatcher operations
Those against enemy small craft in an amphibious objective area.

fly control
The station on a carrier that gives landing and takeoff instructions to flight deck personnel.

flying boat
Type of seaplane which can float on its hull in the water.

flying bridge
Topmost bridge of a ship, usually above the navigating bridge or conning tower.

flying jib
In sailing ships setting more than a single jib, the outer one, farthest forward, is the flying jib.

flying moor
See *moor.*

flying officer
Officer designated as a naval aviator; includes aviation observers and flight surgeons.

foam
Chemical which produces large quantities of smothering suds for fire fighting.

fog buoy
See *towing spar.*

fog lookouts
Special lookouts because of fog. Generally sent to the *eyes of the ship,* since in the thick fog they might well be the first to see another ship or object when danger of collision might exist. The *Rules of the Road* specify that in fog a ship must proceed sufficiently slowly that she can come to a complete stop in half the distance of visibility. Lookouts may also be sent aloft when the fog is dense but close to the surface of the water.

fog nozzle (applicator)
Firehose fitting which forces water into very fine spray or fog.

fog signal, major
Shore signal with normal range of a mile and a half or more.

fogy
Slang for an increase in pay because of length of service. Pronounced "foh-gy."

following sea
Waves moving in the same general direction as the ship.

foofoo
Slang for face lotion or hair tonic.

foot (of a sail)
The bottom edge.

footline
The bottom lifeline.

footrope
The rope attached to the underside of a yard on which sailors stood while loosing or furling sail, now obsolete except for the few sailing ships used for training.

force
A body of troops, ships, or aircraft, or combination thereof; major subdivision of a fleet. Part of a task force. Also a measure of wind intensity, as *force 4.*

forced draft
Air under pressure supplied to the burners in a ship's boilers, characteristic of all ships today except nuclear powered ones.

force tabs
With reference to war plans, the statement of time-phased deployments of major combat units by major commands and geographic areas.

fore-and-aft
Lengthwise of a ship, as opposed to athwartships. A fore-and-after is a vessel rigged with fore-and-aft sails.

fore-and-aft sail
A sail designed to have a leading edge (luff) and a trailing edge (leech), cut in a triangular or a quadrilateral shape, but neither square nor rectangular. Designed to be fitted to booms instead of to yards—except that the lateen sail, as a special and obsolete case, had a yard slung at an angle from the horizontal. Most small craft have fore-and-aft sails because of their far greater versatility than the square sails, but the huge fore-and-aft sails required by large ships were not practical. See *square sail*.

forebody
Ship's hull forward of amidships.

forecastle
Forward section of weather deck. Pronounced "folk-sul." Vicinity of the ground tackle.

forecastle deck
Partial deck over the main deck at the bow.

forefoot
Part of the keel that curves up to meet the stem or where the stem joins the keel of a ship.

fore leech
The luff of a fore-and-aft sail. See *leech*.

Forel scale
Basic scale for measuring color of sea water.

foremast
The forward mast of a ship with two or more masts, unless the second mast is so much smaller than the first that the first is called the mainmast and the second the mizzenmast, or jigger, as in a yawl or ketch.

forenoon watch
The watch from 8 AM to noon (0800-1200).

foresheets
Space in an open boat, at the bow, not occupied by thwarts. Uncommon term. Usually expressed as bow or bows. See *sternsheets*.

foreshore
Portion of the shore or beach lying between low water and the upper limits of normal wave action.

forestay
A stay supporting a mast from forward. See *backstay*.

foretop
Heavy structure supported by a foremast; houses fire-control equipment. Rare in modern warship design. See *top.*

formation
Any ordered arrangement of two or more ships or aircraft proceeding together. Also an arrangement of troops.

forward
Toward the bow.

forward bow (quarter) spring
Mooring lines at the bow (quarter) that lead forward from the ship to the pier or wharf. Both forward and after spring lines are necessary to prevent fore-and-aft movement of the ship. See *spring, after bow (quarter) spring.*

foul
To entangle, confuse, or obstruct. Jammed or entangled; not clear for running. Covered with barnacles, as *foul bottom.* For one ship to *foul* or to run *afoul* of another is to collide broadside or with insufficient force to do serious structural damage.

foul anchor
Anchor entangled in its chain or for any other reason not clear for hoisting all the way up.

foul deck
Aircraft carrier deck that is obstructed and cannot be landed upon.

foul ground
Shallow sea area marked by rocks, reefs, shoals, wrecks, etc.

foul hawse
To have a foul hawse means there is an obstruction or potential obstruction in the hawse hole preventing normal heaving in. This can be something foreign to the ship, a kink or twist in cable or chain, a jammed or tangled swivel, etc. When ship is anchored with two anchors and two chains, foul hawse means that the chains have become twisted together. See *hawse.*

fouling
The attachment of various marine organisms to underwater bodies, a problem in ships because it reduces speed.

foul up
Slang for getting into trouble. Also, trouble, disturbance or confusion.

foul weather
Rainy or stormy weather.

foul-weather parade
An assembly below decks or under shelter.

founder
To sink.

Four-O (4.0)
Perfect; 100%.

four piper
A ship with four stacks. Some cruisers were referred to as four pipers, but the term found general and affectionate use in relation to the very large group of WWI flush-deck destroyers that were the backbone of the U.S. Navy's destroyer force during the between-the-wars years. The fifty destroyers transferred to England during WWII, before US entry, were of this type. Although nearly all appeared identical to anyone but those who knew them, to a destroyerman of that time they exhibited many fascinating differences.

foxer gear (FXR)
Noise-making device towed astern to foil acoustical torpedoes.

foxtail
Short-handled brush for sweeping small areas. Also, short line attached to a jackstay.

Foxtrot
Phonetic word for letter *F*.

fram
Originally, an acronym for fleet rehabilitation and modernization program, now generally signifies a virtual rebuilding of the entire ship with particular attention to adding new and innovative capabilities not in her original design or configuration, but not changing her basic designation. Not the equal of a conversion which would, presumably, alter the fundamental employment or purpose of the vessel. Usually applied to destroyers, for whom the fram program was first created. See *conversion*.

frames
Athwartships strengthing members of a ship's hull, numbered from bow aft and used as reference points to locate fittings, division parades, etc.

frap, frapping gear
To frap is to wrap with line. Frapping gear is the line used.

frapping lines
Lines passed around forward and after boat falls to steady the boat in a seaway as it is being hoisted or lowered.

free
To clear or untangle.

freeboard
Distance from the weather deck to the waterline.

freeing port
A deck-level opening in the ship or in bulwark to permit water to escape.

free surface
Liquid in a partially filled ship's compartment or tank that is free to move from side to side as the ship rolls. Because the liquid always goes to the low side, a large free surface is always dangerous to stability.

frequency
The rate at which a cycle is repeated, originally given in terms of cycles per second (or kilocycles, megacycles, etc.) The term kHz (kilohertz) has replaced kc (kilocycle) and the term mHz (megahertz) has replaced mc (megacycle).

Frescanar
Three dimensional radar used with Talos, Tartar, and Terrier.

freshen the nip
To shift a rope to equalize the wear. Not a drinking term.

freshwater king
Enlisted man in charge of the ship's evaporators and water supply.

freshwater system
Series of freshwater piping to supply galley, washrooms, scuttlebutts, and boilers.

frigate
In days of sail, a full-rigged ship mounting guns on a single gundeck and on forecastle and poop, or spar deck, depending on construction of weather decks, i.e., two decks of guns. Fast and maneuverable, comparable to the cruisers of a later day. The British navy used frigates as adjuncts to their battle fleet, for scouting, signaling, etc. The U.S. Navy designed and used them for ocean raiders, able to defeat anything fast enough to catch them. In modern navies the frigate is smaller and slower than a destroyer, an ocean escort for anything less important than an aircraft carrier. For a time, the U.S. Navy was alone in using the designation *frigate* for its large destroyers (so-called, destroyer leaders) in recognition of the place the early frigates held in our history, but it has now reverted to the common practice of all other navies. The large destroyers have, at the same time, been redesignated as *cruisers*. See *decker, double-banked frigate, razee,* and *Appendix A.*

frogmen
Slang for underwater-demolition team (UDT) personnel.

front
Boundary between two dissimilar air masses marked by turbulence, squalls, rain, and change in temperature or pressure.

fuel depot
A petrolem storage activity designed to provide fuels to other activities and to ships.

full and bye
Said of a square-rigged sailing ship sailing with the wind abeam with all sails set and drawing. She is sailing by the wind, with all sails *full.*

full and down
Said of a ship when all spaces are full of cargo and ship is down to maximum specified draft and drag.

full bag
Complete outfit of uniforms and related gear, required of all enlisted men.

fully rigged ship
A sailing ship with bowsprit and three masts, entirely square-rigged except for the jibs, and the lowest sail on the mizzenmast, the spanker.

full speed
A prescribed speed that is greater than standard speed but less than flank speed. Highest sustainable speed. See *speed.*

funnel
Ship's smokestack; stack.

furl
To make up in a bundle, as in *furl the sail.*

fuselage
Body of an airplane.

fuze
Mechanical, electrical, electronic, or magnetic device for detonating the explosive charge of a weapon.

fuze (projectile)
A fuze of the following types: auxiliary detonating, base detonating, mechanical time, point detonating, or proximity fuze (VT). See *projectile.*

fuze, proximity (VT)
A fuze activated by external influence in close vicinity of target. Also called VT fuze.

G

gaff
Small spar on the aftermost mast from which the ensign is displayed while underway. Also, the upper spar of a four-sided fore and aft sail, as the spanker. In days of sail, the ensign flew from the spanker gaff.

gale
Strong wind, usually described as: a *moderate gale* (28-33 knots); a *fresh gale* (34-40 knots); a *strong gale* (41-47 knots); or a *whole gale* (48-55 knots). See *breeze, storm, hurricane.*

gallery deck
Partial deck below a flight deck of an aircraft carrier.

galley
A shipboard kitchen.

gangplank
Temporary bridge from the ship to a pier or to another ship alongside. See *brow.*

gangway
An order to stand aside or stand clear. An opening in the rail or bulwarks of a ship to permit access on board; not a synonym for accommodation ladder. In the days of sail, ships with raised forecastles and poop decks frequently had walkways connecting the two, one on either side. Originally called gangways, these walkways gradually were constructed of much heavier timbers, until they were indistinguishable from the decks they connected, and the once open area between forecastle and poop evolved into a large hatch. The combination of forecastle, poop deck, and gangways became known as the spar deck. In some particularly heavy warships, guns were mounted along its entire length. See *doublebanked frigate.*

gantline
Line passing through a single block aloft. A single block whip or tackle at the top of a mast or stack for sending men or gear aloft.

garble
Error that makes message incorrect or unintelligible.

garboard strake
The strake next to the keel.

gasket
Strip of sealing material, usually rubber, set along edge of watertight door, port, or hatch. The gasket opposes a knife-edge. Also in pipelines, cylinder blocks, etc. Term originally referred to a short rope.

gate vessel
Ship used to open and close gate. Opening in antisubmarine nets protecting a harbor or narrow passage.

gather way
To gain headway.

gauge glass
Device for indicating water level in a tank or boiler.

Gazetteer
Alphabetical lists of names of geographic features of various locations, published by the Defense Mapping Agency.

gear
General term for equipment, material, supplies, or baggage.

geedunk
Slang for ice cream, soda, etc. Items from soda fountain.

general alarm
The signal for manning battle stations. Nowadays given by musical notes over a ship's general-announcing system. In days past, various other means, such as bugle calls, the fife and drum, the drum alone, a loud rattle, or the boatswain's pipe, were used.

general announcing system
System of loud-speakers throughout a ship or station over which the word may be passed to all hands. Public address or PA system.

general classification test (GCT)
A test for scoring basic capabilities of enlisted men. This test has been replaced by the armed services vocational battery (ASVAB).

general mess
Arrangement for feeding all hands except those whose rations are commuted to a flag, cabin, wardroom or CPO mess.

general message
One having a wide standard distribution, originated by the Navy Department or by a fleet commander. Usually serially numbered, as an ALNAV.

general muster
Massed formation of all hands at a designated place.

general officer
Brigadier general and above. An officer of the Army, Air Force, or Marine Corps whose rank insignia is one or more stars. Equivalent to Navy and Coast Guard flag officer. General officers and flag officers are authorized to fly personal flags of appropriate design and color. In the sea-going services this has become a distinguishing title as well.

general orders
Numbered directives of a general nature and wide application issued by the Navy Department and signed by the Secretary of the Navy.

general prudential rule *(Rules of the Road)*
The general caveat that permits a *privileged vessel* to maneuver to avoid collision or other hazard when in extremis. "In obeying and construing these rules due regard shall be had for all dangers of navigation and collision and to any special circumstance which may render a departure from these rules necessary to avoid immediate danger."

general quarters
Stations for battle. To "sound general quarters" is to give the signal, or the general alarm, which will bring all hands of the crew to their battle stations as quickly as they can get there.

general service rating
Those enlisted ratings normally authorized in peace time. See *Appendix B.*

GEOREF
A geographic reference system used to facilitate reporting and plotting of ships and aircraft.

Gibson girl
Portable radio for sending distress signals, carried on life rafts.

GI can
Trash can.

gig
Ship's boat designated for the use of the commanding officer.

gilhoist
Wheeled vehicle used to transport landing craft overland.

Giligan hitch
Any unseamanlike, unorthodox, knot, hitch, or bend.

gimbals
A pair of rings, one within the other, with their axes at right angles. Usually they support a compass or gyro repeater, in which case their purpose is to keep it horizontal despite motion of the ship. Any gyroscope requires a set of gimbals, however, to give it the requisite three degrees of freedom, i.e., freedom to move its axis in any direction. Almost always used in pairs, hence referred to in the plural.

gipsy, gipsy head
An auxiliary drum on a windless or capstan used for handling lines. See *warping head, capstan.*

give way
An order to begin pulling oars together.

glacier
Field or stream of ice moving down a slope and spreading because of its own weight.

glacon
A fragment of sea ice ranging in size from brash to medium floe.

gland
A seal designed to prevent leakage of water, steam, or oil along a movable shaft, such as propeller shafts, submarine periscopes, or turbine rotors.

gland steam
Steam introduced into shaft gland packing to prevent air leakage into and steam leakage out of a turbine.

glass
Barometer. A hand-carried telescope is a *long glass*. Binoculars are referred to as *glasses*.

gooseneck
The pivot fitting at the base of a boom or gaff, so named because of its shape.

glide bomb
A winged missile, unpowered.

go adrift
To break loose.

gob
Slang for an enlisted man (not good usage).

go by the board
To go over the side; to be swept away; forgotten.

godown
Warehouse or storehouse along the waterfront, especially in the Orient.

goldbrick
Slang for a loafer or to loaf.

Golf
Phonetic word for letter *G*.

gook
Slang for an Asiatic; a derogatory expression to be avoided.

go-to-hell hat
Slang for overseas or garrison cap.

gouge
Slang meaning to cheat. Also, a prepared solution to a problem or examination.

grab rope
A safety line secured along a boat boom or gangplank, hung knotted from the span wire between boat davits. Any line fastened to a lifeboat or life raft. Also called a lifeline.

grade
Graduations in authority and pay among petty officers and officers. Grade can only be used as a noun, but *rank* can be both noun and verb. Generally, rank represents relative position within a specific grade, but this is not rigorously true. Thus one could say, "Lieutenant Jones ranks Lieutenant Smith," meaning that Jones is senior to Smith; grade could not be used in this context. *Rank* can, however, also be used to denote a grade, as, "His rank is captain." It would be equally correct to say, "His grade is captain." The term *seniority* is sometimes used with the meaning of rank within a grade.

granny knot
A false square knot, unsymmetrical. To be avoided because it slips, and if jammed tightly, cannot readily be cast loose.

grape
Small iron ball, an inch or so in diameter, bound together in clusters and fired from smoothbore cannon. A common form of ammunition 150 years ago. See *canister*.

grapnel or **grappling iron**
Small, four-armed anchor used nowadays mainly to recover objects in the water. Also used, especially in days of sail, to secure alongside another ship or dock by force.

grass
Visual image of static on a radar or loran scope.

grating
Metal or wooden lattice work used to cover hatches while still providing ventilation below or to provide a platform for the steersman.

graving dock
Basin with a gate or caisson sealing the entrance, in which ships can be built or dry-docked.

great circle
The intersection of the earth's surface and a plane through the earth's center. The shortest route between two points on the surface of the earth.

great diurnal range
The difference in height between mean higher high water and mean lower low water. Also called diurnal range.

great tropic range
Difference in height between tropic higher high water and tropic lower low water. Also called tropic range.

greens

A pre-WWII uniform worn by aviators and submariners. Heavy woolen material, green in color, with black buttons, black stripes on sleeves, khaki shirt, black tie, and no shoulder boards. Warm weather version was similarly cut cotton khaki (same as now except for black buttons and black stripes). Today, members of the Seabees use the term for their green utility uniform and aviation personnel for their aviation green working uniform.

Greenwich Hour Angle (GHA)

Angular distance west of the Greenwich celestial meridian. In conjunction with declination, identifies position of celestial bodies for navigation. See *declination*.

Greenwich meridian

The meridian through Greenwich, England, near London; the reference meridian for measuring longitude and time. The Prime Meridian.

grid, JAN

Joint Army—Navy grid system covering entire earth adopted to afford secure means of referring to geographical positions.

grid navigation

Navigation by the use of grid directions. Generally used in polar navigation, with grid coordinates on the chart replacing latitude and longitude.

grid variation

In grid navigation, the difference between grid north and magnetic north. Also called *grivation* in aerial navigation.

grinder

Paved area at a shore activity, for drill and parades.

gripe(s)

Device for securing a boat at its davits or in its cradle. *Gripe in* means to secure by use of gripes.

grivation

See *grid variation*.

grog

Slang for any alcoholic drink, particularly rum. In old British navy, it was a mixture of rum and water, invented by Admiral Vernon, whose affectionate nickname was Old Grog. Mount Vernon, Washington's home, was named for him.

grommet

Reinforced hole in a sail or awning. The round metal or fiber stiffener in a flat hat or officer's cap.

groove

Prescribed flight path of an aircraft making a perfect approach for a carrier landing. The pilot is said to be *in the groove*.

ground
To run a ship ashore; to strike the bottom through ignorance, violence, or accident. As a special case, certain amphibious vessels run ashore, or ground, deliberately.

ground-controlled approach (GCA)
Aircraft approach to landing ashore during which the pilot is guided in altitude, speed, and heading by advice from a controller at the airfield.

ground-controlled interception (GCI)
Technique by which a pilot is guided to intercept his target by provision of speeds, headings, and altitudes from a controller ashore.

ground effects machine (GEM)
A vehicle designed to move across the earth's surface supported by a downward blast of air. Now called a surface effect ship (SES).

ground speed
Speed made good over earth's surface along course or track. Aircraft item. See *airspeed.*

ground swell
The sea swell encountered as a result of distant or past storms. Same as swell.

ground tackle
General term for all anchoring equipment aboard ship. Tackle is pronounced "take-ul."

ground waves
Signals of a radio transmission that travel along the ground. Sky waves travel upwards and the ionosphere reflects them back to earth.

group
Several ships or aircraft, normally a subdivision of a force, assigned for a specific purpose. The squadrons assigned to an ASW carrier comprise an air group. The words or collections of letters in a cipher or code message are known as *groups.*

group flashing light
Navigational aid showing groups of two or more flashes at regular intervals.

group grope
Slang for full deck launch of a carrier air group for a specific mission.

group occulting light
Navigational aid showing two or more eclipses at regular intervals, the eclipses being shorter than the flashes.

group-rate marks
Short diagonal stripes worn on upper part of left sleeve by non-rated men: white for seamen, red for firemen, green for airmen, light blue for constructionmen.

grouse
Slang meaning to complain, to find fault.

growler
Small piece of floating ice with two to six feet showing above surface. See *bergy-bit.*

G-suit
See *antiblackout suit.*

guard
Usually refers to *radio guard,* i.e., for a group of ships to maintain a continuous radio receiver watch on applicable frequencies or radio schedules, so that other ships can secure their radio watch. Can also mean *medical guard* (doctor available), *mail guard* (receives and sends ashore U.S. mail), etc. See *guard flag, guardship.*

guard flag
Designated flag flown by the ship or unit having the *guard duty* for the entire group, usually a homogeneous division of similar ships with similar requirements and problems, such as a destroyer division. Occasionally the SOPA will arrange guard assignments for all U.S. Navy ships within his area of jurisdiction, regardless of type and organization. Most frequently, all the various *guard* assignments (medical, mail, radio, etc.) are assumed by a single ship in rotation, but often this is not practicable and special arrangements must be made.

guard mail
Mail delivered by guard mail petty officers between naval activities.

guard of the day
That part of the ship's Marine guard on duty for the day, kept in readiness for a call to the quarterdeck.

guardship
A ship ordered to maintain a readiness to get underway immediately. Also, a ship maintaining a prescribed communication watch on certain radio frequencies, or generally to perform common duties for a group of several ships in port together.

guess-warp, guestwarp, geswarp
Rope rove through a thimble on a boat boom for the convenience of boats making fast alongside. Usually terminated in an eye-splice for simplicity in securing. Also may refer to a rope run along a ship's side as a grab line, guy rope, or additional towline to steady a boat towed astern, or to a hauling-line run by a boat to buoy, wharf, dolphin, bollard, etc. for warping (moving) purposes. "Guess-warp" is the preferred spelling.

gudgeon(s)
Metal loops or rings on the hull of a boat into which the pintles of the rudder fit.

guidance
The process of intelligence and flight control involved in directing a missile to the target. Types of guidance are: base-line, beam-rider, command, homing, or self-control.

guide
Vessel designated in a formation or disposition as the one for others to keep station on.

guided missile
Self-propelled airborne weapon capable of seeking a target or of following a radar beam to the target.

guided missile cruiser, destroyer, or frigate
A surface ship configured and equipped to launch one or more of the current family of surface-to-air missiles as one of the escort ships in an aircraft carrier task force. Generally fitted with other important additions to the basic type design.

guided missile designation system
See *Appendix D.*

guidon
Company identification pennant for naval units ashore.

Gulf Stream
That part of the Gulf Stream system from off Cape Hatteras to the Grand Banks. See *Gulf Stream System.*

Gulf Stream System
Part of a large North Atlantic clockwise circulation of warm water. Starts near the equator as the North Equatorial Current, forms the Antilles and Florida Currents, and is known as the Gulf Stream north of Cape Hatteras as it moves north-northeast off the coast of the U.S. It becomes the North Atlantic Current off the Grand Banks as it continues northeast toward Iceland, the British Isles, and Scandinavia. The current also flows east toward the coast of Europe and then south and eventually west toward the Caribbean along the equator to complete the circle.

Gull
A floating radar target used to simulate surface targets for deception purposes.

Gunar
Electronic fire-control system for ships.

gun bag
First-aid material kept at a gun station.

gunboat (modern)
Small, moderate-speed, relatively heavily armed vessel for general patrol and escort duty. See *armored cruiser* for further discussion.

gun captain.
Petty officer in charge of gun crew.

gundeck
Slang meaning to fake or to falsify something, such as a report. To pretend to be drunk. In a sailing warship, and early steel ones, a covered deck mounting broadside guns. See *smokestack, decker.*

gun house
Visible part of a turret extending above the barbette. An enclosed gun mount is sometimes called a *gun house.*

gun mount
A gun structure with one to four guns, which can rotate and carry them to various points of aim. It may be either open or enclosed in a steel shield. While they resemble turrets and are frequently so-called, enclosed mounts are not so heavily armored as turrets and carry no guns larger than five-inch. Some WWII cruisers had eight-inch guns that were carried in *gun mounts* instead of turrets, according to technical purists of the day, because the mounts did not have all the appurtenances of regular turrets as installed in battleships. The enclosure, whether of a turret or mount, which actually housed the guns was sometimes called a gun house.

gunner
Warrant officer who has normally advanced from aviation ordnanceman, fire-control technician, or gunner's mate.

gunner's mate (GM)
Petty officer who performs upkeep and repair of ordnance.

gunnery
The science of using ordnance.

gunnery officer
Officer ordered to head the gunnery department, responsible for the ship's or squadron's ordnance. Now known as the weapons officer.

gunport
Aperture in the front armor plate of a turret through which a gun projects.

gun salute
Blank shots fired to honor a dignitary or in celebration. The national salute is 21 guns, fired for a chief of state. Lesser dignitaries rate progressively fewer guns, according to rank. The number of guns is always odd.

gun tackle
One using two single-sheave blocks. Tackle is pronounced "take-ul." See *purchase.*

guntub
The cylindrical splinter protection around a deck gun aboard ship.

gunwale
Upper edge of a boat's side. Pronounced "gun-ul."

Guppy
An after-the-fact acronym for *greater underwater propulsive power*. A WWII fleet submarine which has been strreamlined, given a more powerful battery, and fitted with a snorkel.

guy
Line used to steady or support a spar or boom. Also called a vang.

guyot
A flat-topped submarine mountain. See *seamount*.

gypsey
See *gipsy*.

gyrene
Slang for a Marine.

gyro angle
In torpedo firing, angle between axis of own ship and final torpedo track, measured clockwise from own bow.

gyro compass
A compass having one or more gyroscopes properly torqued to indicate true north; pgc means "per gyro compass," and is nearly the same as true direction, because gyro error is normally very small. See *standard compass*.

gyropilot
Automatic steering device connected to the repeater of a gyrocompass; designed to hold a ship on its course without a helmsman. Also called automatic steerer, iron mike, and iron quartermaster.

gyro repeater
An instrument containing a compass card driven by a remotely located gyro compass. Used for steering, taking bearings, azimuths, etc.

H

hack chronometer
Spare or comparison chronometer. Not the principal one on which a ship's navigation is based. As the name suggests, it is the chronometer the navigator takes with him to compare with that of another ship, an observatory ashore, etc.

hack, under
Colloquial for punishment for officers, involving restriction to their quarters. Formal term is *suspension from duty, confined to quarters.*

hail
To address or call to a nearby ship or boat. Also a ship or man is said to hail from such-and-such a home port. See *ahoy* and *boat hails.*

half-breadth plan
Engineering drawing of a ship showing the outlines of horizontal sections of the hull from the main deck to keel. Ship is shown from above, i.e., plan view, and only half the hull is shown since the outlines of the other side are identical.

half deck
A partial deck between complete decks. See *deck.*

half hitch
Usually seen as two half hitches; a knot used for securing a line to a post.

half mast (half staff)
To fly a flag halfway up the mast, as a sign of mourning.

half speed
See *speed.*

half-tide level
Plane midway between mean high water and mean low water.

halocline
Area of rapidly changing water salinity.

halyard (halliard)
The line used to hoist a flag, pennant, or sail.

hammerbox
Noise-making device for sweeping acoustic mines.

hammock
A traditional sailor's bed, made of heavy canvas and swung from a pair of hooks on the underside of the deck above, i.e., "swung from the overhead."

hammock ladder
Non-existent item, as a "bucket of steam," often requested of new men aboard ship. Theoretically, a ladder to help men climb into their hammocks.

hand
Member of the ship's crew. *All hands* means every person on board.

handie-talkie
Ship-to-shore, portable, battery-powered radio.

hand lead
Weight and line used in taking soundings.

handrail
Metal or wood rail on bow, ladder, etc.

hand rope
See *grab rope.*

hand salute
Gesture of respect exchanged between military men and women. See *salute, hand.*

handsomely
Carefully; deliberately; smartly. See *ease, easy.*

handy billy
Small portable water pump.

hangar
Building in which aircraft and airships are stored and serviced. Large compartment in a ship for similar purpose.

hangar deck
Deck, below the flight deck of a carrier, where aircraft are parked and serviced.

hangfire
Delayed detonation of an explosive charge in a gun. See *misfire.*

hank
Loose group of bights of line, secured together with twine. Lifelines on a balsa float are made up in hanks.

happy hour
Period of entertainment aboard ship, including refreshments. Same as *smoker.* Also period at a bar or club ashore when prices are reduced.

harbor defense
Technique or organization for protecting a harbor against enemy ships, submarines, and aircraft.

harbor entrance control post (HECP)
The control and tactical command post from which the harbor defense commander controls and coordinates the harbor defense system.

harbor master
Officer in charge, under port director, of piloting, berthing, and traffic in harbor; responsible for navigational aids and hydrographic information.

hard
Section of a beach especially prepared with a hard surface for amphibious operations. Also, an adjective meaning full or extreme, as in the command *Hard right rudder*.

Harrison cargo gear
Cargo handling system using traveling overhead cranes instead of usual booms and winches.

hash mark
Slang for service stripe.

hatch
Access opening in the deck of a ship, fitted with a hatch cover for watertight closure. Emphasis is on the cover. Compare to *hatchway*.

hatch beam
Steel support for a cargo hatch cover.

hatch coaming
Raised framework around a hatch on which the hatch cover rests.

hatch cover
Wooden or steel cover for a hatch.

hatch hood
Canvas cover rigged over an open hatch to keep out rain, spray, and wind.

hatch list
List and location of all cargo loaded through a particular hatch.

hatchway
Same as hatch, but with emphasis on the opening.

haul
To pull or drag. The wind *hauls* when it changes in direction with the sun, i.e., clockwise in northern latitudes. When a ship changes course so that her head lies nearer to the wind than before, she is said to *haul up* or bear up. *Fall off* means to sail not so close to the wind. *Bear off* indicates intent, as, *after hailing, she bore off to leeward*. With relation to the wind direction, *veers* means the same as *hauls*. *Backs* means it changes direction against the sun. See *haul off*.

haul down
Term used as a directive to execute a flag hoist by lowering it.

hauling part
The part of a tackle to which power is applied, in contrast to a standing part.

haul off
To sail closer to the wind in order to get farther away from another ship, or the shore. *Haul to the wind*, or *haul your wind*, means to sail closer to the wind, usually when the ship has been sailing free. One hauls off to windward and bears off, or falls off, to leeward. See *fall off*.

haul out
To make fast at the boat boom. To move out of a ship's formation.

haven, submarine
Sea area in which no attacks on submarines are permitted, allowing a safe passage for allied submarines in wartime. Submarine havens may be fixed (stationary, defined by navigational or geographic coordinates) or moving at a specified course and speed. See *moving havens* and *submarine haven*.

hawk, anchor
A multipronged device used at the end of an anchor chain, usually by salvage vessels, to recover a lost anchor.

hawse
Area at bow of ship where hawsepipes are located. Also, that space between the bow of a ship and the anchors. See *foul hawse*.

hawse buckler
Metal cover for hawseholes to prevent entrance of water.

hawsepipes
Heavy castings through which the anchor chain runs from deck down and forward through ship's bow plating. Hawseholes are the openings.

hawser
Heavy line of fiber or wire. Any line over five inches in diameter.

head
Toilet and washroom. Derived from days of sail when the comfort station for the crew was forward on either side of the bowsprit. Also, the upper corner of a triangular sail.

header box
An extension of the salt water compensating line that is open to the sea and equalizes fuel tank pressure in a submerged submarine.

headers
Reservoir into which or from which the tubes of a boiler or heat exchanger terminate.

heading
That part of a message or order preceding the text. The direction in which a ship or aircraft is pointed.

head line
Mooring line that is made fast forward of the ship's pivot point.

headroom
Clearance between the decks.

head sails
Those set forward of the mast(s), as jibs, spinnakers, etc.

head stay
Wire support from top of forward mast to bowsprit of a sailing vessel.

headway
Forward movement of a vessel through the water.

heart
Center strand of fiber or wire rope.

heave
To throw, as in *heaving the lead*. Also means to pull, as *heave in*. See *heaving*.

heave around or **heave 'round**
To activate a windlass to which a line or chain is attached. To turn to and work hard.

heave away
An order to start heaving on a capstan or windlass so as to pull on a line.

heave in
To haul in.

heave out (roll out)
Rise and shine: get up out of bed.

heave short
To heave around on the anchor chain until the anchor is at short stay, just short of breaking ground. Done in preparation for getting underway.

heave to
To stop—in an affirmative sense, to bring the ship to a halt, dead in the water. In case of heavy weather, a ship may heave to in order to take the most comfortable and safest heading. She is in this case considered to be *hove to* even though making considerable way through the water from the action of wind and sea.

heaving
The vertical displacement, or up-and-down movement, of a ship in a seaway, as distinguished from pitching, which is essentially a rotation about an athwartships axis. Heave generally refers to an upward movement, bodily, of the entire ship, but is sometimes applied only to bow or stern in a less specific sense, as *her heaving bows*. Also, to come into sight, e.g., *as soon as she heaves into sight* or *when she heaves over the horizon*. See *pitch, roll, surge, sway, yaw*.

heaving line
Light, weighted line thrown across to a ship or pier when coming alongside to act as a messenger for a mooring line. The weight is called a monkey fist.

heavy cruiser
This term has lost its original meaning. None are now in commission. During WWII it was useful only to distinguish cruisers carrying eight-inch guns (heavy) from those with six-inch (light). Size and displacement not a factor. Conversion to missiles with removal of all or part of main battery produced proliferation of types based on the original heavies: CA, CAG, and CG; also, from light cruisers, CL, and CLG. The nuclear-powered guided-missile cruiser *Long Beach* was built from keel up. See *cruiser, destroyer,* and Appendix A.

heavy weather
Stormy weather with rough seas.

Hedgehog
An ASW ahead-thrown weapon; a mortar-type projector mount that fires a contact-fuzed projectile.

heel
To list over; the amount of inclination or list. A ship *heels* because of some external force and does so temporarily, while list is a more lasting condition.

heel and toe
Period of duty (watch) alternating with a period of rest. Also called watch and watch.

helicopter
An aircraft supported in flight by rotating airfoils instead of fixed wings. Used for spotting, rescue, evacuation, transport, and general utility. Also called pinwheel, egg beater, whirly-bird, windmill, copter, or chopper.

helm
The helm proper is the tiller, and thus the order to put the helm to port, for example, is the same as an order to put the rudder right. The term has now developed to mean the rudder and gear for turning it, and the helmsman is, of course, the man who steers. Because of possible confusion as to intended direction, however, orders are today given with respect to the rudder, and never, except in small pleasure craft, with respect to the helm, using *right* and *left*, never *starboard* and *port*.

helmsman
Steersman, a man who steers a ship or boat.

Herald equipment
Sonar and listening devices used in harbor defense.

hermaphrodite brig
Two-masted sailing vessel with the foremast square-rigged and the mainmast fore-and-aft-rigged. See *brigantine*.

hertz (Hz)
A unit of frequency equivalent to one cycle per second. See *frequency*.

H-hour
Term used to designate the time, usually on D-day, for an operation to commence.

higher high water (HHW)
The higher of the two high waters during any tidal day.

higher low water (HLW)
The higher of the two low waters of any tidal day.

highline
A simple line rigged between two ships underway transferring stores. The simplest transfer rig. Stores and personnel are transferred on a wheeled trolley riding on the highline and hauled back and forth between the ships.

highlining
Simple exchange of material or personnel at sea using the highline with associated trolleys and skids, both ships underway.

high performance external gun (HIPEG)
A 20-mm gun pod for aircraft with very high firing rate.

high water
The maximum height of a tide because of tidal and weather conditions.

high water line
The intersection of the plane of mean high water with the shore.

high water stand
Interval of time at high water when tidal level does not vary appreciably. See *low water stand*.

hitch
A knot whose loops jam together in use, particularly under strain, yet remain easily separable when the strain is removed. Method of securing a line to a hook, ring, or spar, e.g., *clove hitch*. Slang for a term of enlistment.

hit the deck
Get up; same as "rise and shine."

hit the sack
Slang meaning to turn in, go to bed. See *rack* and *sack*.

hit the silk
Make a parachute jump.

hobby shop
Recreational workshop.

hogging
Distortion of a ship's hull which results in bow and stern being lower than amidships section; opposite of sagging.

hogging line
Line passed under the keel and secured on the opposite side of the ship. Used for pulling gear (e.g., a collision mat) under a ship's bottom.

hoist
Display of signal flags at a yardarm. To lift. Also, the vertical portion of a flag alongside its staff.

hoist, boom
A whip, or single part of a line, running over a block at the head of a boom and then to the deck where it may be used to handle weights.

hoist in
Hook on, hoist and stow, or secure a boat aboard ship. See *hook on.*

hoisting eye (ring) (rod)
Fittings in a boat to which the boat falls are attached for hoisting.

hoisting pad
Metal plates supporting a pad eye or ring by which a boat is hoisted.

hoist out
To lower a boat from a ship to the water.

hold
Compartment of a cargo ship. A command to a line handler that means to take sufficient turns around his cleat to prevent any more line from running out. See *check, snub.*

holdback
Catapult fitting for holding down the airplane prior to firing.

hold captain
In amphibious operations, an enlisted man who supervises the loading and unloading in a ship's hold.

holding ground
The bottom in an anchorage. Usually described as good or bad, depending on ability to hold an anchor.

holiday
Unscrubbed or unpainted section of a deck or bulkhead. Any space left blank or unfinished through inadvertence or carelessness.

holiday routine
Schedule aboard ship involving no work or drills; normal for Saturday (sometimes Wednesday) afternoons and Sunday. See *rope yarn Sunday.*

Holy Joe
Slang for chaplain.

holystone
Small stone used with sand and water to scrub wooden decks.

home
To be guided by a signal emanating from the target, is to *home* in on it.

home of record
Address which an individual may desire to use as a home or "basic" address.

home port
Port or air station on which a ship or aircraft unit normally bases.

homeward bound pennant
Pennant flown by ships returning to U.S. after absence of year or more.

home yard
Now designated as planning and overhaul yard of a ship.

honey barge
Garbage scow.

honors and ceremonies
Collective term: official guards, bands, salutes, and other activities that honor the colors, celebrate a holiday, or greet a distinguished guest or officer.

hood
Canvas cover, e.g., hatch hood, periscope hood. Also, a metal or plastic cover for a binnacle.

hooker control
A station that assists the landing signal officer for night carrier landings.

hook on
To attach the boat falls to the padeyes at bow and stern of a boat, then hoist it clear of the water. *Hoist in* is a more complete evolution which includes the entire operation of taking a boat out of the water and securing it for sea.

hookmen
Men who disengage the arrester hook from the cable on a carrier flight deck. They wear green jerseys and helmets.

horned scully
Underwater beach obstacle designed to tear holes in boats.

horns
Horizontal arms of a cleat or chock; projecting timbers of a stage to which rigging lines are secured.

horse latitudes
Sea areas on outer margins of trade winds, around 30 degrees north and south where prevailing winds are light and variable.

hospital ship (AH)
An unarmed ship, marked in accordance with the Geneva Convention, staffed and equipped to provide complete medical and surgical facilities.

hostile nonmilitary vessel category
Regarding merchant ships in time of war, a vessel which refuses to be brought to, commits an unquestionably hostile act, offers resistance to the examining party, or flagrantly disobeys orders.

hot caseman
Person who disposes of the ejected cases from a gun using case ammunition. Also called hot shellman.

hot suitman (hot poppa)
Person wearing asbestos suit trained to rescue crews of burning aircraft.

Hotel
Phonetic word for the letter *H*.

house
To stow or secure in a safe place, as to house the anchor. Has a special meaning in connection with ship's awnings: in case of rain, to loose alternate stops from ridge rope, to haul down and secure to rail, lifeline or, most properly, to the housing line, thus creating gutters or valleys to carry off the water.

housing anchor
An anchor having no stock: houses itself in hawespipe when hove in. Compare *old-fashioned anchor*. See also *stockless anchor, patent anchor*.

housing chain stopper
Stopper fitted with a screw turnbuckle and a pelican hook. See *stopper*.

housing line
The middle one of the three lifelines around the perimeter of a ship. From top, they are lifeline, housing line, and foot line. When an awning is housed, gutters to carry off the rain are formed by bringing alternate lashings down to the housing line.

hove
Nautical past tense and participle of heave. The leadsman *hove* the lead—not heaved.

hovering
In submarines, the maintaining of a constant depth with no forward movement by use of ship's pumps controlling on-board ballast. In helicopters, to maintain altitude over a fixed point. See *balancing*.

hove taut
Pulled tight

hug
To keep close. A vessel might *hug* the shore.

hulk
A worn-out vessel, stripped of all useful gear, often used for storage in a port.

hull
The body or shell of a ship or seaplane.

hull board
Group of officers who inspect and report on the condition of the ship's hull.

hull down
Said of a ship visible over the horizon by her upper works alone. If hull is visible ship may be described as *hull up*.

hull report
Result of weekly inspection made of his spaces by a division officer.

hummock
An irregular ridge or hillock on sea ice.

hunter-killer force (HUK)
A naval force consisting of an ASW carrier, associated aircraft and escorts.

hunter-killer operations
Coordinated search-and-destroy ASW activities by surface and/or air units.

hunting
Mechanical self-perpetuating oscillation between two limits, as in a follow-up or servo system. See *mine countermeasures*.

hunting, mine
Branch of mine countermeasures which determines the positions of individual mines and concentrates countermeasures on these positions; includes locating, clearance, and watching.

hurricane
Destructive cyclonic storm with winds more than 65 knots. In the eastern hemisphere it is called a typhoon.

hydro-flap
Planing surface swung down beneath the fuselage of land aircraft to assist in emergency water landings.

hydrofoil
A surface craft designed to "fly" in water. By use of submerged foils, the hull is lifted from the water much as an aircraft is lifted from the ground. Reduction of hull drag permits greater speed.

Hydrographic Office
The office of the Navy Department that produces charts and navigational publications. Now called the Defense Mapping Agency Hydrographic Topographic Center; formerly called the Navy Oceanographic Office.

hydrography
The science of determining the condition of navigable waters.

hydrophone
An underwater microphone.

hydro skimmer
An air cushion vehicle experimental program.

hydrospace
See *inner space*.

hydrostatic pressure
Pressure at a given water depth due to water mass above, normally measured in pounds per square inch.

I

ice anchor
Timber, or deadman, buried in ice, to which ship's lines are secured.

iceberg (berg)
Large ice mass of glacial origin, floating in the sea.

ice blink
White glare on sky produced by reflection from ice.

ice breaker (AGB)
A specially designed U.S. Coast Guard vessel with a spoon-shaped bow, protected propellers, and powerful engines for operations in heavy ice.

ice concentration
The percentage of ice cover, usually expressed in tenths, in a given area of water.

ice fields
Mass of drifting ice, offshore. A form of pack ice.

idler
A crew member authorized not to participate in whatever evolution may be going on. Convalescing members of the binnacle list would be *idlers* while up and about before returning to duty. So would persons whose full schedules of certain duties exempted them from night watches or pre-inspection field days.

IFF
Identification, friend or foe. An electronic system of exchanging identification. With radar and radar-controlled missiles this is a necessity.

immediate message
A category of precedence reserved for messages relating to situations which gravely affect the security of national or allied forces or populace, and which require immediate delivery.

impact, mean point of
Geometric center of all the points of impact of the shots of a salvo or of the bombs in pattern bombing, excluding wild shots.

impulse charge
Propellant designed to start a self-propelled missile, such as a torpedo, on its way.

in
A Navy man serves *in* a ship, not "on" her.

inactivate
To place a ship in the reserve fleet. Slang: put into mothballs.

inactivation
Process of preparing a ship for reserve fleet status.

inboard
Toward the center of a ship or a group of ships, as opposed to outboard.

in bows
An order to bow oarsmen to boat their oars and to prepare to come alongside a vessel or dock.

incentive pay
Extra pay for hazardous duty such as that involving flying or submarines, or for specialists such as doctors.

inclination diagram
Polar coordinate graph used to record roller path data in making a gun battery alignment aboard ship.

incline
To list a ship and compute its stability. See *inclining experiment*.

inclining experiment
Computation of the metacentric height of a ship by use of weights to cause a list. The result is a measure of the stability of the vessel.

inclinometer
Instrument for measuring the roll of a ship. Same as clinometer.

index correction
Correction to sextant altitude in celestial navigation to allow for index error of the sextant caused by the index and horizon mirrors not being parallel.

India
Phonetic word for the letter *I*.

indicator
In cryptography, an element within the text that provides a guide to prompt decryption.

indirect fire
Aiming guns by laying them on a point of aim that is not the actual target, bringing them on by artificial range and deflection corrections. Employed when the real target cannot be seen by the gun layer(s). See *fire, direct*.

inertial guidance
System designed to guide a missile, aircraft, or ship by devices independent of outside information, using the inertial properties of gyroscopes. The system measures and converts minute accelerations experienced by the ship, aircraft, or missile to distance in the direction of the acceleration

inertia reel
Device for automatically restraining a pilot's shoulder harness when a force of two or three G's is applied.

infrastructure
Term used in NATO, generally applicable to all fixed and permanent installations, fabrications, or facilities for the support and control of military forces.

inhaul
Any line used to haul in on something. Opposite is outhaul.

initial provisioning
Process of determining range and quantity of spare repair parts, special tools, test equipment, and support equipment required by an end item during initial service period.

initial velocity (IV)
Velocity of projectiles at start of trajectory.

injector
Device using a jet of steam to force water into a boiler.

Inland Rules of the Road
The *International Rules of the Road*, having been accepted by international convention, are binding on all public and private vessels of the United States and other nations when on the high seas. They do not apply to harbors, rivers, lakes and other inland waters of the United States, where certain special rules are in effect. The boundary lines dividing the areas where the various rules apply are established by the U.S. Coast Guard and are marked on navigational charts. Among the special rules are the Inland Rules (federal law), Pilot Rules for Inland Waters (U.S.C.G.), Great Lakes Rules, Pilot Rules for the Great Lakes, Western River Rules, the Motorboat Act of 1940, Army Corps of Engineers Rules, and others. It is incumbent on the master of any ship operating in U.S. waters to be fully aware of and comply exactly with the applicable *Rules*, foremost of which are the *Inland Rules* which, in case of conflict, take precedence over any other special rules. See *Rules of the Road*.

inland waters
Those areas, shown on most coastal and harbor charts where the Inland Rules of the Road apply. If not so indicated they are those waters inland of a line roughly parallel to the coast drawn through the outermost aid to navigation (buoy, lighthouse, etc.). Not to be confused with territorial waters.

inner bottom
Top of the double bottom of a ship; consists of watertight plating. See *bilge*.

inner space
Popular term used to describe the area below the ocean's surface.

in ordinary
A ship not in commission, maintained by a skeleton crew. Term not used by the U.S. Navy.

in-port watch
See *port watch*.

inshore
Toward land. If already ashore, *inshore* means away from the sea.

inshore currents
The motion of water inside the surf zone, includes longshore and rip currents.

inshore fire support ship
An amphibious warfare vessel of shallow draft capable of providing heavy fire cover for military landings.

inspection
There can be many types, ranging from a careful and critical examination of personnel, material, and record-keeping to the ceremonial captain's, admiral's, or political figure's inspection at a spit-and-polish formation.

instruction
Serially numbered directive issued by commanders ashore and afloat. May contain policies, procedures, orders, doctrine, and information of a continuing or permanent nature. See *notice*.

instrument landing system
ILS radio and radar system enabling aircraft to land in low visibility.

insular shelf
Sea bottom surrounding islands from their point of permanent immersion to about 200 meters, where slope increases rapidly toward greater depths.

insular slope
The sea bottom from the seaward limit of the insular shelf to the sea floor.

Interagency Committee on Oceanography
The top national planning council for oceanographic matters.

intercardinal points
The four points midway between the cardinal points of the compass: northeast, southeast, southwest, and northwest.

intercom
Ship's voice intercommunication system. Also called squawk box.

interdict
To prevent or hinder enemy use of a certain area.

interdiction
Destruction of roads, bridges, railroads, tunnels, supply dumps, etc., to prevent the support of enemy front lines.

interior communications
All telephones, call bells, alarms, and other forms of communications within the ship.

interlock
Safety switch which cuts off high voltage when access covers, doors, or panels on an electrical device are opened.

intermediate waves
Waves with a relative depth (water depth/wave length) of between 0.5 and 0.05. See *deepwater waves, long wave.*

internal waves
Waves that occur along the interface separating two water masses; usually at the thermocline. Wave heights, periods, and lengths are usually large compared to surface waves. Also known as "dead water."

International Ice Patrol
A patrol operated by the Coast Guard in accordance with an international agreement for the prevention of disasters caused by collisions of vessels with ice.

international low water (ILW)
Reference plane below mean sea level calculated by multiplying half the range between mean lower low water and mean higher high water by 1.5.

International Rules of the Road
Officially known as *The International Regulations for Preventing Collisions at Sea.* Rules of the nautical road made effective by agreement of the major maritime powers for use on the high seas and most inland waterways of the world. They are binding on public and private ships of all signatory powers when on the high seas (international waters), and they apply on the inland waters of all such countries unless superseded by duly enacted special rules. Masters of ships operating anywhere in the world are required by law as well as custom to be aware of and comply fully with all applicable rules. See *Inland Rules of the Road, Sailing Directions,* and *Pilot Rules.*

interrogatory
In any naval message, means: *Question; I do not understand; meaning not clear;* etc.

interrupted quick-flashing light
A navigation light showing quick flashes for several seconds followed by a period of darkness.

intertidal zone
Generally, the zone between mean high water and mean low water.

interval (tactical)
Distance between foremasts of adjacent guides of ships in formation.

intervalometer
Device for measuring depth charge interval, used to lay a barrage or pattern.

Intruder
Model designation: A-6; cognizant service: Navy. All-weather, low altitude, carrier-based, two-place attack aircraft. Primary mission is to conduct interdiction close-air-support missions and attacks on land bases and ships under any weather conditions.

inventory control point (ICP)
Organizational unit within a military service assigned primary responsibility for management of a group of items either for inter- or intra-service use.

ionosphere
Layer of ionized air above the earth that reflects some radio transmissions.

Irish pennant
Loose, untidy end of line left adrift. Also called *deadman* or *cow's tail.*

irons
Unable to maneuver. A sailing ship caught with the wind coming from ahead or in any direction in such a way that she cannot cast to either side is said to be *in irons.* Also handcuffs and leg irons. See *aback.*

island
Structure above the flight deck of an aircraft carrier.

isobar
A line on a chart connecting points of equal atmospheric pressure.

isobath
A contour line connecting points of equal depth on a bathymetric chart.

isohaline
Having no change in salt content on the reference plane or line connecting points of common salinity.

isopleths
Lines of equal wave heights on a wave chart used for optimum track ship routing.

isotach
Line connecting points of equal current velocity.

isotherm
Line connecting points of equal temperature.

isothermal
Having no change in temperature.

isothermal layer
A layer of water throughout which a constant temperature exists.

isotherm follower
Device used to study the movement of subsurface layers of sea water.

isovelocity
A phenomenon in which sound velocity is the same throughout a given water layer.

iswas
Slang for any crude or improvised measuring or calculating device. Some of these, the submarine iswas, for instance, used in attack maneuvering before development of the torpedo data computer, attained a high degree of sophistication.

J

jack
Short for union jack, a blue, white-starred flag flown at the bow jackstaff of a vessel at anchor. To jack over the engines is to turn them over. Short for cablejack.

jackass
Cover over hawespipe to keep water out. Also, similar cover over entrance to pipe leading to chain locker, after anchor chain comes off wildcat. See *buckler*.

jackbox
Receptacle into which telephone plugs or jacks are fitted.

jack-of-the-dust
Man in charge of the provision issue room.

jackstaff
Flagpole at the bow of a ship from which the union jack is flown when the ship is not underway.

jackstay
Wire or line rigged for a special purpose, such as hanging seabags.

Jacob's ladder
Portable ladder, with rope or wire sides and wooden rungs, slung over the side for temporary use. See *sea ladder*.

jamming
Deliberate radio or radar interference.

Japan Current
The counterpart of the Gulf Stream System in the western Pacific. Flows north along the coast of Japan. Also called the Kurosiwo or Kuroshio.

jeep carrier
Small aircraft carrier built in great numbers during WWII.

jeheemy
Salvage rig to rescue swamped or stranded boats during an amphibious landing.

jet-assisted take-off (JATO)
An auxiliary rocket device providing short, intense thrust during take-off of an aircraft.

jetsam

Material thrown overboard. The term *flotsam and jetsam* is loosely used to denote floating debris, even though, theoretically, only the flotsam floats. See *flotsam*.

jettison

Thrown over the side, as when emergency reduction of topside weight is required.

jet stream

Relatively narrow wind currents of high velocity (100-300 knots) at 30,000-60,000 feet altitude. Generally from west to east, but meandering. Both hemispheres. The jet stream has a significant effect on world weather (storms), and it is associated with clear air turbulence.

jetty

Any solid structure (such as a breakwater) extending into the water to protect channels or shoreline from erosion, or to form a boat or ship harbor.

jewelry

Gear used to fasten together sections of a pontoon causeway.

jew's harp

Ring or shackle at upper end of shank of an anchor to which anchor chain is secured. Any harp-shaped shackle.

Jezebel

AN/SSQ-38 sonobuoy, passive, used for localization of targets.

jib

A triangular fore-and-aft sail set forward of the foremast. In square-rigged ships it balanced the spanker and assisted the helmsman in maintaining a steady course. The *flying jib* is a sail set forward of the regular jib, almost always in ships with bowsprits. Large ships might carry as many as three or four jibs with their own private nomenclature for them.

jibboom

Once a separate wooden spar extending the bowsprit. It is now considered the most forward part of a bowsprit.

jibe

When the stern of a fore-and-aft-rigged ship passes accidentally through the wind so that her sails catch the wind from the other side, she is said to *jibe*. Even under the most controlled conditions, the weight of canvas and booms which can slam from one side of the ship to the other, with sometimes tremendous velocity, can be very dangerous to rigging and personnel. For this reason, the proper way for a fore-and-aft rigged vessel to come about, in all but the smallest pleasure boats, is by tacking. Wearing can be called a *controlled jibe*, performed by square-riggers for the identical reason: so as not to endanger masts and rigging by suddenly being taken flat aback when passing the bow through the wind. See*wear*

jigger or **jiggermast**
The fourth mast in a four-masted ship, sometimes called the spanker. Yawls and ketches generally call their aftermost (and smaller) mast a jigger instead of a mizzenmast, and most frequently the other mast is called the main. Also, light tackle ("take-ul") for general use.

Jimmy legs
Slang for guard, master-at-arms.

job order
Order issued by a repair activity to its own people to perform a repair job in response to a work request from the unit to be repaired.

joe pot
Slang for coffee pot, short for *jamoke* which was once the naval term for coffee.

joiner door
Conventional non-watertight door aboard ship.

joint
Involving elements of more than one of the armed services. See *combined operation.*

joint command
Similar to *specified command* except composed of all services.

joint long-range strategic study (JLRSS)
Broad appraisal to assist in development of guidance based on military strategies and concepts for the period from eight to 12 years hence. Provides general guidance for military research and engineering objectives. JLRSS is pronounced "jellers." Updated annually.

joint strategic capabilities plan (JSCP)
Annual translation of national objectives into terms of military objectives which becomes directives for conduct of military operations during life of the plan. JSCP is pronounced "jay-scap." Updated annually.

joint strategic objectives plan (JSOP)
Annual mid-range plan for operations anticipated five years hence and extending for the following three years. JSOP is pronounced "jay-sop." Updated annually.

Jolly Roger
Skull-and-crossbones flag flown during crossing-the-line ceremonies.

journal
The part of a shaft, pin, or rotating piece fitted into and working in a bearing.

jubilee pipe patch
Damage-control patch for piping resembling an elongated hose clamp under which a sheet of packing is laid.

judge advocate general (JAG)
The senior legal officer in the Navy.

Julie
The AN/SSQ-23A sonobuoy that releases charges to explode at predetermined depths to provide echo-ranging information.

Juliett
Phonetic word for the letter *J*.

jumbo boom
Heavy-lift boom aboard ship.

jumper
Connecting pipe, hose, or wire for emergency use aboard ship. Enlisted man's blue or white pullover uniform shirt.

jump ship
Slang for leaving ship without authority or permission. See *over the hill*.

junior officer
Technically, lieutenant commanders and below. In practice, usually ensigns and lieutenants are considered junior officers. Lieutenant commanders are often addressed as "commander," following the traditional army practice of addressing lieutenant colonels as "colonel."

jury rig
Any temporary or makeshift device, rig, or piece of equipment, such as a *jury rudder*, *jury mast*, etc. Can be a term of mild derision, but need not be. Many a good ship has been saved by a jury rig.

K

kamikaze ("divine wind")
Japanese suicide aircraft in WWII that crashed into ships. Also, the pilots of such craft. Term is now used to refer to any deliberate suicidal tactic in war.

kapok
Natural, light, waterproof fiber used in stuffing life jackets. From seeds of tropical kapok or silk tree.

karry krane
Mobile, crash-handling crane for small aircraft carriers.

kedge
To carry out an anchor in a small boat, then haul the ship or craft up to the anchor, then repeat. See *anchor* (n), *kedge anchor.*

kedge anchor
Usually an old-fashioned *anchor* for kedging, pulling off when aground, or for warping. Now rare except in salvage work. See *stern anchor* for amphibious adaptation.

keel
Central, longitudinal beam or timber of a ship from which the frames and hull plating rise.

keel depth
For surface ship, the distance of the keel below the waterline; for a submarine, the depth at which operating. Some foreign navies use the depth of water over the deck as the measure of depth in submergence.

keelhaul
Slang meaning to reprimand severely, derived from ancient barbaric punishment: the hauling of a man from one side of the ship to the other under the bottom by means of ropes passed under the keel.

keelson
Originally a timber or steel fabrication bolted on top of a keel to strengthen it. Now any structural member used to strengthen hull or support a heavy weight.

keep
To hold or maintain as in *keep that buoy to port.*

keeping ship
Observing the routine of a ship when not engaged in exercises or operations.

kekle
To dress up mooring lines, wrapping them with small stuff where they come together.

kelp
The largest known seaweed (algae), which grows on rock or stone bottom; may be as long as 600 feet with fronds four feet wide.

Kenter shackle
Patented anchor chain link that disassembles on removal of a pin. Now replaced by connecting shackles of later design.

ketch
A small sailing ship, fore-and-aft rigged, fitted with a tail mainmast and a much shorter mizzenmast or jiggermast, stepped in front of the rudder post. In appearance the ketch is similar to a yawl, but the yawl has its aftermost mast stepped behind the rudder.

keying interval
The elapsed time between successive pings on echo-ranging sonar.

K-gun
Depth-charge projector. See *Y-gun.*

kick (of the rudder)
Swirl in the wake of a ship caused by rudder action when making a turn. Same as knuckle. Used as a reference by ships turning in column, one astern of the other.

kick plate
Bright metal plate, to absorb scuff marks on the vertical parts (steps) of a ladder. Also the dark stripe near the deck of a light-painted bulkhead.

kid (kit)
Small container, such as a mess kid or spit kid.

killer submarine (SSK)
One designed to detect and destroy submarines.

Kilo
Phonetic word for the letter *K.*

king posts
Sturdy vertical posts supporting the cargo booms of cargo ships. Often erected in pairs. Also the centerline pillars in a cargo ship's hold.

king spoke
The spoke of a ship's wheel that is up when the rudder is amidships.

Kingston valve(s)
Large valves admitting water to ballast tanks of pre-war submarines. Had to be open for diving readiness. Obsolete.

kit
See *kid.*

kite
Airborne radar reflector used to simulate a target for deceptive purposes. May be dropped from aircraft or streamed from a ship.

kiyi
Small brush used to scrub clothing.

knee
An angular piece of wood, formerly found naturally, used to connect a wooden ship's frames to her deck beams.

knife edge
The rim of a door frame, hatch, or port that meets the gasket for a watertight fit. Has the appearance of a very dull knife blade.

knock off
To stop; cease.

knot
Unit of speed equivalent to one nautical mile (6,080 feet) per hour. A collective term for hitches and bends (any combination of loops, mostly interlocking) used to attach two or more lines to each other, or to a fixed object such as a post or bollard, or to form an eye or loop. A knob (knot) in a line or rope, used for climbing or any other purpose, including the measurement of a ship's speed through water (the origin of *knot* as a unit of speed) by how many knots were pulled across the taffrail in a given unit of time. See *nautical mile*.

knuckle
See *kick*. Also, a sudden change in curvature of a ship's hull.

kytoon
Helium-filled balloon supporting a temporary radio antenna.

L

labeled cargo
Cargo labeled for special handling, such as explosives and chemicals.

labor
A ship is said to labor when she moves violently in a rough sea, putting heavy strain on her hull and equipment.

Labrador Current
A cold-water current flowing south along the coast of Labrador, which is the principal carrier of icebergs that menace the sea lanes of the North Atlantic. Upon meeting the Gulf Stream drift it turns east and then northeast.

lace, gold
Officer's gold braid, now often synthetic.

lacing
Line that secures canvas by passing through the eyelets or grommets in the canvas.

ladder
Stairs. Also, a succession of salvos with established differences in range, fired to establish hitting gun range.

ladder screen
Canvas or metal sheet secured on the underside of a ladder.

lagging
The insulation around pipes aboard ship.

LAMPS
Light airborne multipurpose system. A helicopter with all its support equipment, including landing platform and the ship carrying it.

land breeze
Breeze coming off the land in the evening. After sunset the land cools faster than the sea and thus cools the air adjacent which then flows to displace warmer sea air.

landfall
The arrival or first sighting of land at the end of a voyage.

landfast ice
Ice of any type that is attached to the shore, beached or stranded in shallow water.

land ice
Any ice floating on the sea that broke from a glacier.

landing craft
Craft employed in amphibious operations, specifically designed for carrying troops and equipment and for beaching, unloading, and retracting. Also used for logistic cargo resupply operations. See *Appendix A.*

landing force
The troops organized for an amphibious assault. Also, a portion of a ship's crew detailed to go ashore in an organized unit for any military operation, a term obsolete since WWII.

landing party
An organized force of infantry from the ship's company detailed for emergency or parade duty ashore. Formerly called landing force.

landing ship
An assault ship which is designed for long sea voyages and for rapid unloading over and onto a beach. See *Appendix A.*

landing signal officer (LSO)
Officer who directs pilots in landing on an aircraft carrier.

landing team
See *battalion landing team.*

landlubber
Seaman's term of derision for one who has never been to sea, hence a lubber, or lubberly.

lands
The raised part of the rifling of a gun between grooves.

langrage
Shot formerly used to destroy sails and rigging. Consisted of metal junk chained or wired together. See *canister, grape, dismantling shot.*

lanyard
Formerly a relatively small line rove between two deadeyes, forming a sort of tackle for setting up the shrouds of a sailing ship and keeping them at the proper stretch. In general, a strong piece of cord fastening something, or to pull something, as a firing lanyard.

lapping head
Abrasive device for removing copper fouling from the bore of a gun.

laser
Light amplification by stimulated emission of radiation. A device that converts light of mixed frequencies to discrete visible radiation.

lash
To secure with line or wire by wrapping and tying with seamanlike knots in the case of line, or with an approved hitch in the case of wire. *Lashing* or *wire-lashing* are the materials used. LASH (Lighter aboard ship) is a new method of shipping in which loaded lighters or barges are transported in a specially designed merchant ship.

lateen sail
A fore-and-aft sail triangular in shape (or nearly so, with one very short side), still used in the near east. It is slung from a *lateen yard*, a very long, drooping spar, sometimes fashioned from two sticks lashed together, which crosses a relatively low mast at an angle of about 45 degrees, the low end being about one third the length of the upper. Also used on mizzenmast of square-riggers until replaced by spanker late in the 18th century.

latitude
The measure of angular distance in degrees, minutes, and seconds of arc from 0 degrees to 90 degrees north or south of the equator.

launch
To float a ship on completion of building, traditionally by sliding down the building ways although many ships, especially big ones, are now launched by floating them out of the drydock in which they were built. Also, an open powerboat.

launcher
Device for holding and firing a rocket, guided missile, or any projectile, such as a depth charge, which does not qualify as being a bullet or projectile.

law officer
Officer member of a court-martial who is a qualified lawyer, a member of the JAG Corps.

lay
To go, as in *Lay aft on the fantail.* The direction of the twist of strands of a rope.

lay before the mast
To assemble or fall in, usually to make reports.

layer depth
The thickness of the mixed layer nearest to surface of the sea; the depth to the top of the thermocline. A term much used in antisubmarine warfare.

lazaret
Storage compartment in the stern of a ship or boat. Also an isolation hospital for people with contagious diseases from vessels in quarantine.

lazy line
General term for a line used for various purposes in securing boats, specifically the line made fast to stern of boats at a boat boom.

lead
Short for hand lead or sounding lead, a device for measuring depth of water. (Pronounced "led").

lead (in ice)
Long narrow passage or lane in pack ice through which a ship can navigate. (Pronounced "leed").

leadership
The art of accomplishing the Navy's mission through people. It is the sum of those qualities of intellect, of human understanding and moral character that enable a man to inspire and manage a group successfully. From General Order 21 as originally promulgated.

leadline
Lead with attached line, used for taking soundings. Also called a hand lead. (Pronounced "led.") Fathoms are indicated by bits of leather and cloth, called marks, at 2, 3, 5, 7, 10, 13, 15, 17, 20, and 25 fathoms. Depths between marks are estimated by eye and called "deeps." See *deep, mark*. Lead weight has a dished-in bottom for arming.

leadsman
Man who takes soundings (measures depth of water) from the chains of a slowly moving ship by swinging the lead forward, letting it go and feeling the bottom as he notes depth and reports by calling out *By the mark two* or *by the deep six*, etc.

lead time
The length of time before end item delivery in which an operation must be performed to meet delivery schedules. Pronounced "leed."

lead yard
Shipyard that builds the first ship of a design class. It furnishes specified services to yards which build other ships of the class. Pronounced "leed."

league
Unit of distance. Three nautical miles. See *mariners' measurements*.

leak stoppers
Wooden plugs and metal fittings designed to stop leaks in the hull of a ship or boat.

leatherneck
Slang for a Marine.

leave
Authorized vacation or absence from duty other and longer than liberty. The term "shore leave" is no longer used. Leave carries with it permission to travel beyond the allowed radius of liberty.

leave rations
Cash payment in lieu of rations in kind while on leave, for enlisted personnel.

leaver (convoy)
A section of a convoy that breaks off from the main convoy to proceed separately to its own prearranged terminal port. When detached, the leaver section becomes a leaver convoy. If it is a single ship, it is referred to simply as a *leaver*.

lee
The direction away from the wind, i.e., toward which the wind is blowing. Opposite of weather. If the wind is blowing from the west, westerly directions are *weatherly*, or to *windward*, while easterly directions are to *leeward*.

leech
The after edge of a fore-and-aft sail or one of the two vertical edges of a rectangular (square) sail.

lee helm
A sailing vessel that carries a lee helm tends to fall off to leeward, and a little helm in that direction (rudder to windward) is necessary to keep her on course. The opposite is weather helm, necessary if the vessel is ardent. Either effect, if pronounced, indicates that centers of pressure of sails and keel are not in balance. Compare *lee helmsman*.

lee helmsman
Assistant steersman. Compare with lee helm.

leeward
Away from the wind. Pronounced "LOO-urd," but only for this specific word. In all other cases, the word or syllable "lee" is pronounced as spelled.

leeway
Drift of an object with the wind, on the surface of the sea. The sideward motion of a ship because of wind and current, the difference between her heading (course steered) and her track (course made good). Sometimes called drift.

left-handed rope
Twisted from right to left. Strands and cables are usually left-handed. Also called left-laid rope.

leg
Portion of a ship's (or aircraft's) track or course on a single heading.

let fall
An order to let oars fall into the rowlocks from the position of toss. Also, when lowering a boat, to let the falls go by the run just before the boat is waterborne.

let go by the run
Allowing a line to run free.

letters of censure
Non-judicial punishment imposed on an officer by his CO or reporting senior and entered in officer's record. Most severe is a letter of reprimand; of lesser severity —letter of admonition; least severe—letter of caution.

liberty
Authorized absence of an individual from place of duty, normally not more than 48 hours. Sometimes incorrectly called shore leave. Liberty sometimes carries geographical limits to provide possibility of quick recall. See *leave*.

lie off
To remain stopped a short distance away.

lie-to (lay-to)
To stop a ship or boat but not anchor or moor it.

lieutenant (LT)
Junior officer ranking above a lieutenant junior grade and below a lieutenant commander. (Identified by two stripes).

lieutenant commander (LCDR)
Officer who ranks just below commander and above a lieutenant. (Identified by two and one-half stripes.)

lieutenant junior grade (JG)
Officer who ranks just above ensign and just below a full lieutenant. (Identified by one and one-half stripes.)

lifeboat
In merchant ships, a boat required by international law, which can be quickly launched for safety of passengers and crew. The number required is determined by the number of persons permitted to voyage in a ship (as a result of the *Titanic* disaster, when there were not enough). In a warship the lifeboat is a ready boat that can quickly be launched with a crew trained and equipped for rescue day or night. The motor whaleboat is traditionally the most seaworthy of all ship's boats and is much the preferred type for this use.

life buoy (ring)
Buoyant device, usually fitted with a light and smoke maker, for throwing to a man in the water.

lifefloat
Same as liferaft.

lifeguard
Aircraft and ships detailed to recover aircraft personnel at sea.

lifeguard submarine
One stationed to rescue downed airmen in an area where surface vessels cannot operate.

life jacket, preserver
Device to keep individual afloat. May be jacket, ring, knapsack, belt, yoke, or vest type.

lifeline
Line secured along the deck to lay hold of in heavy weather; any line used to assist personnel; knotted line secured to the span of lifeboat davits for the use of the crew when hoisting and lowering. The lines between stanchions along the outboard edges of a ship's weather decks are all loosely referred to as lifelines, but specifically the top line is the lifeline, middle is the housing line, and bottom is the footline. Any line attached to a lifeboat or life raft to assist people in the water. Also called a grab rope.

life raft
Float either constructed with a metallic tube covered with cork and naval canvas, or made of balsa wood or other suitable material. Modern life rafts are usually of rubber which automatically release and inflate if submerged. They contain water, emergency radio and provide shelter.

lift
Specified quantity of cargo requiring transportation. To transport cargo or personnel.

lift, amphibious (or assault)
Total capacity of assault shipping utilized in an amphibious operation.

light cruiser
See *heavy cruiser*, also *Appendix A*.

lightening hole
Hole cut in steel plate in order to lighten it without sacrificing much strength. (Note spelling.)

lighter
Barge-like vessel used to load or unload ships.

lighter-than-air (LTA)
Blimps, dirigibles, and other devices whose lifting capability depends on being inflated with a gas of less specific gravity than air.

lighthouse
A building in which an aid to navigation light is located.

light lists
Publications describing aids to navigation maintained by U.S. Coast Guard.

light lock
Double door permitting passage without showing light to the outside.

light, navigation
See *navigational light*.

light off
Start, literally "to start a fire in," as in *light off a boiler*. Slang meaning to *light off* an engine, controversy, investigation, etc.

light period
The length of time in seconds required to complete one cycle of the characteristics of an aid to navigation.

light ship
Command or word passed permitting lights to be shown as the ship is secured from being darkened. See *lightship*.

lightship
An anchored, manned, floating navigational light, in the form of a ship. It has the desirable feature of being able to go to harbor for upkeep. Now rare, being replaced by unmanned buoys or structures.

light ship condition
Ship which is complete, ready for service and has all permanent ballast and spare parts aboard but without variable load.

lignum vitae
Very dense wood used in propeller shaft bearings.

Lima
Phonetic word for the letter *L*.

limb (of the sun or moon), upper or lower
The upper or lower edge as sighted against the horizon in taking sun or moon sights.

limited duty officer (LDO)
An ex-enlisted man who has won a commission because of his high quality. Because of the branch and experience through which he has risen, he is limited to duties of his specialty.

limpet mines
Small explosives attached to the hull of a ship by enemy swimmers. See *mine*.

line
General term for rope; the equator; a formation in which ships or personnel are formed in any direction from the guide. See *rope*.

lineal number
Precedence number for naval officers. Replaces old signal number. Changes with each promotion, becoming smaller as officer becomes more senior. See *number in grade*.

line chief
Aircraft maintenance man, the "straw boss" of the hangar deck.

line of departure
In amphibious assault, the line from which the scheduled boat waves leave, on signal, for the beach.

line officer
An officer of the line, one who is primarily concerned with command and control of forces afloat and who is eligible to succeed to command at sea himself. Distinct from staff officers such as members of Supply Corps, Medical Corps, etc., who may succeed to command only in their own specialties, in posts such as Commanding Officer, U.S. Naval Hospital. Some line officers also are restricted to duties within a specialty, such as engineering duty officers, who may command only naval shipyards and similar activities.

line of fire (LOF)
A straight line joining gun and point of impact (or burst) of the projectile.

line-of-sight
Straight line, used to describe radio frequency transmission that does not follow the curvature of the earth.

lines drawing (of a ship)
The representation of the ship's form in three separate planes. The longitudinal is known as the sheer plan. The transverse section is the body plan, and the horizontal is the half-breadth plan.

line service
Fueling, arming, engine warm-up, and minor adjustments of aircraft.

line squall
A violent windstorm characteristic of a weather front.

line-throwing gun
A .45-cal. gun for throwing a line. The projectile carries a light line which is used to pull a messenger across.

list
Permanent or semi-permanent inclination of a ship to one side or the other as distinct from heel. A ship rolling back and forth would not be listing, unless the middle of the roll were not at the even keel position. (i.e., a ship with a 10-degree port list might roll between zero and 20 degrees port.) Implies a condition less than optimum.

listen
To maintain a continuous radio receiver watch.

listening sweep
Sonar search conducted without sound emanation; passive use of sonar.

littoral
The coastal region, pertaining to the seashore.

littoral currents
Another name for longshore currents.

littoral system
Subdivision of benthic division.

littoral zone
That shore area between low and high water marks.

lizard, traveling
A short section of line with a thimble at one end, through which passes a small wire cable stretched taut between two fixed structures on board ship. The lizard can move freely along the wire, while firmly gripped by a man needing to make the passage safely from one structure to the other in bad weather.

load
Single round of ammunition. Command to put ammunition into the gun. Also, to stow supplies in a boat, vehicle, ship, or aircraft. To *lose the load* is to lose all electrical power in a ship.

loading, combat
Loading assault troops and equipment for rapid debarkation in predetermined priority.

loading, commercial
Loading of troops and/or equipment for maximum use of space.

loading machine
Dummy gun used to train gun crews in loading.

loading, rail
Loading of boats during amphibious assault at the rail of the ship instead of after they are waterborne.

load line marking
An indication of draft (load) limits, displayed by international agreement on all merchant ships as well as on some naval vessels. Also called load waterline marks. See *Plimsoll mark*.

load list
Items carried in a ship of the mobile support force, which supports the fleet underway.

loafer's loops
Slang for aiguillettes.

local apparent noon (LAN)
The instant that the center of the sun is exactly over the upper branch of the meridian of the observer, i.e., the highest altitude to which the sun will climb on that day. Time of LAN, pronounced Ell-Ay-Enn, varies with the time the ship is keeping; thus the instant that the sun "dips," i.e., when its altitude begins to decrease, can be converted directly to the difference in longitude between the actual position of the ship and that of the meridian whose time the ship happens to be keeping. This is why the search for an accurate timepiece was so important for navigation. At this same moment, calculation of latitude from altitude of the sun and its declination is easy. Thus, LAN has long been a favorite of navigators, and a sun unobscured by clouds at noon is always desired.

lock
Compartment in a canal for lowering or lifting vessels to different levels.

locker
Metal cabinet, fitted with a lock, in which men keep their gear. Any small compartment or cabinet.

lodgement area
The area, resulting from a consolidation of several beachheads, which is the base for subsequent operations inland.

log
Device for measuring a ship's speed and distance traveled through the water. To record something is to log it. Short for *logbook*. See *taffrail log*, *pitometer log*, and *electromagnetic log*.

logbook
Any chronological record of events, as an engineering watch log.

log, deck
Official record of a ship in commission submitted to the Chief of Naval Personnel in accordance with Navy Regulations and the BuPers Manual.

log, engineering
Daily record of important events and certain data concerning the machinery of a ship.

loggerhead
A piece of iron on a long handle used for melting pitch in seams to make the seams more watertight. The loggerhead was thus a deadly weapon readily available to fractious members of a ship's crew.

logistics
The science of planning and carrying out the movement and maintenance of forces.

logroom
Engineer's record room on board ship.

long blast
See *blast*.

longevity pay
The increase over base pay that is computed on years of service.

long glass
Medium-powered (up to 16) monocular telescope used on ships, especially for spotting signals. Short term is *glass*. The long glass is the traditional symbol of authority on board ship, and some ships still provide the OOD in port with a ceremonial one to carry about while standing his watch.

longitude
Measure of angular distance in degrees, minutes, and seconds east or west of the Prime Meridian at Greenwich.

longitudinal frames
Frames of a ship that run fore and aft. Most ships are built with transverse framing, that is, frames perpendicular to the keel. Certain types, however, are built with frames parallel to the keel. Generally, these are tankers whose fluid cargoes can accept greater flexing of the hull. See *frames.*

longitudinal wave
A wave in which particles of the transmitting medium are displaced perpendicularly to the wave itself, i.e. sound waves in air or water.

long-range active detection (LORAD) system
A shipboard active long-range sonar system.

long-range objectives (LRO)
Basic guidance for the achievement of ship, aircraft, and weapons goals for period 10 to 15 years, hence using self-imposed fiscal assumptions. It is used internally within the Navy only and is based on *long-range requirements.*

long-range requirements (LRR)
Estimate of the ship, aircraft, and weapons capabilities required during the period to 15 years hence.

longshore currents
Currents within the surf zone that parallel the shoreline and are caused by waves breaking at an angle to the shoreline. Derived from "alongshore current."

longshoreman
Laborer who loads and unloads marine cargo, generally same as stevedore.

long wave
Waves occurring when phase velocity depends on water depth alone and whose relative depth (water depth/wave length) is 0.05 or less. See *intermediate waves.*

loofa sponge
Formerly sponge used in the hot well of a feedwater heater aboard ship.

look alive
Meaning be alert, move quickly.

lookout
Man stationed as a visual watch; air, horizon, surface, fog, etc. See *reports, lookout.*

loom
The shine of a light that is below the horizon. Also, the rounded part of an oar from blade to handle, also known as the shaft.

Lorac
A short range hyperbolic navigation system used principally for survey operations.

Loran
A system of electronic navigation in which the time difference in the reception of pulse signals originated simultaneously at a master and slave station is used to locate the ship as being on a charted hyperbolic curve that is the focus of all possible positions which would observe the identical time difference. The intersections of two such lines gives a fix. (Derived from: LOng-RAnge electronic Navigation).

lower high water (LHW)
The lower of the two high waters on any tidal day.

lower low water (LLW)
The lower of the two low waters during any tidal day.

lowest low water
Plane of reference lower than mean sea level by an amount equal to the difference between mean sea level and the lowest low water of any normal tide.

lowest normal tides
Reference plane lower than mean sea level by half the maximum tide range without consideration of wind or barometric pressure influences.

low-order burst (detonation)
Incomplete, less destructive detonation of an explosive.

low water (LW)
The minimum height reached by a tide. Can be due solely to tidal action or may include weather factors as well.

low water datum
The approximation of mean low water used as a standard for limited areas.

low water stand
Interval of time at low water when level of water does not vary appreciably. See *high water stand.*

LSO
Landing signal officer.

lubberly
Unseamanlike; clumsy. A lubber is an unseamanlike person. See *landlubber.*

lubber's line
Reference mark on a compass or radar scope corresponding to ship's head.

lucky bag
Container or stowage for articles found adrift. Unclaimed articles aboard ship are periodically sold at auction.

luff
To head into the wind so that the upwind edge of the sail ripples with wind passing on the back side. The leading edge of a fore-and-aft sail. See *leech.*

luff tackle
A tackle having one single- and one double-sheave block. See *tackle, purchase.*

lug sail
A small boat rig, a four-sided sail whose head (top) is supported by a yard or spar fastened obliquely to the mast.

lunar day
Time for one rotation of the earth with respect to the moon, approximately 24.84 hours.

Lyle gun
Gun used in lifesaving to throw a lifeline to a ship in distress. Same as line-throwing gun.

M

machinery index
Comprehensive listing of all machinery and related equipment, other than electronic, installed on board.

machinery spaces (engineering spaces)
The part of a ship containing propulsion and auxiliary machinery and under the cognizance of the engineer officer.

machinery trials
Tests of main propulsion plant of a ship.

machinist
A warrant officer advanced from machinist's mate.

machinist's mate (MM)
A petty officer who maintains and operates machinery.

mach number
Ratio of an object's speed to that of sound in air.

MacNamara lace
Fancy curtains and trimmings for barges and gigs worked from unlaid canvas threads. Nautical corruption of macrame lace. See *sennet, square knotting, coxcombing, fancy work.*

Mae West
Pneumatic life jacket.

magazine
Compartment aboard ship or ashore fitted for the stowage of ammunition.

magnetic airborne detector: (MAD)
A device that detects a submerged submarine from low-flying aircraft making use of the magnetic field of its submerged mass.

magnetic compass
A compass using the earth's magnetic field to align the compass card. See *compass.*

magnetic storm
Worldwide magnetic disturbance that usually starts suddenly and lasts a minimum of several hours. Interferes with electronic communications.

magnetometer
Device for measuring magnetic force on the sea bottom.

mailbuoy
An ancient sailor's joke: the mid-ocean buoy in which mail is kept for delivery to passing ships. See *bucket of steam, hammock ladder, relative bearing grease.*

Mailbuoy
Communications satellite for UHF relay.

mailgram
Dispatch transmitted by mail.

main battery
The largest caliber guns carried by a warship, which make up her *main battery.*

main body
The major part or the important ships of a formation or disposition.

main brace, splice the
Braces are the lines attached to a square-rigger's yards by which they may be trimmed to the wind. The main yard braces (port and starboard) might thus be called the main braces, although it would be more likely and logical that they would be called mainsail braces, matching the terms, main topsail braces, fore topgallant braces, and the like. Although specifics are lacking, it appears that the main brace in antiquity was the principal fore-and-aft support of a ship's masts, running from an extremely strong fastening at the bow to the tops of her lower masts and finally to the deck abaft the mizzenmast. Splicing this fundamental line was one of the most difficult chores on board ship, and one on which her safety depended. Thus, it became the custom to give out or drink spirits after completion of the job. Nowadays this is done to honor a special occasion or after great hardship or effort on the part of all hands.

main deck
Uppermost complete deck of a ship, except in aircraft carriers.

main drain
Suction line for pumping out engineering spaces.

mainmast
The second mast of a ship with two or more masts, except when the first mast is much the larger of the two. See *foremast.*

main radio
Main radio room; radio central aboard ship.

maintop
A top in the mainmast, not necessarily at the highest point. See *top, foretop, masthead.*

make

A ship *makes headway, makes good* a course steered. A line is *made up* ready for use, and is *made fast* to an object. To the report from the OOD, *"12 o'clock, sir"* the CO replies: *"make it so."* A lookout *makes out* a light before reporting it. A leaking boat *makes water.* A man being promoted *makes a rate.*

make and mend (clothes)

British equivalent of rope yarn Sunday. Any day or part of a day free of work and drills aboard ship. Admiral David Beatty's famous signal to the Grand Fleet at Scapa Flow at the end of World War I ended with this order.

make it so

Response by captain to 12 o'clock report at sea. See *make.*

make-up feed

Water of required purity with boiler compound added ready for use in ship's boilers. It is the water needed to replace that lost in the cycle between the boiler and the condenser.

Mameluke sword

Cross-hilted type worn by Marine officers.

man

To assume station, as in: *man your planes.*

maneuver

The operation or movement of a ship or aircraft.

maneuvering board

A compass rose containing polar coordinates printed on a sheet of paper used in solving problems of relative motion involved in ship maneuvering.

maneuvering rudder

See *pilot rudder.*

manhelper

A paint brush lashed to a long wooden handle.

manhole

Round or oval hole cut in deck, bulkhead, or tank top to provide access. Often placed in watertight door or hatch. Barely big enough to squeeze through. Fitted, of course, with means for closure when appropriate. See *scuttle.*

manifest

A list of all cargo with details as to shippers, consignee, etc.

manifold

A piping complex with many valves and pipes permitting suction or discharge into various pipelines. Sometimes designed in the shape of a large waterproof or pressureproof chest with valves built in.

manila

See *rope.*

manned and ready
Report made by a gun or station when all hands are present and ready for action. See *ready*.

manning level
Mathematical percentage of personnel actually on board as opposed to allowance. Not presently figured against complement, though this might be done in wartime. Thus has only a second-order relation to combat effectiveness of unit. See *complement, allowance*.

manning the rail
All-hands evolution in which the men line up along the ship's rail to honor some personage or occasion.

man-of-war
Fighting ship; armed naval ship. A warship. Most commissioned vessels of the Navy are men-of-war, but not all, e.g., a hospital ship.

manrope
Side rope to a ladder, used as a handrail; a rope used as a safety line anywhere on deck; a rope hanging down on the side of a ship to assist in ascending the ship's side.

mare's nest
Slang for any mess or disarray.

Marine
A member of the U.S. Marine Corps. If the word is not capitalized it refers to anything relating to the sea.

Marine Corps
An elite, sea-going soldier corps of the Department of the Navy, first of the armed services to be founded. Mission is to be available on short notice for tough combat and police duty, worldwide. Slang: leathernecks.

Marine Corps air station
Provides operating, testing, overhaul, and personnel facilities for Marine aviation.

Marine Corps Institute
An official training activity charged with the educational development of Marine Corps personnel.

Marine division/wing team
Marine Corps air-ground team consisting of one division and one aircraft wing.

Marine expeditionary corps
Marine air-ground task force built around two Marine divisions and two Marine aircraft wings.

marine railway
A device on tracks leading into the water on which a ship can be hauled out.

mariners' measurements

fathom	6 feet
cable	120 fathoms
statute mile	7 1/3 cable lengths (5280 feet) (880 fathoms)
nautical mile	8.4444 cable lengths (6080 feet)
league	3 nautical miles (For a workable approximation, use 8.5 cables to the mile.)

(NOTE: The British navy uses a 100-fathom cable; ten to the nautical mile.)

mark

An exclamation used in taking a reading of an amount, dial, etc., when it is necessary that the reading be marked by time. *Mark! Bearing is 279 degrees,* or, as in celestial observations, *Stand by—Mark! Altitude is 46 degrees, 27.6 minutes.* Also the marked fathoms on a hand lead: *By the mark seven.*

mark (MK)

Term used to identify specific type of weapon or equipment always followed by a number to indicate the specific equipment and frequently followed by a MOD (Model) number to indicate variety of equipment, e.g., Torpedo MK 46, MOD 1.

marker ship

In an amphibious operation, a ship that takes accurate station on a designated control point. It may fly flags by day and show lights to seaward by night. (NATO term is marker vessel.)

marline

Small stuff (cord), formerly tarred now usually made of synthetic fiber. Used for mousing, etc.

marlinespike

Tapered steel tool for separating strands of rope or wire in splicing. See *fid.*

marlinespike seamanship

Skill with rope, line and related gear topside.

marry

To join, as an LDT is married to a pontoon causeway, or two lines such as boat falls are laid out side by side and handled together. Also to set together the unlaid strands of each rope end when splicing.

martinet

A very strict officer who goes by the rule book and never permits any deviation. Not necessarily always harsh: *"He's a martinet, but he's fair."* Similar to a *sundowner* but to a lesser degree.

Mary Anne

Floating crane used to salvage aircraft in the water.

maser

Microwave amplification by stimulated emission of radiation.

maskee or **moskee**
Slang for an expression of Asiatic origin, meaning, O.K. or all right.

mast, captain's
Actually a sort of court held in a designated place at which the commanding officer awards punishment, listens to requests (request mast), or commends men for special services (meritorious or commendatory mast). Derived from the old practice of actually holding this court publicly at the mizzenmast, which, in a three-masted ship, separated officers quarters from those of the crew. Such terms as *before the mast* also relate to the significance of the mizzenmast.

master-at-arms (MAA)
Ship's police, headed by a chief MAA. There may be special MAA, such as the one in charge of the mess decks. In the old Navy the chief MAA had custody of the ship's hand weapons and trained the crew in their use.

masthead
Highest point of a mast to which the rigging is attached. Does not include staffs, poles, etc., which might project above that point. Traditionally, a midshipman might be *mastheaded* for training or discipline. See *top, cap.*

masthead light
White 20-point light required by *Rules of the Road* to be carried on the foremast of a ship.

material condition
State of damage-control security within a ship. Designated X, Y, Z depending on number and type of closures made. The order "Set condition Yoke" refers to the material condition desired and designates the closures (all these marked with "Y") to be made.

material history
Loose-leaf card system for keeping a record of ship's machinery and hull.

mayday
International distress signal, voice radio. Derived from the French *"M'aider"* (help me).

meaconing
System of receiving enemy beacon signals and rebroadcasting them to confuse enemy navigation.

meal break or **meal pennant**
Echo flag hoisted from port yardarm of a naval vessel at anchor when the crew is at mess. Significance is that only routine honors may be expected at such times. Also called bean rag or chow rag.

mean depth of the sea
Depth above and below which half of the earth's submerged surface lies, usually considered to be 3,800 meters.

mean higher high water
Average height of higher high waters.

mean high springs
The average height of the high waters at *syzygy*.

mean high water
The average height of high waters.

mean high water neaps
The average height of high water calculated at the first and last quarters of the moon. See *neap tides, spring tides.*

mean lower low water
The average height of lower low water.

mean low water
The average height of all low waters at a given place. The tidal datum used for most charts.

mean low water neaps
The average height of low water at the first and last quarters of the moon.

mean range
The average difference between mean high and mean low water.

mean river level
The average height of the surface of a river at a given point for all tide stages. Calculation is usually based on hourly readings with unusual variations excluded.

mean sea level
Surface level determined by averaging all stages of the tide.

mean sounding velocity
Average velocity of sound through a vertical column of water based on velocities in different sections of the column.

mean tide level
The average of the high waters and the low waters.

mean water level
The mean surface level determined by averaging the height of water at equal time intervals over a long period.

measure black, blue, green, white
Lighting conditions used for night landings on carriers.

measured mile
An exact nautical mile delineated by beacons or markers ashore used in calibrating pit logs and propeller shaft revolutions per minute.

meatball
The battle efficiency pennant.

Mechanical Mule
A half-ton carrier, designated the M-274, for light infantry weapons and cargo.

mechano decking
Portable aluminum decking for a tanker.

Mediterranean moor
Mooring a ship with stern to seawall and bow kept from swinging by anchor(s) placed ahead while maneuvering in. Brow is rigged from fantail to seawall. Called *Med moor*, and much used by ships of the U.S. Sixth Fleet.

meet her
An order to the steersman to apply opposite rudder to check or stop ship from swinging.

mend clothes
See *make and mend*.

merchant ship broadcast system (MERCAST)
System providing communication with a merchant ship under government lease or charter.

mercator chart
Most commonly used chart for marine navigation. Mathematically compiled but often illustrated as projection from the center of the earth onto a cylinder tangent to the earth.

merchant ship report (MEREP)
Daily report indicating total number of merchant ships arriving or departing a specified port.

meridians
Great circles of the earth that pass through the poles. Used for measuring longitude.

mess
To eat. A group of people eating together. Crew's mess is called the *general mess*.

message
Any thought briefly expressed in plain or secret language in a form suitable for rapid transmission.

messboy
Old term for wardroom waiter. Obsolete.

messcook
Old term for messman.

messenger
Light line used to carry across a larger line or hawser. Man who carries messages for OOD or other officers of the watch.

messenger mail
See *guard mail.*

mess gear
Knives, forks, spoons, etc. Also, the word passed before meals to clear the messing decks.

messman
An enlisted person detailed to serve food to the crew. Slang: bean jockey.

mess treasurer
Person who administers finances of any mess.

metacenter
The mathematically computed instantaneous center of the arc generated by the center of buoyancy as it changes when the ship rolls is called the *transverse metacenter.* That generated when the ship pitches is called the *longitudinal metacenter.* Location of the appropriate metacenter with regard to the ship's center of gravity is a measure of her stability against roll or pitch. For surface ships, the transverse metacenter is the only one of concern, unless there has been serious damage adversely affecting the longitudinal metacenter. For a submerged submarine the entire calculation is different because the center of buoyancy cannot shift, no matter what the ship's attitude. See *metacentric height.*

metacentric height
Distance between the metacenter and the center of gravity of a ship: a measure of stability. See *metacenter.*

microseismograph
Instrument for detecting distant storms by minute movements in earth's crust.

mid-channel buoy
A buoy placed in the middle of the channel, to be passed on either side. In U.S. waters it has black and white stripes.

mid-ocean ridge
A great median arch or sea-bottom swell extending the length of an ocean basin and roughly paralleling the continental margins. The Atlantic Mid-Ocean Ridge is a most prominent example.

midshipman
A student officer, enrolled at the U.S. Naval Academy or at a civilian university under the NROTC program who is commissioned as a Navy or Marine Corps officer upon graduation. Unlike a cadet, he or she wears gold braid and has a legal status between CPO and warrant officer. Acceptable slang: "mid," "middie" is term of derision.

midwatch
The watch from midnight to 4 AM (0000 to 0400).

Mike
Phonetic word for the letter *M*.

mil
Unit of angular measurement defined by the Navy as the angle whose tangent is 1/1000 of the radius and equivalent to 3.44 minutes of arc. The Army defines the mil as 1/6400 part of the circumference of a circle. The Navy mil is 0.065 minutes greater than the Army mil.

mile, nautical
A minute arc of the earth's circumference measured at the equator. Thus, the circumference of the earth at the equator is 60-times-360, or 21,600 *nautical miles.*

military
Marine Corps slang for anything rough or uncomfortable.

military occupational specialty (MOS)
Numerical system used by the Marine Corps and Army to identify special skills of an individual.

Military Sealift Command (MSC)
Ocean freight and passenger service, operated by the Navy for the Department of Defense. Includes specially equipped ships for support of ocean, missile, and space research. Formerly known as the Military Sea Transport Service (MSTS).

military specifications (MILSPECS)
Used primarily in procurement to provide clear, accurate descriptions of technical requirements.

military standards
Document setting engineering and technical limitations to assure uniformity in materials and products. Military standards can also refer to the general naval qualifications (knowledge and practical factors) that naval personnel must have concerning discipline (UCMJ), ceremonies, regulations, first aid, etc. See *occupational standards.*

MILSTRIP
Military standard requisitioning and issuing procedures.

mind your rudder
A caution to the steersman to steer a more precise course or to be alert to some special circumstances such as meeting a current.

mine
An explosive charge, submerged and designed to explode against or beneath a ship. Automatic mines are self-actuating; controlled mines are fired from afar. Mines may be dropped from the air, moored, or allowed to drift. Firings may be acoustic, contact, influence, or pressure. Sometimes called sea mines to distinguish them from land mines, which are usually antipersonnel mines.

mine countermeasures
The branch of naval warfare that embraces all methods, procedures, and techniques for preventing or reducing damage to ships from mines. It includes: channel conditioning, clearance, disposal, hunting, loading, sweeping, and watching.

minefields
Minefields are classed according to their location. Defensive minefields are planted in one's own or in friendly waters. Offensive fields are placed in enemy waters, generally at choke points carrying heavy ship traffic. They are classed as: attrition, countered, nuisance, strategic, sustained attrition, and transitory attrition.

mine sterilizer
Device to make a mine harmless after a pre-set number of days.

minesweeping
Procedure of removing or destroying mines to permit safe passage of friendly ships.

minesweeping boat (MSB)
Specially constructed boat used for sweeping mines.

mine tracks
Tracks fitted on the deck of a minelayer to permit mines to be dropped over the stern.

mine vessels
Those designed to plant or sweep mines. Principal types are: minelayer, destroyer minelayer, minesweeper, and destroyer minesweeper.

minimize
A condition where normal high-speed communications are drastically reduced so that high-priority messages will not be delayed.

mining effect
Destructive effect of an explosion under water.

minute-guns
Saluting guns fired at intervals of a minute as a sign of mourning in military funerals for officers and officials entitled to gun salutes.

misfire
Propellant charge that fails to fire when the trigger has been pulled. See *hangfire.*

missile designation system
See *Appendix D.*

mission
The objective or purpose of a military operation, usually stated in general terms.

mission, call
Type of air support operation in which a specific request is made for an attack against a target.

miss stays
In tacking, if the head of the ship will not come around through the wind, she is said to *miss stays*. The result may be to put her in irons, or flat aback, or she may fall off to the original tack, gain headway, and try again.

mizzen, mizzenmast
The third mast of a ship with three or more masts, except when the vessel has only two masts and the first is much taller than the second, as in yawls and ketches. See *foremast*.

mizzentop
Top in the mizzenmast. See *top, maintop, foretop, masthead*.

MO
Radio signal—a series of dashes sent from a scene of action or emergency for aircraft or ships to home on.

mobile noise barge
A ship especially instrumented for recording noise emanations.

mock-up
Model or replica, sometimes life-sized, of a machine or device, used for planning, design, instruction, or training purposes.

model basin
Large tank or basin for testing models of ships for speed, power, and general behavior at sea.

moderate speed
Maximum speed allowed by the *Rules of the Road* to be made in a fog. Speed at which a vessel can stop in half the distance of visibility.

modification (MOD) number
Part of equipment identification, always follows mark number. See *mark*.

mole
A large, solid-fill nearshore structure of earth, masonry or large stone; used as a breakwater or a pier.

monkey drill
Slang for physical drill, usually setting-up exercises.

monkey fist
Weighted knot in the end of a heaving line.

moor
To secure a ship alongside a pier. To secure to a *mooring buoy*. To anchor with two anchors and a *mooring swivel*. To make a regular moor, the ship drops the upstream anchor first, then backs down and drops the second. Then the second anchor chain is paid out while the first is hove

in—until the ship is centered between the two, for insertion of the mooring swivel. In a *flying moor*, the ship drops the downstream anchor first as she approaches her anchorage, pays out the chain as she steers for the spot to drop the upstream anchor, then veers the upstream chain and heaves in on the first one dropped until centered. The most spectacular maneuver of all was a simultaneous flying moor by a squadron of battleships entering a harbor on a strong flood tide. See *mooring swivel*.

mooring
Securing a ship to a pier or wharf or to a mooring buoy. Anchoring with two anchors connected to a single chain by means of a mooring swivel. See *Mediterranean moor*.

mooring buoy
A heavy round buoy anchored with several extremely heavy and strong anchors, usually concrete blocks known as sinkers, and fitted with a swivel and link in the center of the buoy's top surface. Mooring buoys are numbered and marked on harbor charts, and of course are always in the center of their berths. To moor to a buoy, the ship first unshackles the anchor, then leads the chain, with shackle, to the mooring link on the buoy. The process of mooring is complete when the chain is properly shackled to the buoy, and the stoppers put on it on deck in the usual manner. When mooring to a buoy, of course, much less chain is used, and the ship's swing around the buoy is much smaller in radius than it would be to a single anchor.

mooring line
Line used to secure a ship to a pier.

mooring swivel
A huge swivel fitted into the ground tackle to restrict the ship's swing in her berth by using two anchors some distance apart, generally one upstream and one downstream so that as the current shifts from ebb to flood the ship will alternately ride to each. Anchor chains are usually fitted with regular swivels, inserted in the chain near the anchor to prevent kinks in the chain as the ship swings to the current. The mooring swivel differs from these in that it has two links to which an anchor chain can be attached instead of only one. After the two anchors are down, their chains are broken and both shackled to the swivel; then a single chain is led from the other end of the swivel through one of the hawse pipes and stoppered on deck in the usual manner. See *moor*.

morning call book
Blank book listing locations of persons requiring early reveille, such as navigators, cooks, etc.

morning-order book
Book in which the executive officer writes his instructions for the next morning's ship's work. See *plan of the day*.

morning orders
Published schedule of activities for the day aboard ship. A part of *plan of the day*

morning watch
The watch from 4 to 8 AM (0400-0800).

Morse code
Code of dots and dashes used in radio and visual signaling.

mosaic
An assembly of overlapping aerial photographs used in intelligence. A controlled mosaic is rectified to fit known reference points.

mothball fleet
Slang for ships out of commission, but maintained in good condition. Same as reserve fleet.

motor launch
Large, sturdily built powerboat used for liberty parties and heavy freight.

motor torpedo boat
A 100-foot long, high-speed (60 knots) boat armed with torpedoes and machine guns.

motor tube
The part of a rocket that contains the propellant charge.

motor whaleboat
A small, double-ended, diesel-powered ship's boat, sometimes called the life boat if held ready for quick lowering.

mount
To assemble, organize, and prepare for embarkation a unit of Army or Marine Corps troops.

mount (gun)
System of gun-supporting parts, elevating and training mechanisms, and recoil and counter-recoil equipment.

mounting
All preparations made to load personnel and material for an amphibious operation.

mounting area
A general locality where forces of an amphibious expedition are assembled, trained, and loaded.

mourning badge
Three-inch band of black crepe worn on left arm by officers when prescribed as a mark of official mourning.

mousetrap
Ahead-thrown ASW weapon used on small ships. Similar to *hedgehog*, but smaller.

mousing
Small line strung across a hook to prevent a sling from slipping off.

movement report center (MRC) or office (MRO)
Both are part of the movement report system which accounts for all ship and command movements.

movement report system
System established to collect and make available to certain commands information on the status, location, and movement of flag commands, commissioned fleet units, and ships under operational control of the Navy.

movement, ship-to-shore
Act of debarking troops and their equipment from assault shipping via assault craft and vehicles to the assigned landing area.

moving havens
Restricted areas established to provide a measure of security to submarines and surface ships in transit through areas in which the existing attack restrictions would be inadequate to prevent attack by friendly forces.

moving surface ship haven
Normally a circle with a specified radius centered on the estimated position of the ship or the guide of a group of ships. Established by "surface ship notices."

moving target indicator (MTI)
A device that enables a moving target to be distinguished on a radar scope.

mud drum
See *drum, water.*

mushroom anchor
A large anchor having the general shape of an upside down mushroom, used on lightships and modern submarines. When housed it fits snugly into its receptacle under the ship's bottom.

mustang
Slang for an officer who was a former enlisted man.

muster
Roll call.

muster on stations
Roll call taken aboard ship while the men are at work or drill.

muster out
Discharge or release from active duty.

mutiny
Rebellion against constitued authority aboard ship, a crime that, when committed at sea in a civilian ship, comes under the jurisdiction of the Coast Guard.

muzzle bag
Canvas cover fitted over the muzzle of a gun to shield the bore from water.

N

nadir
That point on the celestial sphere vertically below the observer, or 180 degrees from the zenith. See *zenith*.

Nancy
A system of visual communications using a special light visible only by means of special equipment.

Nansen bottle
Oceanographic water-sampling bottle.

napalm
Jellied gasoline for use in flame throwers and incendiary bombs.

Nasty
Class name given to group of Norwegian-produced, high-speed patrol boats used in the Vietnam war. Derived from the building firm name: Naste.

national agency check
Cursory review of individual's background usually restricted to search of police and security records for derogatory material.

National Ocean Survey (NOS)
Formerly the Coast and Geodetic Survey, an office of the government that produces navigational charts and publications.

nautical mile
Length of one minute of arc of the great circle of the earth; 6,080 feet compared to 5,280 feet of a statute mile. The U.S. and United Kingdom standard is 6,080 feet, most other maritime countries use 6,076 feet. See *mariners' measurements, mile, nautical.*

naval activity
Unit of the naval establishment established under an officer in command or in charge.

naval air base
Collective term comprising all naval and some Marine aviation shore facilities in each naval district.

naval air facility (NAF)
Provides operating aid in some cases and maintenance facilities to meet special requirements.

naval air station (NAS)
Provides operating, testing, overhaul training, and personnel facilities for naval aviation.

naval alteration (NAVALT)
Specific alteration affecting the military characteristics of a ship.

naval attache
A naval officer on duty at an embassy abroad whose major tasks are advising and representing his ambassador on naval matters and collecting intelligence. See *ALUSNA*.

naval auxiliary air station (NAAS)
Provides facilities similar to an air station but less extensive. Requires logistic support from its parent NAS.

naval barracks
An activity to house, clothe, pay, and administer nontransient enlisted personnel.

naval base
A shore command in a given locality which includes and integrates all naval shore activities in the assigned area.

naval beach group
Permanently organized naval command, within an amphibious force, comprised of a commander, his staff, a beachmaster unit, an amphibious construction battalion, and boat unit.

naval control of shipping officer
Officer who controls and coordinates the routing and movements of merchant convoys and independently sailed merchant ships subject to the directives of the operational control authority.

naval control of shipping organization
Organization within the Navy that carries out specific responsibilities to provide for the control and protection of movements of merchant ships in time of war.

Naval Establishment
Unofficial term for the entire Navy, consisting of operating forces, the Navy Department, and the shore establishment. See *Navy Department.*

naval gunfire team
Men organized to control and direct naval gunfire from the shore.

naval landing party
Part of ship's complement organized for military operations ashore. Formerly called the landing forces.

Naval Material Command
Activated in May 1966, successor to the Naval Material Support Establishment. Command includes six functional commands: Air Systems, Ship Systems, Electronic Systems, Ordnance Systems, Supply Systems, and Facilities Engineering. Commander, Naval Material Command, reports directly to CNO.

naval mission
Group of officers and men who assist a friendly foreign power in the administration of its navy.

Naval Ordnance Laboratory (NOL)
Test and research facility for naval weapons, located at White Oak, Maryland.

Naval Port Control Office
An authority that coordinates logistic support and harbor services for any services for any ships under naval control.

Naval Research Advisory Committee
Advisory committee of private civilians reporting to the Secretay of the Navy to provide advice on all research matters to the Secretary of the Navy.

naval research requirement
Prepared by the Chief of Naval Research to start basic and applied research in support of future needs.

Naval Reserve
A force of qualified officers and men available, in an emergency, to meet the needs of an expanding Navy while an adequate flow of new personnel is being established. Component parts are Fleet, Organized Volunteer, and Merchant Marine Reserves.

naval ship maintenance facility
See *reserve fleet.*

Naval Ship Research and Development Center
Activity formed in 1967 from integration of David Taylor Model Basin, Carderock, Maryland, and Marine Engineering Laboratory, Annapolis, Maryland, to single command.

naval shipyard
An industrial activity charged with building, repairs, alterations, overhauling, docking, converting, or outfitting of ships, together with necessary replenishment.

naval station
Naval shore activity, having fixed boundaries and a commanding officer.

naval stores
Oil, paint, turpentine, pitch, and other items traditionally used for and in ships.

naval tactical data system (NTDS)
Computerized system for assembly and evaluation of all available tactical information for tactical commanders. British version is called action data automation system (ADAS).

navigable waters
Waters that can be used for passage of ships.

navigation
The art and science of conducting a ship or aircraft from one position to another.

navigational light
A light with fixed characteristics, marked on charts and described fully in light lists so that passing navigators can use it to fix their positions. May be in a lightship but most frequently mounted in a lighthouse or on a buoy. Among the given characteristics are height above sea level, arc of visibility, color, period of repetition, etc. Known as alternating—showing color variations; fixed—a steady light; flashing—off more than it is on; occulting—on more than it is off; group flashing—flashing in groups of two or more flashes followed by a period of darkness.

navigation head
A transshipment point on a waterway where loads are transferred between water carriers and land carriers. A navigation head is similar in function to a railhead or truckhead.

navigation, pressure pattern
The selection and control of a flight path or track for aircraft by considering the atmospheric pressure pattern in order to take advantage of the most favorable wind conditions. See *optimum ship routing*.

navigator
Officer who is head of the navigation department, responsible for the safe navigation of the ship.

Navol
Solution of hydrogen peroxide in water, used as a fuel in MK 16 torpedo.

NAVSTAR
Part of the Global Positioning System, an advanced worldwide navigation system using high-altitude satellites to broadcast signals. Thus, distances can be measured instantly to solve the navigation equation rather than measuring angles as in celestial navigation. NAVSTAR when completely operational will provide secure, rapid, all-weather, all-purpose position fixing.

Navy capabilites plan
This plan with its annex, the Navy logistic capabilities plan, supports the joint strategic capabilities plan and covers the short-range period.

Navy Department
The executive part of the Navy located in Washington, D.C. Differs from Department of the Navy in that by long usage it refers only to the administrative offices at the seat of government. See *naval establishment*.

Navy enlisted classification (NEC) code
A system for identifying and designating special skills and knowledge for enlisted personnel. Every sailor has at least two of the four-digit NEC codes: a primary code and a secondary code. Details are contained in the Manual of Navy Enlisted Classifications.

Navy exchange
A store for naval personnel and their dependents that sells at a small profit for the benefit of the welfare and recreation fund.

Navy League of the United States
A national organization that believes in and works for a strong Navy; headquarters, Washington, D.C. Completely independent of the Navy; active duty officers may not belong.

Navy long-range strategic study (NLRSS)
An appraisal of the strategic environment with consideration given to scientific and technological factors likely to affect naval warfare.

Navy mid-range objectives (NMRO)
Provides mid-range force structure goals (10 to 11 years) based on the NMS, NLRSS, etc. Considers alternate force goals in relation to threats and assesses risks involved in each case to serve as a base for Program Objective (PO) and JSOP submissions based on a balanced force goal.

Navy mid-range study (NMS)
Provides internal planning guidance for the portion of the mid-range period between five and 10 years hence.

Navy navigation satellite system (NAVSAT)
Navigational system using the doppler shift from signals transmitted by the satellite to establish position.

Navy objective plan (NOP)
Covers strategic concepts and objectives during the next 10 years.

Navy oceanographic and meteorological automatic device (NOMAD)
A 20-by-10-foot platform moored at sea to monitor and report weather and oceanographic data automatically.

Navy Oceanographic Office (NAVOCEANO)
Produces navigational charts and publications. Now called the Defense Mapping Agency Hydrographic Center.

Navy program objectives (PO)
Contains annual increments of the Navy and Marine Corps force levels required for orderly progress towards objectives in the Navy mid-range objectives.

Navy Relief Society
The quasi-official relief agency operated for the benefit of naval personnel and their dependents.

Navy technical data office (NTDO)
An element of the Office of the Chief of Naval Material reponsible for implementing, reviewing, and monitoring policies for handling technical data and keeping the authorized data list (ADL).

Navy Unit Commendation (NUC)
An honor accorded a naval unit for distinguishing itself in combat or other operations, of lesser degree than Presidential Unit Citation.

neap range
Average diurnal range of tide occurring during the first and fourth
quarter points of the moon.

neap tides
Tides of decrease~~d~~   ~~a~~rring at the first and fourth quarter points
of the moon   ~~n~~ture. Opposite from spring tides.

negative
In any nav~~a~~   ~~n~~o; not granted; do not concur; not
approved; etc.

nekton
Ocean life form~~s~~   ~~n~~eous swimming.

Neptune
Mythical god of th~~e~~

nest
Two or more ships moored together, side by side. Also, a boat stowage
on board ship in which one boat is placed inside, or partially inside
another.

net
A group of connected radio stations. A steel mesh to protect ships and
harbors from torpedoes, submarines, and surface craft.

net-laying ship
Ship designed for laying and tending submarine or anti-torpedo nets.

nets and booms
Combination of underwater steel mesh nets and surface floating booms
for harbor defense against submarines, torpedoes, and small surface craft.

netting
Same as snaking.

NEWRADS
See *nuclear explosion warning.*

night order book
Official ship's record in which the commanding officer writes his
orders to the officers of the deck for the night's activities. The engineer of
a ship uses a similar book to leave directions for the engineering officers of
the watch.

night stick
A short wooden club carried by men on shore patrol duty.

night vision
Faculty of seeing well at night. See *dark adaptation.*

nip
Sharp bend or turn in a line or wire. See *freshen the nip.*

nipple
Short connector; a short length of tubing in a boiler.

no bottom
A notation appearing on nautical charts indicating that the sounding did not reach bottom. Also, a leadsman's report: *No bottom,* meaning the same.

NOL
Naval Ordnance Laboratory, White Oak, Maryland.

nonjudicial punishment
Punishment by a commanding officer imposed on men and officers without trial by court-martial. Specified and limited by the Uniform Code of Military Justice.

nonmilitary vessel category
Nonmilitary vessels entering a controlled port in wartime are given one of four initial classifications for purpose of determining examination procedures. They are: clean, doubtful, hostile, and suspect.

North Atlantic Current
A continuation of the Gulf Stream after its juncture with the Labrador Current in the vicinity of the Grand Banks off New England. Movement is generally eastward in an irregular flow, with components that flow northeastward as well as southeastward.

North Equatorial Current (Atlantic)
The major westerly flow across the North Atlantic in the trade wind belt, pushed by the northeast trades and fed by southeast currents off the western coast of Africa providing the source in the Caribbean Sea of the Gulf Stream System. A comparable current in the Pacific provides the source of the Japan Current. A North Equatorial Current also exists in the Indian Ocean.

NOTAL
Not to (nor needed) by all, a term used in messages.

nothing to the right (left)
An order to the steersman not to steer to the right (left) of the given course.

notice
A specially numbered announcement or one-time directive. Not permanent. Also, notice for getting underway; required material and personnel condition of readiness (e.g., *four hours' notice*).

Notices to Airmen (NOTAMS)
Information, issued perodically, concerning any facility or aid relating to air navigation.

Notice to Mariners
A publication giving latest changes to navigational charts and other aid.

not under command
Said of a ship when she is disabled and uncontrollable through some exceptional circumstance and is unable to maneuver as required by the *Rules of the Road.* During the day the ship shows two shapes and at night two red 32-point lights, both in a vertical line. Lights are called breakdown lights.

now do you hear there
Traditional preface to *the word* when passed by the boatswain's mate throughout the ship. Usually shortened to *now hear there (this).*

no wind position
Last well-determined position of an aircraft advanced along the heading for the true air speed, (i.e., assuming the aircraft had maintained constant heading and speed, and the wind had suddenly died). Application of known winds should give a fairly accurate position.

no-year appropriation
Appropriation available for incurring obligations for an indefinite period. See *appropriation, annual* and *appropriation, continuing.*

nonrated man
Enlisted man in the first three paygrades. Not a petty officer.

notional ship
An imaginary, arbitrary ship used in naval logistic plannning.

November
Phonetic word for the letter *N.*

NSFO
Navy standard fuel oil. Known in the naval service as *black oil.* More refined than *bunker crude* of the merchant service.

nuclear explosion warning and radiological data system (NEWRADS)
Program to provide fleet commander with information on radiological hazards which might affect operations.

nuclear yields
Energy released in the detonation of a nuclear weapon, measured in terms of the kilotons or megatons of TNT required to produce the same energy release.

Very low	less than 1 kiloton
Low	1 kiloton to 10 kilotons
Medium	over 10 kilotons to 50 kilotons
High	over 50 kilotons to 500 kilotons
Very high	over 500 kilotons

null
A symbol in cryptography having no plain text significance. Also, the least signal where intensity varies with orientation antenna (RDF).

number
A merchant ship's four-letter identification flown either as a signal or used as a radio call is known as her number.

numbered document
See *registered matter.*

number in grade
Precedence number assigned Marine Corps officers annually, corresponding to the lineal number of a naval officer.

number one
British naval slang for a ship's first lieutenant, especially when he is also executive officer.

nun buoy
Cone-shaped buoy used to mark channels; it is anchored on the right side of the channel, as seen from a ship entering the harbor from seaward, and is painted red. See *red, right, returning.*

O

oakum
A caulking material made of old, tarred, hemp rope fiber.

oarlock
Device to hold oars when pulling a boat; also called rowlock.

oars
Command given to crew of a pulling boat, directing them to stop rowing and stand by with oars in rowlocks, extended horizontally, ready for the next order.

OBA
Oxygen breathing apparatus.

objective area
Geographically defined area around the assault beaches of an amphibious operation in which the commander of an attack force directs the operation of all ships and aircraft.

Ocean Shipping Procedures
A joint manual for merchant shipping control during wartime.

occulting light
A navigational aid in which the period of light is equal to or more than the period of darkness. See *flashing light*.

occupational standards
Formerly "technical requirements." The skills and knowledge expected of a man in his rate and rating. See *military standards*.

octant
See *sextant*.

office
Slang meaning the cockpit of a large aircraft.

office hours
Marine term for mast.

Office of Naval Material Command (ONM)
Since December 1963, the staff of the Chief of Naval Material concerned with supporting CNM in his role as commander of the Naval Material Support Establishment. Now more properly referred to as the Office of the Chief of Naval Material.

officer candidate
Person under instruction at the officer candidate school. Has status of an enlisted man.

officer conducting the exercise (OCE)
A senior officer who plans and directs the exercise without necessarily having tactical command of the forces involved.

officer in charge (OIC or OinC)
Generic term describing an officer, not a commanding officer, who has responsibility of directing special units or activities.

officer in tactical command (OTC)
The senior officer present or one who has been designated by him or by a common senior to exercise tactical control.

officer of the deck (OOD)
An officer on duty in charge of the ship representing the commanding officer. His assistant is the junior officer of the watch (JOOW) or junior officer of the deck (JOOD). The officer on watch under instruction is the assistant officer of the watch.

officer of the watch (OOW)
Officer on duty in the engineering spaces. Also called the engineering officer of the watch (EOOW).

officer's call
A bugle call (or word passed) for officers to take their stations. Precedes general call for all hands.

officer service record
Record of the nature of the duties that an officer performs. Includes his periodic evaluation by seniors in the form of fitness reports, any awards, commendations, or records of punishment or censure.

official visit
A formal visit of courtesy requiring special honors and ceremonies. See *call.*

offshore
The region seaward of a specified depth, usually the three- or five-fathom isobath. Opposite is inshore or nearshore.

offshore currents
Nontidal currents outside the surf zone independent of shoaling or river discharge influence.

offshore winds
Winds blowing from the land seaward.

ogive
The forward, curved section of a projectile.

oil canning
The snapping in and out of the hull plating of a ship in heavy seas, accompanied by the characteristic noise. Experienced only by small, lightly built ships. See *panting.*

oiler (AO)
A tanker specially configured to replenish combatant ships of all types underway at sea. Heavily outfitted with booms and hoses rigged and ready.

oil flat
An oil-carrying, single-crew yard craft. Also, oil barge.

oil king
Petty officer aboard ship who keeps fuel oil records.

oilskins
Waterproof clothing.

old-fashioned anchor
The traditional hook anchor. Fitted with a stock—axis of which is at right angles to the plane of the flukes, and also at right angles to the axis of the shank of the anchor. When the ship tugs at her anchor, the action of the chain is to drag the stock flat along the bottom, and this causes the flukes to stand upright with the maximum "bite" into the ground. The stockless anchor accomplishes the same thing by a type of hinge built into the flukes. See *anchor* (n).

Old Man
Slang for the commanding officer of any activity. (Almost always capitalized.) The corresponding expression for an admiral is old gentleman. (Usually not capitalized.)

Omega
A highly accurate sub-surface or surface VLF worldwide radio navigation system using phase differences for positioning.

omnidirection range (ODR)
A navigation system for aircraft based on radio beacons that provides true headings.

ONM
Office of Naval Material Command.

one-time code
A code destroyed after one use.

onshore winds
Winds blowing from sea to land.

on soundings
Traditionally said of a ship that is near enough to land so that soundings with a deep-sea lead can be taken. Now considered to be within the 100-fathom curve.

on the bow
Said of an object somewhere ahead on one bow or the other. Stated more specifically, e.g., *on the port bow*. The expression *broad on the port bow* means that the object is 45 degrees on the port bow, or the relative bearing is 315 degrees.

on the double
Quickly; with speed; as: *"Man your stations on the double."*

on the line
Operational aircraft ready for use are said to be on the line.

on the quarter
Said of an object somewhere astern but not directly astern. Almost always is stated more specifically, e.g., *on the starbard quarter. Broad on the starboard quarter* means that the object bears 135 degrees relative.

on the wind
Close hauled.

OP
Short title for an office or individual within the Office of the Chief of Naval Operations; when so used it is always followed by a number or number and letter designation, e.g., OP 50, OP 09D.

open purchase
Purchase of materials on the open market, instead of by requisition through government channels.

open water
Water with less than one-tenth ice coverage.

operating forces
Fleet, seagoing, sea frontier, and naval district forces, and such other activities and forces as may be assigned by the President of the U.S. or the Secretary of the Navy.

operating ratio
The ratio of the number of hours of operating time to total possible operating time in a given period. Down-time includes scheduled and unscheduled time out of service. Expressed as a percentage.

operation
A military action or the carrying out of a training or administrative measure.

operational
Pertaining to operations; capable of operating; in contrast to administrative.

operational control authority
Naval commander responsible for the movement of ships.

optimum ship routing
Ship routing technique based on consideration of currents, weather, and wave conditions to reduce transit time.

orbit
To fly a circular path, as aircraft do about an orbit point or as satellites about the earth.

orbit point
Geographically fixed or a moving reference point for stationing aircraft.

order
An order directs that a job be done but does not specify how. See *command.*

order of battle
The identification, strength, command structure, and disposition of the personnel, units, and equipment of any military force.

orderly
Messenger or personal attendant, usually for a senior officer.

ordinary, in
Status of a ship not in commission but maintained with a skeleton force. Obsolete term.

ordinary tides
Mean tides. See *mean tide level.*

ordnance
Collective term for guns, missiles, torpedoes, bombs, and related equipment.

ordnance engineering duty officer (OEDO)
See *engineering duty officer.*

Ordnance Systems Command
Functional command replacing Bureau of Naval Weapons in the 1966 Navy Department reorganization. Component of Naval Material Command.

ORE
Operational readiness evaluation.

originator
The command by whose authority the message is sent.

ORI
Operational readiness inspection.

Orion
Model designation: P-3. The P-3 is a 10-crew, turboprop, anti-submarine patrol aircraft developed from the commercial Lockheed "Electra" design. Replaces the Neptune. See *Appendix C.*

orlop deck
Lowest deck of a four-deck merchant ship. No longer used in the Navy.

Osborne shackle
Used in underway replenishment at the end of the first messenger line. It carries a bight of the hose messenger for alongside fueling.

Oscar
Phonetic word for the letter *O*.

otter
A device used in minesweeping that keeps sweep wire extended laterally.

outboard
In the direction away from the center line of the ship. Opposite is inboard.

outhaul
Any line used to pull out something, as a boat boom is pulled into position perpendicular to the ship. Opposite is inhaul.

outreach
Horizontal distance from mast or kingpost to end of boom.

overfalls
Turbulent water surface caused by strong currents flowing over shoals or by conflicting currents.

overhang
Projection of the ship's bow or stern beyond the stem or sternpost.

overhaul
Repair, clean, inspect, adjust. To overtake. Also to separate the blocks of a tackle. Opposite of round in.

overhead
The ceiling of a compartment as viewed from the inside, e.g., *the overhead needs painting.* Also, less common, the roof, as *he is on the overhead.*

overlay (chart)
Transparent sheet to be used with a chart, providing special operational or navigational information such as gunfire support stations, etc.

over leave
See *unauthorized absentee.*

overt
In intelligence work, means open and above board. Opposite of covert.

overtaking vessel
One that overhauls another (the overtaken vessel), approaching from more than two points abaft the beam.

over the hill
Slang for deserting. To desert is to *go over the hill.*

over the side
Over the ship's side; in the water.

oxygen-breathing apparatus (OBA)
A device that supplies oxygen to anyone who must enter closed spaces or compartments.

P

pack ice
Offshore ice moving with wind and current. May be close, open or drift and in the form of fields, floes, or blocks.

padding
Words or phrases unrelated to the text of a message.

pad eye
A metal ring welded to deck or bulkhead.

padre
Slang for chaplain.

painter
A line in the bow of a boat for making fast. The corresponding line in the stern is the stern fast. See *bow painter, sea painter.*

pallet
A portable platform used in handling cargo on fork-lift trucks or slings. Palletized cargo is made up to fit the pallets.

palm and needle
Sailor's thimble made of leather, which fits over most of his palm, and a large needle; used for sewing heavy canvas or leather.

pan (ice)
A piece of ice varying in diameter from a few yards to several hundred yards, formed by the action of wind and sea on field ice. Pancake ice is newly formed ice, usually between one and six feet in diameter.

panel
A large cloth used by ground personnel for visual signaling. An electric switchboard or instrument board.

pant, panting
Series of pulsations caused by minor, recurrent explosions in the fire of a ship's boiler. Usually caused by a shortage of air. Also the rhythmic bulging in and out of a ship's hull plating because of wave pressure.

pantry
Place where officers' food is prepared for serving; may be a wardroom, captain's or admiral's pantry.

Papa
Phonetic word for the letter *P.*

parade
An area aboard ship where the divisions fall in for muster or inspection. Fair weather parades are topside; foul-weather parades below. See *all-hands parade.*

parallel middle body
That length of the ship over which the midships section remains constant in area and shape.

parallel of latitude
A circle on the surface of the earth parallel to the plane of the equator and connecting all points of equal latitude.

parallel ruler
A double, connected ruler used on charts to transfer courses and bearings to and from the compass rose. See *protractor, drafting machine, compass rose.*

pararaft
A combination parachute and one-man life raft worn by pilots.

paravane
Torpedo-shaped device towed on either side of a ship's bow to deflect and cut adrift moored mines.

parbuckle
Method of raising or lowering a heavy object along an inclined or vertical surface. A bight of rope is thrown around a secured fastening at the level to which the object is to be raised or from which it is to be lowered. The two ends of the rope are then passed under the object, brought all the way over, and led back toward the bight. The two ends are then hauled or slackened together to raise or lower the object, the object itself acting as a movable pulley. Parbuckling works best with cylindrical objects, such as a barrel or cask, but any solid object can be handled in this manner.

parcel
To wrap a line or wire with strips of canvas. See *serve, worm.*

parking harness
Device fitted over the controls of a parked aircraft.

part
To break, as to *part a line* or hawser.

party
Group organized for a special task such as repair party, working party, liberty party, recreation party, etc.

passageway
Corridor or hall aboard ship.

pass a line
Throw or project a line. To carry a line to or around something.

pass down the line book (PDL Book)
A notebook for the officer of the day or the officer of the watch in which instructions or information of a temporary nature are recorded.

passing honors
Those honors, except gun salutes, rendered by a ship when ships or embarked officials or officers pass close aboard.

passive acoustic torpedo
Torpedo that homes in on noise generated by its target.

passive sonar
Gathers its target information from the sound emanations of the target only.

pass the word
Broadcast of information.

patching
The plugging in or connecting of required radio frequencies in the transmitter room upon request by radio central.

patent anchor
General term for stockless anchor.

patent log
Device for measuring ship's speed through the water. See *taffrail log*.

patrol vessel
Small man-of-war used for general escort and patrol duties. See *Appendix A*.

paulin
Short for tarpaulin, a cloth (canvas) used to cover and protect. Also called tarp.

pay
Slang for disbursing or supply officer of a ship; short for paymaster. Also, to fill the seams of a wooden vessel with pitch or other substance. *The devil to pay and no pitch hot!* (Devil was the longest and toughest seam to pay.)

pay clerk
Warrant officer, usually advanced from storekeeper or disbursing clerk.

paygrade
Level of military pay, from E-1 (recruit) to E-9 (master chief petty officer); from W-1 (warrant officer) to W-4 (commissioned warrant officer); and from 0-1 (ensign) to 0-10 (fleet admiral).

paymaster
General term for any disbursing officer.

pay off
To turn the bow away from the wind. Not used as a command. A ship *pays off* as necessary to keep her sails filled.

pay out
To slack off or ease out a line.

PCO
Prospective commanding officer.

peacoat
The heavy topcoat worn by seafaring men in cold weather. Cut short, well above the knees. The coat was originally made of material called pilot cloth; so it is probable that the name was successively pilot-cloth coat, pilot coat, P-coat, and finally peacoat. Also called reefer in the old Navy.

peak
Topmost end of the gaff; from this point the ensign is flown while the ship is underway. Also, to adjust for optimum performance, as for a radio or radar.

peak tank
Tank low in the bow or stern of a ship, usually kept empty and dry, but sometimes designed for carrying potable water. So-called because one end of the tank is at the very bow or stern and therefore comes to a peak.

pelican hook
A quick-release device made in various sizes, ranging from an anchor chain stopper to boat gripes. Released by pulling a toggle key or pin, or knocking off a bail shackle. The hook has a shape resembling a pelican's beak.

pelorus
Device for taking bearings with a ring fitted with a telescope that can be rotated over a gyro repeater on a stand. Same as alidade. See *azimuth circle, bearing circle.*

pendant
Length of line or wire, often fitted with an eye or block at one or both ends. One end usually made fast to mast, yard, spar, etc.

pennant
A flag that is longer in the fly than in the hoist, and usually tapers to a point. Some pennants terminate in a swallow-tail (two points). Examples are commission and broad command pennants, etc.

per diem
Additional expense money for a person on temporary additional duty or in a travel status.

perigee
The point at which a missile trajectory or a satellite orbit is closest to the center of the gravitational field of the controlling body or bodies. See *apogee*

period of roll
Time it takes for a ship to roll from one extremity to the other side and back again. Can be used to determine metacentric height, which is a measure of initial stability.

periscope
An optical device of mirrors and prisms used to project one's vision over an obstacle, as in a submarine periscope.

periscope feather
The spray formed by the periscope of a submerged submarine moving through the water at moderate to high speed.

personnel diary
A daily record, by name, of all personnel assigned to an activity.

Personnel Management Information Center (PERMIC)
Computer installation used in personnel administration. Originally called Personnel Accounting Machine Installation (PAMI).

per standard compass (psc)
Phrase used in describing a course, e.g., "steering 090 degrees psc." The *standard* compass is the most reliable magnetic compass. *pgc* correspondingly, means *per gyro compass.* Today courses are given pgc whenever possible.

petty officer
Non-commissioned officer in the grades of master chief, senior chief, chief, and first, second, and third class. See *Appendix B.*

petty officer of the watch
Senior enlisted assistant to the officer of the deck.

phonetic alphabet
Words that identify letters so that they will be clearly understood; for example, A is Alfa, B is Bravo, etc.

photograph, oblique
Any photograph other than a vertical one. May be low (angle between camera axis and horizontal is less than 45 degrees), high (angle greater than 45 degrees), or flat (axis of camera horizontal).

photograph, vertical
One taken with optical axis of the camera pointed vertically downward.

picket
Ship or aircraft stationed away from a formation or in a geographic location for a specific purpose, such as air warning.

picket boat
Armed boat that performs sentry, security, and patrol duty, usually at night.

pier
Structure for mooring vessels which is built out into the water perpendicular to the shore line. See *dock, wharf.*

pier head jump
An immediate departure from a ship as it arrives in port or a last-minute embarkation as the ship departs, viewed with mixture of disdain, amusement and admiration.

pig
The float at the end of a minesweeping cable.

pigboat
Slang for an old-type submarine.

pigstick
Small spar at top of mainmast from which the commission pennant flies.

piling
Wooden, concrete, or metal poles driven into the river or sea bottom for support or protection of piers or wharves. Singular: pile.

pilot
An expert on local harbor and channel conditions who advises the commanding officer in moving a ship in or out of port; one who operates an airplane; a book of sailing directions.

pilot charts
Monthly charts of oceans showing winds, currents, and weather conditions to be expected.

pilot house
The compartment in the bridge structure that contains the ship controls and from which the ship is normally controlled. See *wheelhouse.*

piloting
Navigation near land using landmarks, aids to navigation, and soundings.

pilot rudder
A small additional rudder forward of the propeller of a landing craft. Also called maneuvering rudder.

Pilot Rules
Special rules governing piloting and pilots in inland waters of the United States or in any country enacting such rules. There should be no conflict with the *Inland Rules*; if so, the *Inland Rules* have precedence as far as the U.S. is concerned. Of course, each nation makes up its own *Pilot Rules*, if any. See *International Rules of the Road, Sailing Directions.*

ping
Acoustic pulse signal of an echo-ranging indicator.

ping jockey
Slang for sonarman.

pink lady
Slang for cleaning alcohol, not fit for drinking.

pintle
Fitting on a rudder that secures it to the hull of a ship by fitting into a gudgeon.

pip
Visual indication of a target on an electronic indicator screen. Also blip.

pipe, boatswain's
Distinctive silver whistle used to sound calls when passing the word aboard ship or during quarterdeck honors. Also used to direct the men as when hoisting in a boat or handling cargo. Sometimes referred to as a boatswain's call, although this term is also used to designate a tune played on the pipe.

pipe down
An order to be silent or reduce noise, when used alone. In combination with other instructions, means to take down *(pipe down aired bedding)*, carry below *(pipe down chow for the crew)*, or terminate an activity *(pipe down sweepers). Pipe down chow* is used to announce crew meals no matter where the galley is.

pipe the side
Render honors with sideboys and boatswain's pipe. See *side honors.*

pipe to
Pass the word and pipe the appropriate call to an evolution, such as *pipe to dinner.*

piping the side
Name of a boatswain's call on the pipe used during side honors. See *pipe the side.*

pitch
The vertical motion of a ship's bow or stern in a seaway about the arthwartships axis. Of a propeller, the axial advance during one revolution. See *roll, yaw, heaving, sway, surge.*

pitometer log
Device for indicating the speed of a ship and distance run by measuring water pressure on a pitot tube projected outside the ship's hull.

pitot tube
Sensing element used to measure static and dynamic pressure for ship or aircraft speed indicators.

pivot (pivoting) point
The point about which a ship pivots when turning, usually in the vicinity of the bridge.

pivot ship
The wing ship in a line around which a wheel is being made in a convoy maneuver.

plaindress
Message having its address in the heading.

plane
Said of a seaplane or boat when it gains enough speed to ride on the step of the hull.

plane captain
Enlisted person responsible for the material condition of his assigned aircraft.

plane director
The person who hand-signals the pilots for taxiing aircraft on an aircraft carrier or ashore.

plane guard
A fast ship (destroyer) that accompanies a carrier to pick up downed personnel. Helicopters also perform this duty.

plane handler
Enlisted person who handles aircraft on a carrier flight deck. Also called plane pusher.

plan, entry (sortie)
Plan for entry (sortie) of a task force to (from) a port with the greatest possible security.

plankowner
Person who has been on board since ship was commissioned.

planning and overhaul yard
Shipyard responsible for design work and maintenance of records of ships assigned to it for planning or overhaul. Formerly these functions were assigned to the *home yard,* now an obsolete term.

plan of the day
Schedule of the ship's activities for the day including work, training, meals, recreation, etc. Also called morning orders.

plan position indicator (PPI)
A radar screen that exhibits a chart-like picture of the surrounding land and sea.

platform deck
Partial deck of a ship below the lowest complete deck.

Plimsoll mark
Mark on a merchant ship's side indicating by international agreement how deeply she may be loaded under various expected sea conditions, depending on season and geographical area. Plimsoll is capitalized because it is a man's name. See *load line marking.*

plot
A diagram of ship movement (surface plot), aircraft movement (air plot), or submarine movement (underwater plot). Also, tactical and operational control center aboard ship: air plot, flag plot, etc. To record the courses of ships and aircraft, to diagram movements.

plumb (a hatch)
To rig a tackle directly over it.

pneumercator
An instrument for measuring the level and thus the volume of liquid in tanks.

pod
Group of whales. Projecting streamlined container usually located under the wing of a aircraft.

pogey bait
Slang for candy, also soda fountain items. Same as geedunk.

point oars
A pulling boat order given when the boat is aground; oarsmen thrust their blades forward and downward at an angle of about 30 degrees. At the command *shove off*, the crew push together, lifting the boat and forcing it back off the shoal.

pointer
Man who controls a gun in elevation (range). See *trainer*.

point oboe
An arbitrary point, sometimes in motion, used in gunfire target designation and carrier aircraft operations.

point of tow
Device on the forefoot of a ship to which the paravane wires are attached. See *clump, shoe*.

points, compass
The 32 directions of the compass card, equal to 11¼ degrees of arc each.

points, retirement and promotion
Credits earned by Naval Reserve officers and enlistees attending school, serving on active duty, taking correspondence courses, etc.

Polaris
Model designation: UGM-27 (series). Submarine-launched, two-stage ballistic missile powered by solid-fuel rocket motors and guided by a self-contained interial guidance system. Only the A-3 remains in service—range 2,880 nautical miles. Can be launched from surfaced or submerged conditions. See *Poseidon, Trident*.

polar lights
The aurora australis and aurora borealis of the southern and northern hemispheres, respectively. Displays, usually associated with sunspots activity or magnetic storms, are seen at night only.

police
To inspect and to clean up.

polliwog
One who has not crossed the equator. See *shellback.*

polynya
An open water area in the pack ice other than a lead.

pontoon
Steel boxes 5 by 5 by 7 feet, many of which are bolted together to form causeways, barges, etc. Loosely, any watertight structure (box, barrel, etc.) used to float something.

pontoon barge
A barge made of pontoons bolted together and propelled by an engine driving an outboard propeller. See *warping tug.*

pontoon causeway or **pier**
A floating, movable pier made up of pontoons bolted together. Used in amphibious assaults to expedite unloading.

pool, electronics
A receiving, stock and issue point for electronic materials.

poop deck
A partial deck, aft above the main deck, in wooden men-of-war. See *spar deck.*

pooped
Said of a vessel when a following sea breaks over the stern. Slang meaning tired, worn out.

poopy bag
Slang for a lighter-than-air craft, a blimp.

poopy suit
Slang for an aviator's anti-exposure suit worn on overwater flights.

porpoise
A small sea-going mammal related to the whale. Also (v), to break the surface of the sea and immediately go under again, as the porpoise does.

port
Seagoing term for left as opposed to starboard, which means right. A coastal city accessible to sea commerce. Short for air port, cargo port, etc.

port capacity
Estimated capacity of a port or an anchorage to clear cargo in 24 hours. Usually expressed in tons.

port commander
An officer who is responsible for and has authority over all activities of a port.

port director
Officer who controls the water operations of a port. Now called naval port control officer.

portfolio chart
A group of charts for a specific geographical area.

porthole
Round opening in the side of a ship. Also an air port. British term is *sidelight*.

port watch or **in-port watch**
Watch set when a ship is in port in contrast to the underway watch. Also, if a ship is in a watch-and-watch condition, the watches are usually named port and starboard.

Poseidon
Model designation: UGM-73A. Successor to Polaris. Poseidon is outfitted with multiple warheads, each of which can be separately targeted. Their range is about 2,900 nautical miles. See *Trident*.

position
The location of an object relative to a reference point or in accordance with recognized coordinates as longitude and latitude.

position angle
The number of degrees an object seen in the sky is above the horizon.

position buoy
A marker towed astern in formation. Same as *towing spar*.

post shakedown availability (PSA)
Period in the shipyard after a ship's shakedown cruise during which she is brought to full operational condition. Length of PSA varies with type of ship.

powder hoist
A device to lift powder charges from the magazine to the gun mount, or turret.

practical factors
Items a man must be able to do, in addition to what he must know, in order to win advancement in rating.

pratique
Permission granted in a foreign port for a ship to communicate with the shore after a certification that she is free of contagious disease. Usually granted by radio.

precedence
The relative order in which messages should be handled.

pre-dreadnought
A battleship mounting several calibers of big guns (12-inch, 8-inch, 6-inch, and 3-inch was typical), built prior to HMS *Dreadnought* and much inferior to her. See *dreadnought*.

Presidential Unit Citation (PUC)
An honor accorded a naval unit for distinguishing itself in combat or other operations. Of higher degree than Navy Unit Commendation.

pressure hull
The cylindrical, pressure-resistant core of a submarine that encloses its operating spaces.

preventer
Any line used for additional safety or security or to keep something from falling or running free.

pricker
Small marlinespike.

primary loop
The heat transfer medium of U.S. Naval reactors is highly pressurized water, driven constantly, and at high speed, between reactor and steam generators by the main coolant pumps in a completely closed loop. This is the primary loop. In the steam generators, heat is transferred to the secondary loop, so-called, where steam is generated under less pressure to operate the machinery. See *reactor*.

prime contract
As used by DOD, any contract entered into directly by a military department or procurement activity of DOD.

prime contractor
Any contractor who enters into a contract with the government to produce, assemble or deliver specific items or material, or perform a service. He may negotiate subcontracts which are his responsibility.

Prime Meridian
Meridian from which longitude is measured. The meridian of the original site of the Royal Observatory at Greenwich, England.

priming
The carryover of water with steam from a boiler. A good watertender will not permit this.

prisoner at large (PAL)
Person under arrest whose restraint to certain specified limits is morally enforced.

privileged vessel
Ship having right of way under *Rules of the Road* and required to hold course and speed. The other ship, the burdened vessel, must take avoiding action. See *general prudential rule*.

prize, or prize of war
Merchant vessel captured during wartime and retained for legal prize proceedings. The term can also be applied to a captured warship.

prize master
Officer placed in command of the prize to bring it into port. He is provided with a *prize crew*.

prize money
Paid to enlisted men for the award to their unit of the Battle Efficiency Pennant. No longer paid for the capture of a prize.

proceed time
Time allowed between day of detachment and the date of reporting to a new duty station, not considering travel time and leave, if any.

program for afloat college education
Cooperative college-Navy extension program offering up to two years of college credits. BUPERS sponsored.

program torpedo
Torpedo designed to follow a pre-planned course.

projectile
The missile fired by a gun. Major classes are penetrating, fragmenting, and special-purpose.

projectile flat
Stowage space for projectiles in a magazine. Also called shell room.

projectile hoist
Elevator mechanism for lifting projectiles from storage space to guns.

prolonged blast
See *blast*.

propeller guard
Protective framework over projecting propeller of a ship.

property pass
Written permission for an enlisted man to take private property out of ship or station.

proportioner
A firefighting device that produces foam by mixing a chemical and water.

proprietary information
Privately owned information not previously disclosed or made available to the public.

prospective commanding office (PCO)
Officer who is ordered to assume command of a ship. Normally used when the ship is not in commission at the time of his assignment. Can also refer to an officer preparing to relieve someone else of command.

protective deck
An armored deck. In ships fitted with more than one armored deck, the protective deck is the more heavily armored of the two, the other being the splinter deck, fitted above the protective deck.

protest flag
International alphabet flag B flown by a yacht during a race if it considers itself fouled. Race committee must arbitrate the matter before the winner is declared.

protractor
A transparent plastic semicircle marked in degrees of arc with an attached swinging arm or rule for inscribing bearing and course lines, or transferring them from the compass rose on a chart. Easier to use than parallel ruler, more difficult than drafting machine but has the advantage of being easily carried from place to place with the chart. A three-arm protractor has three swinging arms for finding position with sextant angles between navigational aides, tangents of land, etc. if three or more are in sight.

prow
Part of the bow above the water line. Acceptable naval usage, but not favored.

proword
A word or phrase in condensed form representing certain frequently used orders and instructions in voice radio communications.

proximity fuze
See *fuze.*

PSA
Post shakedown availability.

public reprimand
A rare but legal form of punishment upon an officer issued pursuant to the sentence of a general court-martial.

public works
Buildings, grounds, utilities, other structures, and land improvements at a naval shore activity.

puddening (pudding)
Chafing gear used to protect, for example, a towline or a spar. Also used as a bumper along the gunwale of rearming boat.

pull
Proper nautical term for row. A sailor pulls on an oar.

pulling boat
Any boat designed to be propelled by oars. Generally used with reference to a fairly large boat with several oarsmen. The coxswain steers and is in command.

pulse length
The duration, in microseconds, of a radar transmission.

pulse-jet
Type of jet engine that uses a flapper valve alternately to compress and then eject air. Also called aerojet.

punt
Rectangular shallow boat used in painting the ship's side at and above the waterline.

purchase
General term for any mechanical arrangement of blocks and line for multiplying force. Blocks can be single, double, or triple, according to how many sheaves ("shivs") they have. After the line is rove around the sheaves and the standing part is made fast to one of the blocks, the entire assemblage is known as a tackle ("tay-kul"). The tackle is designated according to the number of sheaves in the blocks or the purpose of the tackle. Some of the latter can be quite exotic in derivation, such as gun-tackle, luff-tackle, and the like, but it is useful today to classify the tackle according to its mechanical advantage. Thus a *two-fold purchase*, made of two double blocks and four falls (lines between the blocks), has a four-to-one multiplication. A *three-fold purchase* (two treble blocks, six falls), has a six-to-one advantage. This is the biggest purchase commonly used on board ship. A luff tackle, with one single and one double block, has a three-to-one advantage because of its three falls. A double luff (a triple and a double block, five falls), has a five-to-one advantage. Friction neglected, the power advantage of any tackle can be figured by counting the falls.

pure water
A term used in nuclear operating machinery. Means water so heavily distilled as to be purer than ordinary distilled water, of quality fit to be used in the primary loop of the nuclear plant.

pyrotechnics
Ammunition, flares, or fireworks used for signaling, illuminating, or marking targets.

Q

Q-ship

Disguised man-of-war used for decoying enemy submarines into close gun range. Highly controversial during WWI, because the Q-ship tactic was to force the German submarine to adhere to the "cruiser rules" promulgated by international law and convention (come to close range on the surface, order crew and passengers into boats, etc.), while the supposed merchant ship obeyed no rules at all. British use of Q-ships was one of the factors leading Germany to declare unrestricted submarine warfare in WWI. In WWII, even though international convention signed by all participants prescribed the same cruiser rules, they were immediately disregarded by both sides.

quadrant

A portable device for measuring angles having an arc length of 45 degrees or less (1/8 of a circle). Forerunner of the larger and more accurate sextant. Also called octant, but the more common usage of octant today is for the bubble octant, an instrument used most generally in aircraft.

quadrantal correctors or spheres

Two iron balls at either side, athwartship, of the binnacle to help compensate for ship's magnetic effect on the compass.

quadrantal davit

One in which the lower end of the arm is a steel quadrant fitted with gear teeth and appropriate mechanism for cranking out the arm and lowering the boat.

quadrantal deviation

A deflection of the magnetic compass caused by the induced magnetism of the ship's horizontal iron. Corrected by quadrantal spheres.

quadrature

Relation between two celestial bodies when they are 90 degrees apart. They are then said to be "in quadrature" with each other. When the sun and moon are in quadrature, at first and last quarters of the moon, there is a significant effect on the tides. See *neap tides.*

qualification code number (officers)

A four-digit number that marks an officer as having certain basic qualifications for duty.

quarter

One side or the other of the stern of a ship. To be *broad on the quarter* means to be 45 degrees away from dead astern, and starboard or port quarter would have to be stated to be more specific. *Quarters* refers to assigned places for military purposes, ranging from general quarters to living areas or quarters for muster. Also, an old term referring to surrendering. To *cry for quarter* is to ask to have one's surrender accepted. The term comes from the ancient custom of permitting a captured officer to be ransomed at one-fourth of his annual pay (or estate, if wealthy). To *give quarter* means to accept the other party's surrender. See *quarters.*

quarterdeck
Ceremonial area of the main deck, kept especially neat and clean. The specific domain of the officer of the deck while in port. Always located near the accommodation ladder or brow—or the principal one if more than one is rigged. In days of sail the ship would be conned from the quarterdeck.

quartering sea
A sea on the quarter. That is, waves are approaching from about 45 degrees on one side of the stern.

quarterly marks
Periodic evaluation (quarterly) of enlisted men in proficiency in rate, seamanship, mechanical ability, leadership and conduct.

quartermaster (QM)
An enlisted person who is general assistant to the officer of the deck underway or in port. A person well qualified in deck and bridge routine, intelligent and able to give meaningful support to the OOD. A navigating quartermaster is one designated as assistant to the ship's navigator, a position of some prestige and responsibility. The helmsman during important evolutions, such as battle stations or entering port, is almost always a quartermaster. Originally the quartermaster was the man assigned to look after troops' quarters, and the Army and Marine Corps still use the term in much of its original meaning.

quartermaster's notebook
A pencil log maintained by the quartermaster on watch to provide material for the deck log. It is an official document; entries may be crossed out, but not erased.

quarters
An assembly, as *quarters* for inspection or a gathering on stations as *fire quarters.* Government-owned houses or apartments assigned to naval personnel. Living spaces aboard ship.

quay
A solid stone or masonry structure built along the shore of a harbor to which boats and ships make fast, load, unload, etc. See *dock, pier, wharf.*

Quebec
Phonetic word for the letter *Q.*

quenching
The significant drop in underwater sound transmission or reception due to air bubbles trapped in the sonar dome. Roll and pitch of a ship in rough water is a primary cause.

quick-closing
Special doors and hatches that can be closed quickly to preserve watertight integrity.

quick-flashing light
A navigational light, such as a lighthouse, that flashes continuously at least once a second.

R

rack
A framework aboard ship from which depth charges are dropped. Slang for bunk or bed. *Rack out* means to nap. See *sack*.

racon
Radar beacon that transmits in response to signal from ship's radar. See *ramark*.

radar
Radio Detection And Ranging; an instrument for determining, by radio echoes, the presence of objects and their range, bearing, and elevation.

radar countermeasures
Actions taken to reduce effectiveness of enemy radar.

radar frequency
P-Band, 200 mc; L-Band, 100 mc; S-Band, 300 mc; C-Band, 5000 mc; X-Band, 10,000 mc; K-Band, 30,000 mc; V-Band, 50,000 mc. See *hertz*.

radar picket
Ship or aircraft stationed at a distance to increase radar detection range.

radar picket escort ship
Escort ships modified to give increased CIC, electronic countermeasures, and electronic search facilities. Now called radar picket frigate (FFR). See *Appendix A*.

radar reflector
Device to increase radar target signal, used in life rafts and yachts.

radar trapping
Atmospheric distortion of radar signals due to their refraction in air masses of different characteristics.

radar wind sounding (RAWIN)
A determination of winds aloft by the radar observation of a balloon.

radar wind sounding and radiosonde (RAWINSONDE)
Radiosonde and RAWIN combined, an observation of temperature, pressure, humidity and winds aloft, made by electronic means.

radiated noise
Underwater sound energy emitted by ships, submarines, and torpedoes.

radioactivity detection, indication, and computation (RADIAC)
Term that designates various types of radiological measuring instruments or equipment.

radio-acoustic range finding
Determining distance by a combination of radio and sound, radio being used to indicate the time of transmission and of reception of a sound wave.

radio and television aid to navigation (RATAN)
An aid to navigation in which a central station transmits radar map to ship's receivers, usually UHF television.

radio beacon
An electronic aid to navigation that sends out radio signals for reception by a directional antenna.

radio central
Major radio room aboard ship. Also called *main radio* and *radio one*.

radio countermeasures (RCM)
Actions taken to reduce effectiveness of enemy radio.

radio data and flight information book
Flight planning and flight information required by air crews that is stable in nature and does not need frequent revision.

radio direction finder (RDF)
A radio receiver with a directional antenna to determine bearings of radio signals.

radio electrician
Warrant officer advanced from an electronics rating.

radio facility chart
Information on radio aids to navigation in graphic and tabular form for use by air crews in flight operations.

radio frequency
VLF, below 30 kc; LF, 30-300 kc; MF, 300-3000 kc; HF, 3-30 mc; VHF 30-300 mc; UHF, 300-3000 mc; SHF, 3000-30,000 mc; EHF, 30,000-300,000 mc. See *hertz*.

radio guard
Ship or station assuming radio communications responsibility for another ship or station.

radiological defense
The means taken to minimize and control damage from radioactivity.

radio sextant
An electronic sextant that receives radio waves emitted by the sun and other celestial bodies as compared to light waves in standard celestial navigation.

radiosonde
Balloon that automatically transmits meteorological information to a weather station.

radioteletype (RATT)
A rapid communication system in which a radio circuit actuates a teletype machine that produces a message in printed form.

radmail
Administrative messages handled by radio and by regular, air, or guard mail.

radojet
Device for removing the air from a condenser by means of steam jets.

radome
Dome on an aircraft or airship containing radar gear.

raft kit
First-aid gear secured to a life raft.

rail
An open fence aboard ship, made of pipe or other rigid material as opposed to lifelines, usually along the edge of the weather deck. Also used below in large spaces such as enginerooms. Also a plank, timber, or piece of metal forming the top of a bulwark. A hand rail, ladder rail, or safety rail associated with ships' ladders. Rail screens of canvas are sometimes rigged along a ship's rail.

rail loading
Loading of boats while hanging from falls at rail of a ship instead of when waterborne.

rainmaker
Coil used to condense steam from the pier. Slang for a meteorologist.

raise
To come within sight of, as a lookout *raises* land when the ship makes a landfall. To establish contact on a radio circuit.

rake
A fall of shot observation in range. *To rake* is to make such observations. Also, angle that stack, masts, etc., make with the vertical.

rakish
Having a pronounced rake to the masts, probably more for appearance than utility. Smart, speedy appearance, but also dashing, jaunty.

ram
Aircraft-carried antitank rocket. Also, an underwater ice projection from an iceberg or a hummocked ice flow. In the old Navy, an armored projection of the bow below the waterline, intended for use in combat.

ramark
A radar lighthouse that transmits independently of a ship's radar. See *racon*.

ram-jet
Type of jet engine which uses inlet air velocity as compressor.

rammer
Part of gun mechanism that seats the projectile.

ramp
Hinged forward section of a landing ship or craft over which its cargo is unloaded when craft is beached.

ram, rudder
Part of the mechanism for turning a large rudder. Older ships used a steam engine with a system of gears, but newer ones employ steel connecting rods, attached to the rudder yoke, which are pushed or pulled by hydraulic pistons in response to commands by the steering wheel. The combination of hydraulic piston and connecting rod is called a rudder ram. See *yoke.*

ram tensioner
A large hydraulic cylinder containing a piston or ram that maintains tension on the highline wire during replenishment underway.

range
An area for shooting, as a rifle range or a sea area for ship's gunnery. When safe for firing, a range is said to be clear; when not safe for firing it is foul, or fouled. Distance to the target is also called *the range.* Two or more objects on shore, marked on a chart to indicate a safe course or a measured distance, are known as a *range.* Also, to lay out anchor chain in even rows. See *range, navigational.*

range alongside
To come close aboard, abeam, of another vessel, without making fast.

range finder
An instrument to measure range or distance to the target. Optical range finders are either steroscopic or coincidence type. Radar provides most accurate range finding.

rangekeeper
Instrument which automatically receives and computes information necessary to fire the guns. A computer does a similar job for bombing.

range light
A second, sometimes optional, white light which, with the masthead light, forms a range which reveals the course of the vessel.

range, navigational
A pair of lights or day beacons used to mark a line of definite bearing. When on the line, a navigator reports the range closed; when off the line, the range is open.

range tables
Elements of the trajectories of specific guns and projectiles, compiled in convenient form.

rank
Relative position of officer or petty officer within a particular grade. See *grade* for usage.

RATAN
See *radio and television aid to navigation.*

rate
Level of proficiency within a rating. Radioman, third class, is a *rate*. Also means a privilege or to deserve, e.g., *he rates liberty*. A chronometer's *rate* is the number of seconds it gains or loses daily. See *rating*, also *Appendix B.*

ratey
Slang meaning presumptuous; impertinent.

rat guard
A conical metal shield secured around mooring lines to prevent rats from coming aboard.

rating
General grouping of enlisted personnel according to military skills, i.e. boatswain's mate, photographer's mate, etc. See *Appendix B.*

rating assignment officer
An officer assigned to the Bureau of Naval Personnel with the responsibility of detailing enlisted persons to sea and shore assignments. Formerly called a detailing officer.

rating badge
Insignia of rating and rate worn by petty officers.

ration
An allowance for provisions in money or kind, for one man for one day.

rations
Food. May be abandon ship, flight, aircraft, emergency, landing party, travel, or leave rations.

ratline
Three-strand, tarred hemp used for snaking on destroyers, formerly seized to shrouds to form ladders.

RATT
Radioteletype.

rat tail
Tapered braid that finishes off a stopper.

RAWIN
Radar wind sounding.

raydist
An accurate electronic system of navigation using range information from two portable stations. Used principally in surveying.

Raymond releasing hook
Quick-release hook used on boat falls.

razee

Can be either verb or noun. To cut down the spar deck and associated sides of a sailing man-of-war, thus reducing her freeboard while at the same time reducing her draft because of the reduced weight. As a result, such a ship, henceforth called a *razee,* carried her lower deck of guns higher out of water and they were by consequence more effective, particularly in blowing weather. One of the reasons for the great success of the big frigates of the early U.S. Navy was that they carried their gundecks so high. To compete with them, the British navy *razeed* a number of their 74's, two-deckers, which were then rated at 44 or 50 guns. Since she still could carry the masts and canvas of the two-decker she had been, such a *razee* was usually fast as well as powerful and heavily built. Only one ship-of-the-line was razeed in the U.S. Navy, USS *Independence,* built in 1814 as a 74, razeed to a huge frigate in 1836, and finally broken up in 1914 after an extraordinarily useful career. Several 44-gun frigates were razeed to sloops-of-war, among them USS *Cumberland* which fought CSS *Virginia* in the first day's fighting of the Battle of Hampton Roads in 1862 and went down with guns firing and colors flying.

reach rod

A long handle by which valves can be operated from a distance.

reactivate (activate)

To restore a preserved ship to service. Slang: unzipper or de-mothball.

reactor

An apparatus in which nuclear fission may be sustained in a self-supporting chain reaction. It comprises the fissionable material, a moderator, a reflector to prevent the escape of neutrons, measuring and control elements, and a means for taking off the power produced in the form of heat. The first nuclear reactor on board ship was installed in USS *Nautilus,* and had an effective full power life of about 1,000 hours. Since then the technology has so improved that reactors now being built are expected to last the entire useful life of the ship in which they are installed. The heat transfer medium in the naval reactor is water at high pressure; therefore the entire reactor must be contained in an extraordinarily strong pressure vessel. The water is prevented from flashing into steam in the primary loop by the high pressure. Steam is produced in the secondary loop, at lesser pressure and is not radioactive. The pressurized water in the primary loop is refined (distilled) to an extreme degree of purity and hence retains its induced radioactivity for only a short time.

readiness, conditions of

Comprehensive term which includes: material—what closures have been made; engineering—maximum speed immediately available; armament—what weapons are manned. A ship's battle and damage control bills will indicate the strictures and nomenclature for each of the conditions. In addition, *Condition I* is general quarters, the maximum readiness attainable; *Condition II,* half the crew on stations and ready; *Condition III,* normal cruising. See *condition watch.*

readiness for sea period
Number of days, at end of vessel's overhaul, for loading ammunition, fueling, calibrating, testing, cleaning, painting, and stowing gear.

ready
Report made by a gun station when enough men are there to fire the guns. See *manned and ready*.

ready about
An order to the crew to be at their stations for putting a sailing ship about. See *come about*.

ready room
Compartment on carriers where pilots gather for briefing and to stand by.

ready service ammunition
Ammunition at gun and ready for use.

rear admiral
Rank senior to commodore in the Navy; the junior rank among admirals.

rear commodore
Navy or merchant marine officer designated as convoy commander if the convoy commodore and vice commodore are lost.

rearming boat
Boat with padded gunwales; formerly used to service seaplanes.

receipt
Communication indicating that a message has been received.

receiving station (RECSTA) or ship (RECSHIP)
An activity to receive, process, house, mess, clothe, pay, and transfer transient enlisted personnel.

reclama
A request to superior authority to reconsider its decision or its proposed action.

recognition
Process for determining friendly or enemy character of a ship, plane, or other object or person.

recoil system
System, usually hydraulic, which absorbs the force of the gun as it is driven back in recoil by the explosion.

recreation committee
Enlisted men, appointed or elected, who make recommendations concerning welfare and recreation activities.

recreation council
Board of officers and enlisted men who administer the welfare and recreation activities of ship, squadron, or station.

recruit
Newly enlisted man, still in basic training.

Red Cross flag
The distinctive mark of a hospital ship. Also flown by boats and shore activities engaged in medical services.

red lead
Slang for catsup. Red anticorrosive priming paint.

red, right, returning
An expression used to remind navigators that red buoys are on the right-hand side of the channel when returning to port from seaward.

red tide
A marine phenomenon occurring in subtropical waters during which the sea turns reddish and fish are killed. Caused by an overabundance of plantlike flagellate protozoans called dinoflagellates. Their pigment makes the water appear red, and they produce the toxin that kills marine life. Red tide occurs worldwide in warm seas and can be irritating to human respiratory systems. Coastal resorts sometimes must close when breaking waves release the toxic substance into the air.

reducer
A coupling or fitting that connects two pipes or hoses of different sizes.

reduction gear
Gear used to reduce the economical high speed of a ship's turbine to the necessarily slower shaft and propeller speed. See *bull gear*.

reef
Rock, coral, sand, or any bottom material extending so near the surface of the water that boats or ships can not pass over safely. To reef a sail is to reduce its effective area, either by tying its reef points and rolling or folding it up at the head, if a square sail, or at the foot if a fore-and-aft sail. In modern yachts it may be rolled around the boom or even taken into a split metal mast with a roller built into the mast's hollow interior. The part of the sail that can be reduced is a reef, as in "take in a reef," or "shake out a reef." In days of sail it also meant to lower or take in a portion of a spar such as topgallant masts, topmasts, and the outer end of a bowsprit.

reefer
Short, blue woolen coat worn by midshipmen and enlisted men. Fresh-provision cargo ship or a refrigerated compartment. See *peacoat*.

reef knot
Same as a square knot, except that one of the ends is pulled back through the knot as in a bowknot. To shake out *reefs*, the topmen need only pull the end so treated, which immediately releases the knot.

reeve
To pass a line or wire through a lead; nautical past tense is *rove.*

reference points (harbor)
Lettered geographical points on which sortie and entrance plans of a harbor are based.

reference position
The OTC's announced estimate of his navigational position. Usually signaled daily to the formation.

reference station
Tide or current station for which constants have been determined which is used for comparison of simultaneous observations at other stations.

refit book
A complete submarine material maintenance check-off list, compiled at the end of a war patrol in preparation for the next one.

regimental combat team
Task organization of troops for amphibious operations.

registered matter
Classified matter to which a number is assigned and which is accounted for at prescribed intervals. Documents numbered for administrative convenience only are "numbered documents."

registry, certificate of
Merchant ship's certificate showing ownership and nationality. Short term is "registry."

regular
Member of the regular Navy instead of reserve components.

regulation clothing
Articles of uniform prescribed by uniform regulations and sold as *small stores.*

relative bearing
The direction of an object relative to the ship's head, expressed in degrees or by points. *Relative bearing grease* is a non-existent item for which new men are sometimes sent (all over the ship, of course).

relative plot
Diagram representing the positions of ships or aircraft, relative to each other and not by true (compass) direction.

relay
To forward a transmission through an intermediate station; the message so forwarded.

release
To authorize the transmission of a message.

relieve
To relieve a man on watch or on duty is to take his place. To change, as *relieve the watch, relieve the wheel and lookout.*

relieving tackle
Tackle to reduce strain on a piece of equipment as on a steering engine during heavy weather.

remote underwater manipulator
A seabed recovery vechicle.

Renae
A weather satellite.

repair officer
The head of the repair department of a tender or repair ship.

repair party
Group of specialists organized to control damage and make repairs throughout the ship during battle.

repeater
Flag used to repeat another in a hoist, now called *substitute.*

repeater, gyro
Remote compass driven by a master gyro.

replenishment group
Fleet oilers, supply, and ammunition ships and assigned screen.

replenishment at sea
The process or procedure of supplying fuel, food, stores, ammunition, and personnel to fleet combatant units while underway. If helicopters are used it is called *vertical replenishment.*

reporting point
Geographical location relative to which the position of an aircraft is to be reported.

report, to place on
To record a man's name for appearance before his commanding officer on a charge of infraction of rules or regulations under *Uniform Code of Military Justice (UCMJ).*

reports, lookout
When sighting land, lookout says "Land ho." A vessel or light elicits "Sail ho" or "Light ho." Proper reply is "Where away?" On every bell during the night, the lookouts port and starboard. Report: "Port sidelight, main truck light, bright lights , sir" and "Starboard sidelight, masthead light, bright lights, sir." Acknowledgment is "Very well."

reprogramming
Process of revising previously established programs or previous budget estimates.

request mast
Process by which men can submit requests to the commanding officer or executive officer.

rescue and assistance party
Group of specially qualified men sent off the ship with special equipment to assist in rescue, firefighting, and salvage operations. Formerly called fire-and-rescue party.

rescue basket
Device for lifting an injured or exhausted man out of the water.

rescue breathing gear
Face-fitting device that provides oxygen for use in smoke or gas.

rescue chamber
A two-compartment diving bell, transported to the scene of a submarine disaster by a submarine rescue vessel. The bell can make a watertight seal with a submarine's escape hatch and escape trunk and can then be hoisted to the surface with rescued personnel. See *deep-submergence rescue vehicle.*

rescue combat air patrol (RESCAP)
Air patrols that cover rescue submarines and rescue aircraft. Subdivisions are SUBCAP (rescue submarine combat air patrol) for lifeguard submarines and BIRDCAP (rescue aircraft combat air patrol) for aircraft on rescue duty.

reserve buoyancy
The non-submerged watertight volume of a ship. This is of crucial importance to ships engaged in battle, since a damaged ship taking on water will sink deeper in order to maintain equilibrium between weight and displacement. Once she sinks entirely beneath the surface there is no further volume to displace water, and she will continue directly to the bottom of the sea. A submerged submarine must be (and remain) in neutral buoyancy; her total weight must always exactly equal her submerged displacement, which of course cannot vary; therefore, a complex trimming system is necessary. When a submarine is surfaced, the volume of her now empty ballast tanks equals the total of the above water volume and is, of course, her reserve buoyancy.

reserve fleet
Group of naval vessels in an inactive status, organized into the Naval Ship Maintenance Facility. Slang: mothball fleet.

Reserve Officer Candidate (ROC) program
Program for commissioning, as reserve ensigns, those college students who take certain summer courses at Navy schools.

Reserve Officers Training Corps (ROTC) program
Program in which student officers at various colleges and universities take naval training and may be commissioned and ordered to active duty on graduation. Has greater benefits than ROC program, and longer obligated service.

reserve on board
Classified publications not effective until made so by proper authority.

responsibility
The obligation to carry out an assigned task successfully. The obligation for the proper care and custody of property or funds is *accountability*. The two terms should not be used interchangeably.

restrict
To keep on board: a man may be restricted because of misconduct or illness.

restricted area
Ocean area or seaspace in which there are special restrictive measures to prevent interference between friendly forces, e.g., joint zones, blind bombing zones, submarine havens, danger areas, etc.

restricted data
All data concerning the design, manufacture, or utilization of atomic weapons or the production or use of special nuclear material. Differs from classified matter in that restricted data specifically refers to nuclear information as defined in the Atomic Energy Act.

restriction
Restraint similar to arrest but not involving relief from military duties.

retirement
Planned tactical withdrawal, as of a task force for replenishment.

retract
To back off a beach, as a landing craft retracts.

retraining command
Activity that confines and at the same time tries to rehabilitate men sentenced by courts-martial to long terms of imprisonment.

retreat
Bugle call or word passed that means fall out (disband) from a formation e.g., *retreat from inspection*. Also sounded at *evening colors*.

reveille
Arousing the ship's company in port for work and breakfast. At sea, *idlers* are called, and the expression *reveille* is not properly used.

reverberation
Sound scattering toward its source. Major types are surface and bottom, from surface and bottom respectively and volume, from air bubbles or suspended solids in the water. See *volume reverberation*.

reverberation index
Valuation of the ability of echo-ranging equipment to distinguish target echo from reverberation.

reverse slope
Terrain that because of intervening high ground can only be reached by high-angle fire. Normally refers to the back side of a hill or mountain.

reversing thermometer
Thermometer designed to separate its mercury column on sudden temperature inversion. This gives a reading of temperature at that point.

reviewing authority
A commander in the chain of command who reviews the sentence of a court-martial.

rhino barge (ferry)
A self-propelled lighter made up of pontoons bolted together.

rhumb line
A line on the earth's surface making the same angle with all meridians. It is a straight line on a Mercator projection chart, and is the standard way of laying down a ship's course.

ride
A vessel *rides* to her anchor and may *ride* out the storm there. A turn of the line may *ride over* another on a winch or capstan and jam it.

ride the vents
An expression used in older submarines whose ballast tanks were equipped with flood valves or Kingston valves. The condition of being ready to dive, with flood valves open for entry of water as soon as main vents are opened permitting trapped air to escape. Modern submarines have ballast tanks open to sea at the bottom and are always *riding the vents*.

ridge rope
The backbone line or wire of an awning.

riding lights
Lights required for a ship at anchor, in contrast to running lights. Also called "anchor lights."

rig
To devise, set up, arrange. An arrangement or contrivance. General description of a ship's upper works; to set up spars or to fit out. A distinctive arrangement of sails (rigging), as in a schooner rig. An arrangement of equipment and machinery, as an oil rig.

rig for red
An order to permit only red lights, providing quick dark adaptation for those who may have to assume topside watch stations at night.

rigging
The ropes, lines, wires, turnbuckles, and other gear supporting and attached to stacks, masts and topside structures. Standing rigging is more or less permanently fixed. Running rigging is adjustable, e.g., cargo handling gear.

right-handed
Twisted from left to right or clockwise; yarn and rope are usually right-handed.

righting moment
The force which tends to right, or move back to an upright position, a vessel which is heeled over. See *stability*.

right-laid
Lay of line or wire rope in which the strands spiral in a clockwise direction (as one looks along the line). Same as right handed.

rig in
To unship and stow, as a boat boom or accommodation ladder is *rigged in*.

rig ship for visitors
Word passed to all hands to have ship prepared for expected visitors. This involves closing off restricted areas, stationing sentries, providing guides, etc.

ring
With reference to an anchor, the heavy ring at the top of the *shank* to which the hawser or chain is attached.

rip
Turbulent water produced by conflicting currents, or water flowing over a shoal or an irregular bottom. Sometimes called a rip tide. Short for rip current.

rip current (tide)
Off a beach on which moderate to heavy surf is breaking a rip current is a strong, relatively narrow, seaward-flowing current caused by the escape of water pushed ashore by the breaking surf. If caught in a rip current one has only to swim parallel to the shoreline and he will soon be out of it. This should not be confused with *undertow*, which is the short and relatively harmless downward thrust of a wave when it breaks. See *undertow*.

rise and shine
To get up, go to work, get going. See *show a leg*.

riser
A vertical pipe leading off a larger one, e.g., *firemain riser*. Also, lines from parachute harness to the shrouds.

roadstead
Off-shore anchorage with good holding ground and usually some protection from the sea.

roaring forties
Area between 40 degrees and 50 degrees south latitude in which the stormy westerlies are encountered. This area develops very high seas because of an absence of land masses and consequent unlimited fetch.

rocket designation system
See *Appendix D.*

rocket ship
Landing ship used in close support of the landing assault waves during an amphibious landing. Capable of heavy and rapid rocket firing. Abbreviated LSMR for "landing ship, medium, rocket."

rocketsondes
Rocket sent aloft to register and transmit weather data.

Rocks and Shoals
Extracts from the Uniform Code of Military Justice periodically read aloud to all hands.

roddle
That part of a wire rope clip against which the U-bolt is secured.

rodmeter
The pit sword or part of a pitometer log that projects from the ship's hull.

roger
Used in voice radio, meaning *I have received your transmission.* Not to be confused with wilco (*I understand and will comply*).

roger dodger
Slang for "affirmative," "yes," "OK," "will do."

roll
Side-to-side motion of a ship about its longitudinal axis. See *yaw, pitch, heaving, sway, surge.*

roller
A long usually nonbreaking wave generated by distant winds and a source of big surf, which is a hazard to boats and a delight to surfers.

roller chock
A chock fitted with a roller to permit easy passage of line or wire.

roller path
A precision-machined circular roller surface on which the roller bearings of a turret, mount, or director describe a circular path as it rotates. The inclination of a roller path is of paramount importance to director fire. See *inclination diagram.*

rolling chock
Antirolling bilge keel.

roll-on/roll-off (RO/RO)
Method in which the cargo is loaded into vehicles that drive on board ship and remain, to drive off at destination.

Romeo
Phonetic word for the letter *R.*

room to swing a cat
A very old Navy expression referring to the amount of space required to swing a cat-o'-nine tails. If there is not room to swing a cat, it means in naval terms that the ceiling or overhead is very low, and there is little space around.

root valve
One located where a branch line comes off the main line.

rope
Term used in the Navy for special items such as *manrope* and *bellrope, wheel rope*, and *wire rope. Line* is used in general sense for all cordage and fiber rope, and for such special ones as mooring line, heaving line, shot line, etc. Fiber rope is made of natural fibers (manila, hemp, sisal, cotton) as well as synthetic fibers (nylon, polyester, etc.). Strips of metal foil used in radar countermeasures also are called *rope.*

rope yarn Sunday
Any afternoon, except a weekend, that is free of work and drills. Usually Wednesday afternoon is rope yarn Sunday if no work is scheduled at sea or if liberty is granted in port. British equivalent is *make and mend*, or *mend clothes.*

RO/RO
See *roll-on/roll-off.*

rose box
The strainer at the foot of the suction pipe of a bilge pump.

rotary current
A tidal current flowing continually but changing direction through all compass points during a tidal cycle. Changes clockwise in the northern hemisphere and counter clockwise in the southern hemisphere.

rotating band
Strip of metal around a projectile for sealing the bore, positioning the rear of the projectile, and imparting rotation. See *bourrelet.*

rough log, or rough deck log
Original handwritten and (most) legal version of the ship's log. Incorrect entries may be lined out, but not erased. Copied on a typewriter for official submission, but in case of any legal question the rough log controls. See *log, deck* and *quartermaster's notebook.*

round
With down, in, or up means to haul on a specified line or tackle. *Round in* means to bring the blocks of a tackle closer together. Opposite of overhaul. *Round to* means to turn a ship into the wind.

round line
Three-stranded, right-handed small stuff, used for fine seizing.

round turn
To take a turn around a bitt or bollard to check a strain or weight. To *bring up with a round turn* is nautical phraseology for a calldown or reprimand. Literally, it means a complete twist in the anchor chains at the hawse when two anchors are down in moor.

rouse in
To haul in, especially by hand, with maximum speed and force.

rouse out
Arouse; break out; bestir; e.g., *rouse out the duty boat's crew; rouse out the starboard chain. Rouse and shine,* meaning to awaken, to get up and turn to, has been corrupted to *rise and shine.* See *show a leg.*

route
To forward a message by prescribed path and method.

routing
Process of determining the path or method of forwarding a message or of directing a ship, formation, or convoy.

rove
Nautical past tense of reeve. Likewise, hove is the nautical past tense of heave.

royal (sail)
See *sail nomenclature.*

rudder
A flat surface rigged vertically astern used to steer a ship, boat, or aircaft.

rudder post
The after post of the stern frame to which the rudder is hung. Also called sternpost.

ruffles and flourishes
The roll of the drum (ruffles) and short burst of music (flourishes) that make up one of the honors rendered to high-ranking military and civil officials.

Rules of the Road
Regulations designed to prevent collisions of ships at sea and in inland waters. Proper full term is *International Regulations for Preventing Collisions at Sea.* See *Inland Rules* and *International Rules.*

runner
Line fastened at one end to a fixed object, such as an eyebolt, and rove through a single block. It has an eye on its other end to which a tackle is clapped on. The term is also loosely applied to any line rove through a block.

running bowline
Bowline made over the standing port of its own rope so that it forms a free-sliding noose.

running fix

Geographical position determined by two lines of position obtained by observations at different times. First line is advanced by dead reckoning.

running lights

Required lights carried by a vessel or aircraft underway between sunset and sunrise. See *riding lights*.

running mate

A line officer whose eligibility for promotion results in a certain staff officer's eligibility for promotion is known as the staff officer's *running mate*.

running rigging

See *rigging*.

S

sabot
A bushing, used in firing sub-caliber projectiles or missiles. It falls away as the assembly leaves the muzzle or missile launcher.

sack
Slang for *bunk* or bed. To *sack out* is to take a nap. Slightly earthier derivation than the synonym, rack.

saddle
Any device used to support something such as a spar or boom (also called a boom crutch), or a boat stowed on deck, or a heavy piece of machinery below decks. A special-shaped saddle is used to support a fuel hose from a *span wire* when fueling ships underway. See *boat chock, boat skids*, and *span wire*.

sagging
Distortion of a ship's hull in which the keel droops downward in the middle. Opposite of hogging in which keel is bent downward at the ends.

safety factor
A multiple representing extra strength over maximum intended stress. If *boat falls* having a breaking load of 9 tons are used to hoist a 3-ton boat, they have a safety factor of three.

sail
A large piece of fabric, usually canvas, by which the wind can be used to drive a vessel. The part of a modern submarine extending above the main deck or hull, housing the periscope supports, various retractable masts, and the surface conning station or bridge. Modern yachts use a variety of light, synthetic materials for their sails, nearly all of which are fore-and-aft with leading edge, the luff, fast to a mast. The bottom edge of the sail is its foot, and the after edge is the leech. If the sail is a quadrilateral the upper part attached to the gaff, is the head. If triangular (Marconi rig) the upper corner is called the head. Square sails (actually rectangular) are seldom seen today. Each of their vertical edges is a leech, the top is the head, and the bottom the foot.

sail area
The vertical hull surface of a ship on which the wind exerts force.

sailer
A boat or ship propelled exclusively by sails (archaic).

sail ho
See *reports, lookout*.

sailing
Today a navigational term meaning to voyage on the sea. Involves selecting courses and finding position. One may sail by mercator, rhumb line, mid-latitude, great circle or traverse courses.

Sailing Directions
Books issued by the Navy Department to supplement charts of the world. They contain descriptions of coast lines, harbors, dangers, aids to navigation, applicable *inland* or special *Rules of the Road*, or *Pilot Rules*, and other data that cannot conveniently be shown on a chart.

sail locker
Stowage for awnings, cots, and related gear aboard ship.

sailor
An officer or man who has spent time at sea and is accustomed to the ways of the sea and ships.

sail nomenclature
In a full-rigged ship the sails on each mast are, from bottom to top: On the foremast: foresail, fore topsail, fore topgallant, fore royal, fore skysail. On the mainmast: mainsail; main topsail; main topgallant; main royal; main skysail. On the mizzenmast: spanker (a fore-and-aft sail with gaff and boom); mizzen topsail; mizzen topgallant; mizzen royal; mizzen skysail. Topsail is pronounced "topsul," topgallant is "tuh-gallant," and skysail is "skysul" in the sailor's vocabulary. Royals became common late in the 18th century (most of our revolutionary warships carried none) and skysails in the mid-19th century with the tall-masted clippers. At the same time, topsails had become so large that small merchant crews could not handle them well; therefore, they were split into upper and lower topsails. Jibs, of course, were rigged between the foremast and the bowsprit. The spritsail was rigged under the bowsprit on a small yard, but was abandoned as a man-killer.

sally ship
Evolution aboard ship during which the crew runs from side to side together, causing the ship to roll slowly. Used to extricate a ship in ice or aground or to determine ship's period of roll, a measure of her stability.

saltwater service system
Series of pipes that provide saltwater for flushing and firefighting aboard ship.

salty
Nautical; seagoing; sometimes means raffish, cocky, unconventional, earthy.

salute, gun
A number of blank shots fired to greet some personage or to celebrate an occasion.

salute, hand
A gesture of mutual respect exchanged between persons in military service (except prisoners). Usually accompanied by a greeting, as "Good morning, Sir."

saluting battery
Guns used to fire a salute.

saluting ship or **station**
One so designated by the Secretary of the Navy as being capable of rendering such an honor: in general, only major warships and large naval activities.

salvage
Cast off, discarded material. To save or rescue material that has been discarded, wrecked, sunk, or damaged. The act of salvaging a ship, usually carried out by highly professional crews of salvage vessels. These are powerful, seaworthy tugs prepared to tow anything, anywhere, under any conditions. They carry powerful pumps, can pump out flooded compartments and fight fires. Salvage is their business and quick reaction their stock in trade.

salvage group
In an amphibious operation, a naval task organization designated and equipped to rescue personnel and to salvage equipment and material.

salvage money
Money divided by the crew of a ship that has salvaged another and brought it into port to be sold. No longer paid to naval personnel.

salvo
One or more shots fired simultaneously by the same battery at the same target.

salvo latch
Device to prevent unintentional opening of the breech of a loaded gun, until after the gun has been fired.

Samson post
Vertical timber on the forward deck of a boat used in towing and securing. Sometimes used as synonym for king post.

sand table
Device for constructing a scale model of an amphibious assault landing beach. Used for training purposes.

sandblower
Slang for a short man. Low-level flight, or an aircraft designed for same. Reference is to blowing sand away from one's face, or (aircraft) blowing it astern.

Santa Ana
A violent, dry offshore wind, common in coastal southern California.

save-all
Net spread under cargo handling operations between ship and pier. Any receptacle rigged to catch dripping oil, water, etc.

savoir
Slang for a brainy or clever person. Derived from French verb, "to know."

scale
Undesirable deposit, mostly calcium sulfate, which forms in the tubes of boilers.

scaling hammer
Hand or power tool for removing paint and rust from metal plating.

scanning
Sonar echo-ranging system employing a constantly transmitted outgoing signal over the range of search.

scarfing
Adhesively or mechanically locking together two members of the same material (generally a wooden beam or spar) with a long diagonal joint so as to form a single long piece with no sacrifice in strength. The joint is the *scarf*.

scarp
Bank cut into the shore by surf.

schooner
A fore-and-aft rigged sailing vessel, originally and still typically having two masts, the foremast somewhat shorter than the main, although multimasted schooners were tried for a short time late in the days of sail. See *fore-and-aft sail*.

scope
Number of fathoms of chain out to anchor or mooring buoy. If to anchor, scope is increased in strong winds for more holding power.

scouting
A mission involving search, patrol, tracking, or reconnaissance by surface ship, submarine, or aircraft.

scour
The movement of bottom sediments from their resting place by currents or wave motion.

scow
Large, open, flat-bottom utility boat for transporting sand, gravel, mud, etc. Small scows are also called *punts* or *prams*, and may be sailed. Large ones are also called *barges* or *lighters*, depending on local usage.

scram
A nuclear-power term indicating that some difficulty in reactor operation has arisen, causing automatic or deliberate activation of reactor protective features shutting it down. To *scram* is to lose all reactor power suddenly, necessitating elimination of the difficulty and then carrying on a programmed restart.

scramble
Emergency launching of lighter aircraft. In cryptography, to mix at random.

scramble nets
Cargo or disembarkation nets rigged over the side for picking up survivors.

scraper
Hand tool used to scrape paint and woodwork.

screamer
A magnetic device attached to the hull of a target submarine, to transmit sound for location of the sub by ASW forces.

screen
Ships stationed to protect a unit, as an antisubmarine screen. To examine and evaluate, as *screening* of applicants.

screw
A water screw: the propeller of a ship. *Screws* may also refer to the water in the vicinity of the propellers. Thus something happening near the propellers might be described as *in the screws*. A man could fall overboard *into the screws* and (by good luck) not be injured. If he fell *into the propeller* or *into the starboard screw* (thus a specific), he assuredly would be.

screw current
A movement of water caused by turning of the propeller.

screwing
Dangerous rotary motion of ice floes caused by wind and ice pressure.

scud
Loose, vapory fragments of low clouds moving rapidly.

scudding
Driving before a gale. Scudding under bare poles means with all sails down or furled, all upper yards lowered, and the rest secured.

scull
To propel a boat by working an oar from side to side over the stern; to propel oneself in the water by working hands and forearms in a figure-eight motion.

scullery
Compartment in a ship where general mess dishwashing is done.

scupper
Fittings along the waterways on the weather decks and below to lead water over the side. They resemble small troughs perpendicular to the waterways and downward tending. Scupper pipes through the side of the ship do the same below decks.

scupper lip
Extension to prevent scupper discharge from running down the ship's sides.

scuttle
Small, quick-closing access hole. To sink a ship deliberately.

scuttlebutt
Shipboard drinking fountain. Slang for rumor or gossip.

sea
A wave generated locally by wind action. Depending on the wind and fetch, seas are generally unsymmetrical in slope, have steep crests, and show white caps.

sea anchor
Device, usually of wood and/or canvas, streamed by a vessel or boat in heavy weather to hold the bow up to the sea. Also called a drogue.

sea bag
Canvas bag in which an enlisted person transports his gear.

seabed
Bottom of the sea, beyond the continental shelf.

SeaBee (CB)
Naval construction battalion. ACB stands for amphibious construction battalion and MCB for mobile construction battalion. Also a system of ocean cargo carrying using loaded barges that are raised aboard and lowered by elevators. Similar to *LASH.*

sea breeze
Breeze blowing off the sea toward the land, caused by land heating more quickly as sun rises. See *land breeze.*

sea buoy
The buoy farthest to sea of those marking a channel or entrance. Often called a farewell buoy or departure buoy.

sea chest
Sailor's trunk, usually made of wood. Also, intake between ship's side and sea valve or seacock.

seacock
Valve in the ship's hull connected to the sea.

sea daddy
Slang for an older man who takes a recruit or younger officer in hand and teaches him his trade or profession.

sea dog
An old sailor.

seadopod
Surface barge-mounted capsule maintained at sea bottom pressure to house divers engaged in bottom work. Men are delivered to a work site by a submersible delivery capsule.

seadrome
Area designated and marked for the safe operation of seaplanes on the water.

sea duty
Assignment afloat in ships, aircraft, or overseas bases or on foreign stations.

Seafarer
Submarine extremely low frequency (SELF) radio communication system to reach deeply submerged submarines. Also an ASW blimp.

sea frontiers
Essentially defensive commands closely corresponding to Army defense commands. They also function as operational commands for forces assigned by the CNO.

seagoing
Capable of going to sea. Salty or nautical in nature. See *seaworthy*.

seagull
Slang for chicken served in the general mess; also a girl of poor reputation.

Sealab
An undersea laboratory development program.

sea ladder
Metal rungs welded to the ship's side above the waterline. See *Jacob's ladder*.

sea lawyer
An argumentative person; one who too frequently questions orders and regulations.

sea legs
Adaptation to the motion of a vessel in a seaway. To get or find one's sea legs is to have recovered from seasickness.

seaman (SN)
Enlisted person in paygrade E-3 who performs general deck and boat duties. Anyone familiar with ships and the sea. See *Appendix B*.

seaman apprentice (SA)
Rate to which a person is advanced shortly after completion of recruit training. See *Appendix B*.

seaman guard
Enlisted person who performs guard duty in the absence of Marines.

seaman recruit (SR)
Lowest enlisted rating. See *Appendix B.*

seaman's eye
The ability to judge distances and maneuvers at sea. To have a good seaman's eye is the ambition of all professional sailors. Officers pride themselves on their possession of this quality.

seamount
An isolated mountain structure rising from the bottom of the sea to a point near the surface. One having a flat top is a tablemount.

sea painter
Line used for towing a boat alongside a ship underway. Led from well forward in the ship to the near bow of the boat, where it is secured with a loop and a toggle, for quick release. Not to be confused with bow painter, which is secured to the stem of the boat and cannot be used for towing alongside.

sea power
The ability of a country to use and control the sea and to prevent an enemy from using it.

search-and-attack unit (SAU)
Two or more ships or aircraft teamed for coordinated search and attack on submarines.

searchlight sonar
Echo-ranging system using the same narrow beam pattern for transmission and reception.

sea return
Interference on a radar screen caused by reflections from the sea.

sea room
Far enough from land for unrestricted maneuvers. Also, enough room between ships for maneuvering.

sea slick
Surface area markedly different in appearance from surrounding water, usually caused by plankton.

sea state
Numerical or written description of sea roughness.

sea stores
Cigarettes and other luxuries sold at sea and abroad free of federal tax.

seaway
A moderate to rough sea.

seaworthy
Capable of putting to sea and meeting any usual sea condition. A seagoing ship may for some reason not be seaworthy, such as when damaged.

Secchi disc
A white, black, or varicolored disc, usually about a foot in diameter, that measures water transparency.

secondary conn
Conning station for use if the main conn (the bridge) is damaged.

second dog watch
The watch from 1800 (6 PM) to 2000 (8 PM). Also called the last dog watch.

secret
Information or material whose disclosure would endanger national security or cause serious injury to the interests or prestige of the U.S. See *classified matter.*

section
Applied to ships or naval aircraft, a tactical subdivision of a division. Normally, half of a division in the case of ships, and two aircraft in the case of aircraft. Subdivision of a division of men.

sector center
The true or relative bearing of an ASW search sector.

sector, geographic (relative)
One limited by bearings from a fixed or moving point.

sector width
The width in degrees of a search sector.

secure
To make fast in a permanent sense as to *"Secure the forward hatch for sea."* Well-fastened or safe. To cease or stop, e.g., *"Secure from fire drill."* To quit, give up, or knock off.

seiche
Periodic wave oscillation (rise and fall of the water's level) whose period varies from a few minutes to nearly a tidal period, found in enclosed bodies of water or superimposed on tide-induced waves in open ocean. Caused by harmonic vibration in response to storm or tidal wave disturbances at sea. Pronounced "sayshe."

seize
To bind with a small rope.

seizing stuff
See *marline, small stuff.*

selection board
Panel of officers who review records and recommend for promotion. Used for all grades above that of lieutenant, junior grade. Also called promotion board.

SELF
See *Seafarer*.

self-sustaining
Said of a nuclear reactor when it is producing enough power to run all associated auxiliaries and hence the load on the ship's auxiliary power equipment, such as diesel engines or battery, has been removed. This phrase is generally used during start-up procedure. See *critical*.

semaphore
Rapid method of short-range visual communications between ships, using hand flags.

semi-diurnal
Having a period of cycle of approximately half of a lunar day, roughly 12.42 hours.

senior officer present afloat (SOPA)
The senior line officer of the Navy on active service, eligible for command at sea, who is present and in command of any unit of the operating forces afloat in the locality or within an area prescribed by competent authority.

sennet, sennit
Braided cordage made from rope yarns or spun yarn, plaited by hand. There are many varieties, such as rounded sennet, square sennet, flat sennet, French sennet, etc. Used for mats, stoppers, manropes, etc., and may have ornamental functions. See *coxcombing, fancy work, MacNamara lace, square knotting*.

sequence number
Number assigned a ship by the unit commander to indicate its position in the line.

serial number
One of a consecutive group of numerals assigned a specific piece of correspondence for identification purposes. Not to be confused with the service number assigned each enlisted person, although sometimes the term "serial" is used when service, signal, lineal, or file number is meant.

serve
To wrap with continuous, contiguous round turns. Wire rope is *wormed, parceled*, and *served*.

service ammunition
That used for combat, as distinct from target ammunition.

service craft
Naval craft too small to be commissioned. See *Appendix A*.

service force (SERVFOR)
A naval task organization that performs logistic support of fleet units.

service line
Logistic support vessels formed on a line to conduct replenishment.

service medal
Medal for service in specific campaign or theater of operations.

service message
Brief message incidental to the correction, verification, or handling of another message, or the exchange of information between stations.

service number
Record identification number for Navy and Marine Corps enlisted and for Marine Corps officers. Has been replaced by social security numbers. See *file number* and *serial number*.

service rating
See *Appendix B*.

service record
Document recording an enlisted person's conduct, performance of duties, tests, etc.

service schools
Schools offering advanced technical training for enlisted personnel.

service stripe
Sleeve marks worn by enlisted men and women to denote length of service. Each stripe denotes four years. Slang: hash mark.

serving
Additional protection over parceling consisting of continuous round turns of small stuff. See *serve*.

setback
The force of inertia that tends to move certain fuze parts to the rear as a projectile is fired. Used to arm a fuze.

SES
See *surface effect ship*.

set (of a current)
The direction toward which the water is flowing. A ship is *set* by the current. A southerly current and a north wind are going in the same direction.

set taut, set up
To remove the slack; to tighten. An order to take in all the slack on running gear before heaving in.

set the watch
To establish the regular routine of watches on a ship or station.

set the course
To give the helmsman the desired course to be steered.

settle
To sink deeper into the water.

sextant
Navigational device used to measure the angular distance between two objects, usually between the earth's horizon and a celestial body. Another instrument with a similar purpose is an octant. See *radio sextant*.

shackle
U-shaped metal fitting, closed at the open end with a pin, used to connect wire and chain. Also to encode a message on voice radio.

shadow zone
Region in which refraction limits effectiveness of echo-ranging sound signals.

shaft alley
The space in a ship through which the propeller shafts extend from the engine room to the propeller.

shakedown
Period of adjustment, clean-up, and training for a ship after commissioning or a major overhaul. After commissioning, a ship also makes a shakedown cruise, usually including a visit to several foreign ports.

shank
The central shaft of an anchor to which the flukes are attached.

shape
Small structure or object, of various descriptions and colors, displayed aloft by a vessel fishing, dredging, at anchor, etc.

shark chaser
Small bag of shark-repelling matter usually attached to life jackets.

sheave
The pulley or grooved wheel in a block over which a line or wire passes. Pronounced "shiv."

sheer
Excess of freeboard of a ship forward or aft over that amidships. Longitudinal curvature of the main deck between bow and stern with low point amidships. Also a sudden change of course, sometimes, accidental, as that due to shallow water or *bank effect*, or a steering casualty.

sheer off
To steer away from; to bear off.

sheer plan
Drawing of the ship showing the vertical sections of the hull form at various sections from amidships to the outer hull as viewed from amidships, superimposed on one drawing. See *lines drawing*.

sheet
A line that regulates the angle at which a sail is set in relation to the wind. See *three sheets to the wind,* and *sheet home.*

sheet anchor
The main or heaviest anchor, formerly carried in the *waist* of a sailing ship. Sometimes the term was used interchangably with bower, but bower came into more general use with large steel ships that no longer carry an extra anchor in the location of what would have been their waist. Long after the stockless anchor came into general use, the sheet anchor, or bower, continued to be of the old-fashioned type because of its greater holding power for the same weight.

sheet home
To extend a square sail by hauling on the sheets until the sail is set as flat as possible. A term used most frequently when the sail is first set, or when reefs are shaken out.

shelf
The area of sea bottom from the point of permanent immersion to the point where steep descent to great depths occurs. The seaward line is usually regarded as 100 fathoms or 200 meters. See *continental shelf.*

shell
Projectile fired from a gun. Originally the word distinguished an explosive projectile from a solid round shot, since the shell was hollow and full of gun powder. The Battle of Sinope in 1853 was the first instance when shells were used in combat, and a numerically superior Russian fleet totally annihilated a Turkish fleet equipped with only solid shot. Today, shell refers to projectiles from large guns, all of which are loaded with explosive charges. Also: the casing of a block within which the sheave revolves; a light, very narrow pulling boat with oar outriggers and sliding seats, used for competitive rowing (crew).

shellback
One who has crossed the equator and was accepted by Davy Jones.

shell room
Projectile stowage in a ship's magazine, or in base of barbette. See *projectile flat.*

sheriff
Slang for master-at-arms.

sheriff's badge
Slang for command insignia worn by line officers.

shift colors
To shift the ensign and jack between the steaming and in-port positions, and vice versa.

shifts
Work periods in shipyards. First shift (daylight) is morning and afternoon; second shift (swing) is late afternoon and evening; third shift (graveyard) is from midnight to breakfast.

shift the rudder
Command to the steersman to apply the same amount of rudder in the opposite direction.

ship
Any large, sea-going vessel. Specifically, in days of sail, a vessel with bowsprit and three masts, entirely square-rigged, except for the jib(s) and the lowest sail on the after-most mast, or mizzenmast, which was fore-and-aft rigged and called the spanker. Also called a full-rigged ship. In days of sail each type of rig had its own name, such as brig, schooner, sloop, snow, brigantine, hermaphrodite brig, bark or barque, barkentine, topsail schooner. Sloop-of-war was a full-rigged ship mounting guns on only a single deck. Also, to set up, to secure in place, e.g., ship the rudder. To re-enlist, as to *ship over*. To take something aboard, as to ship a sea, or to send freight. See *sloop, vessel*.

ship aboard
To enlist. See *ship over*.

ship alteration (SHIPALT)
Authorization to make an alteration on specific machinery or on specific parts of particular ships.

shipboard
Pertaining to a ship.

ship characteristics
All qualities and features that permit a ship to accomplish her mission. Includes complement, their battle stations, and all material for fighting the ship.

ship designations
See *Appendix A*.

shiphandling
The art and skill of directing the movements of a ship in formation, tactics, and maneuvers, in restricted waters or in docking and mooring.

Ship Improvement Guide (SIG)
A catalog of all items, maintained by the ship's characteristics division, submitted for inclusion in the class improvement plan.

shipmate
Person with whom one is serving or has served, particularly at sea.

ship-of-the-line
The battleship of the days of sail. Mounted guns on three or more decks. Slow and cumbersome, but very heavily built and designed to "lie in the line of battle." Thus, a "line-of-battle-ship," and the term gradually became simply "battleship."

ship over
To re-enlist. See *ship aboard*.

shipping board clamps
U-shaped fittings, threaded and provided with an end piece that is secured with two nuts. Used to join wire or to make a temporary eye.

shipping-over chow
Any particularly good meal, supposedly served to encourage re-enlistment.

ship rider
Member of a fleet training group who goes to sea in a ship to assist in its shakedown or refresher training.

ship's bell
Struck every 30 minutes. At seven bells the next watch is called. At eight bells the new watch should be entirely in place. Also used to sound fog signals and as a fire alarm. See *watch.*

ship's clerk
Warrant officer advanced from journalist, personnel man, or yeoman.

ship's company
All hands; everyone on board who is attached to the ship. Does not include passengers.

shipshape
Neat, orderly, as a ship should be.

shipshape and bristol fashion
Neat, clean, all rigging coiled and flemished down, everything in perfect condition as it should be. Term implies a condition superior to merely shipshape.

ship's orders
Written directives upon specific subjects signed by the commanding officer and having the authority of lawful regulations.

ship's organization book
Administrative and organizational guide for a particular ship, based on a standard issued by the type commander. Full title is the *ship's organization and regulation manual.*

ship's secretary
Officer who assists the executive officer with ship's correspondence.

ship's service store
The ship's retail store. Carries supplies for health, comfort, and personal cleanliness of the crew.

Ship Systems Command
Functional command replacing Bureau of Ships in 1966 Navy Department reorganization. Component of Naval Material Command.

ship-to-shore movement
Debarkation of troops from assault shipping to landing area.

shipworm
A marine mollusk resembling a worm which burrows into a wooden ship's bottom planking and, over a short time, can be very destructive. Columbus was forced to abandon the *Santa Maria* because of the depredations of the toredo, one of the most common such "worms." Poisonous bottom paint and coppering were the best defenses in days of wooden ships.

shipyard
Shipbuilding and repair facility. Naval Shipyard is one maintained by the Navy.

shoal
An area of shallow water.

shoaling effect
The change in a wave as it proceeds from deep to shallow water; its length decreases and its height increases.

shoe
Fitting on the stem of a ship from which paravanes are towed. Same as *clump*. See *point of tow*. More generally, a protecting member under keel or bottom of ship.

shole
Flat plate to distribute the force under the end of a shore.

shoot the sun
Measure the sun's altitude with a sextant.

shoran
An accurate short-range navigation system often used for aerial surveying and mapping. Uses pulse transmissions, transponders, and a receiver.

shore
Portable wooden beam used in damage control, or to help hold up a ship in drydock. To *shore up* is to brace up. The land at the edge of the sea. A sailor "goes ashore" on liberty.

shore boat
Civilian-operated harbor passenger boat, also known as a water taxi.

shore duty
Assignment ashore in the U.S. or its possessions.

shore establishment
All activities of the naval establishment not included in the operating forces or in the Navy Department.

shore fire-control party
Specially trained unit for the control of naval gunfire in support of troops ashore.

shore leave
Obsolete term. See *leave*.

shore patrol (SP)
Personnel ashore on police duty.

shoring
Process of placing props against structure or cargo to prevent breaking, sagging, or movement in a seaway, or to hold ship upright in drydock.

short arm inspection
Slang for medical inspection for venereal disease.

short blast
Whistle, horn, or siren blast of about one second's duration. See *blast*.

short-handed
Without enough people to do a job properly.

short stay
Said of an anchor when it has been hove in just short of breaking ground. See *up and down, underfoot*.

short timer
Person nearing the end of his enlistment, service, or tour of duty.

shot
A length of anchor chain, usually 15 fathoms.

shot line
Light nylon line used in line-throwing gun.

shoulder mark
Device indicating rank worn on an officer's overcoat and the jacket or coat of summer uniforms. Also called shoulder board.

shove off
Slang for depart; leave; go. Proper naval usage as in *"shove off, coxswain, on the bell, make the liberty landing and return."*

show a leg
An expression used in rousing out sleeping men. The call *show a leg* is derived from the days when seamen's "wives" were allowed to sleep on board ship. Women who put out a stockinged leg for identification were not required to turn out at first call, although their men were. Nowadays it simply means "wake up, show signs of being awake." The term bears no relation to "shake a leg," a nonnautical phrase meaning to bear a hand, or hurry. See *son of a gun*.

shrouds
Lines or wires that give athwartships support to a mast. Also lines attaching parachute canopy to the jumper's harness, and the close-fitting casing around propeller and turbine blades. See *stay*.

shuttle
Device on an airplane catapult that transmits motion to the airplane.

sick bay
Infirmary or first-aid station aboard ship.

sick call
A call (and word) passed daily aboard ship for those who require medical attention to report to sick bay. A scheduled time each day at all medical facilities when patients may be seen without appointment.

side arms
Pistols or revolvers.

side boys
Non-rated men stationed in two ranks at the gangway on the arrival or departure of officers or officials for whom side honors are being rendered. Number varies from two to eight, depending on rank of visitor.

side cleaners
Men detailed to scrub the sides of the ship.

side honors
Ceremonious greeting for important officers and officials as they come aboard ship. May include piping the side, side boys, the ship's band and guard, and gun salutes.

side lights
The red and green, 10-point, port and starboard running lights required of all ships by the *Rules of the Road.* Also, sidelight, British term for *air port* or *porthole.*

sidereal
See *time, sidereal.*

Sierra
Phonetic word for the letter S.

sight
An accurately timed observed altitude of a heavenly body by use of a sextant.

sight the anchor
To heave an anchor up far enough to see that it is clear, then again let go. Necessary when holding ground is very soft; anchor may sink beyond easy recovery.

signal
Short message using one or more letters, characters, flags, visual displays, or special sounds. Any transmitted electrical impulse.

signal book
The standard publication governing flag communications between naval vessels. Formerly called the *General Signal Book,* now *Allied Naval Signal Book.*

signal bridge
Area of navigating bridge adjacent to flag bags, used by signalmen. Not a part of flag bridge, but taken over by the flag when the ship is employed as a flagship,

signal flags
All flags used in visual communications.

signal number
Old term for officer's precedence number. Replaced by lineal number and number in grade (Marine Corps). Has since been replaced by the social security number.

signal record book (log)
A record of all general signals transmitted or received.

silence!
Command given by any member of a weapons crew who observes a serious casualty that requires immediate attention.

silent running
Condition of quiet operation of machinery in a submarine to deny detection by an enemy listening for noise.

silica gel
Mositure-absorbent chemical used in tanks, voids, magazines, etc.

sill
Submerged elevation separating two ocean basins.

sill depth
Greatest depth at which there is free horizontal communication between two ocean basins. See *sill, of a dock*.

sill, of a dock
The timber or beam at the entrance gate of a drydock over which a vessel must pass. The drydock's "sill depth" is of course a limiting factor.

sing out
To announce or call out.

single-service procurement
Procurement of designated supplies or services by one military department to satisfy its own requirements and those of other departments on agreement by the departments concerned or on assignment by DOD.

single up
A command given before unmooring a ship from a wharf or pier. Means to take in the double sections of line between the ship and the pier, leaving her moored by only single strands of line to the bitts, bollards, or cleats.

single whip
A tackle using a single fixed block. No mechanical advantage, but direction of pull may be changed. See *purchase*

sinuating
Series of curving variations from the base course steered by a ship. See *evasive steering*.

siren
High-pitched, noise-making device used aboard ship when an emergency (collision, grounding, etc.) is imminent.

sister hooks
Pair of hooks that fit together to make a closed ring.

sister ships
Ships built to the same design. Sometimes used loosely to refer to ships in the same employment or organization.

situation report (SITREP)
A special report, generally of informal nature, required to keep higher authority advised. Prescribed under certain predictable circumstances, but may also be required at any time.

skeg
Continuation of the keel aft under the propeller and supporting the rudder post.

skids, boat
Fittings on deck designed to hold and support a boat, composed of saddles making up a cradle and gripes to hold the boat down. See *saddle*.

skipper
Slang for commanding officer, or any captain of a ship or boat. In the United Kingdom "skipper" is the title of a duly certified fishing vessel captain.

skip zone
Area between ground waves and sky waves in which no radio waves are received.

skivvy
Slang for underwear.

Skyhook
System for rescuing of personnel from the sea or isolated areas by aircraft. Also, a large unmanned balloon sent aloft to record meteorogical data. Slang for a mythical gadget sometimes wished for by sailors to handle awkward or heavy items.

skylark
A distinctly nautical expression meaning to play or to have fun, i.e., *to have a lark*. Derived from the practice of young sailors laying aloft and sliding down the back stays. Thus, to engage in horseplay, noisy banter, or friendly scuffling.

sky pilot (slang)
Chaplain on board ship, sometimes also called padre.

skysail
See *sail nomenclature.*

sky waves
Radio waves reflected by the ionosphere.

slack
Ease out, as a line. The loose part of a line that takes no strain.

slack water
Period of no tidal motion between flood and ebb.

sled
Towed surface gunnery target, smaller and faster than a raft.

sleeve
Fabric tube towed by an airplane, used as an antiaircraft target.

slew
To rotate rapidly, as a gun director *slews* to get on a new target.

slice
An average logistic planning factor used to obtain estimates of requirements for personnel and material. A personnel *slice* generally consists of the total strength of the stated basic combatant element, plus its proportionate share of all supporting and higher headquarters personnel.

slick
A smooth area on the surface of the sea, caused by oil, variable winds, the sliding stern of a ship turning, etc.

slide
The sleeve part of the mount which directly supports the gun.

slings
Gear for hoisting something aboard, e.g., *boat slings.*

slip
To part from an anchor by unshackling the chain. The lost motion in a propeller. A narrow stretch of water between two piers.

sloop
Sailing vessel with a single mast, rigged fore-and-aft. See *cutter, ship.*

sloop-of-war
A fully rigged ship mounting her main battery on only a single deck, usually the spar deck, as distinguished from a frigate, which mounted guns on two decks. Smaller than a frigate, and faster in light airs or moderate breeze.

slop chute
A chute hung over the side for the discharge of garbage. Slang for anyone who is dirty and disorderly in appearance or habits.

slops
Clothing and small stores sold to seamen on merchant ships. In early days, the *slops chest* was a locker belonging to the officer who sold articles of clothing to crew members, charging it against their wages. Since such an officer—usually the ship's purser—sometimes considered his slops chest as a device to augment his income, his stock had a tendency to be of poor quality and very expensive, and the whole institution was much resented even when honestly run. Today such stores are a required benefit regulated by law and union agreements.

sludge
Sediment in fuel oil tanks.

slush down
To treat standing rigging with a preservative.

small arms
Rifles, shotguns, pistols, and carbines.

small-craft warning
Red pennant indicating weather conditions unfavorable or dangerous for small-craft operations.

small stores
See *clothing and small stores.*

small stuff
Small cordage aboard ship such as 12-thread stuff, marline, seizing stuff, or spun yarn.

smart
Neat; shipshape; efficient; military; quick.

smoker
Shipboard entertainment, including food, boxing, humorous skits, and movies. Same as happy hour when used at sea.

smoke-pipe
Stack on a ship.

smokestack
Slang meaning to pretend to be drunk.

smoking lamp
A lamp aboard old ships, used by men to light their pipes; now used in phrase *"The smoking lamp is lit"* to indicate when men are allowed to smoke. Today it is entirely a figurative term.

smooth-bore gunner
Officer who specializes in gunnery duties, although not a postgraduate student of ordnance and gunnery.

snake out
To break out specific items of cargo.

snaking
Netting rigged between the housing line and the footline or waterway bar to prevent objects on deck from going overboard.

snatch block
Single-sheaved block with a hinged strap. It can be quickly opened to take the bight of a line, thus not requiring the end of the line to be led through the block. A great convenience for handling line on deck.

Sniffer
Airborne equipment for detecting exhaust gases from a snorkeling submarine.

snipe
Slang for a person of the engineering department. See *black gang.*

snivel
Slang meaning to avoid a training flight.

snooper
An aircraft that is shadowing or observing.

snorkel
Device used by a submarine to enable it to draw air from the surface while submerged. Also to operate submerged with snorkel showing.

snow
A three-masted square-rigger with a lateen sail instead of a spanker mizzenmast. Pronounced to rhyme with "cow." Differs from a ship by having a smaller than usual mizzen stepped closer than usual to the mainmast, with a large lateen sail on it and perhaps a smaller than usual topsail above. In appearance it resembled a large brig with an additional small mast aft. When a "full-size" mizzen was used the vessel was no longer a snow, even though she retained the lateen sail. Most Revolutionary War frigates of our Continental Navy were of this latter type. Only a few carried a spanker instead of the lateen sail.

snow blink
A bright white glare on the underside of clouds, produced by the reflection of light from a snow-covered surface.

Snowflake
General term applied to requests from DOD for additional justification, information, or comment on budget items during preparation of the budget. Specifically, in the latter stages of this preparation, when deadlines are short and the demands are many.

snub
To reduce firmly, but not absolutely, the payout of a running line, allowing only enough movement so that it will not part. Similar to check, but implies a much stronger resistance to allowing the line to run. See *check, hold.*

snug down
To make preparations to weather a storm at sea.

SOFAR
Sounding, Fixing And Ranging.

solar still
An item of survival equipment that distills fresh water by use of the energy from sunlight.

soldier
Slang meaning to loaf on the job. One who loafs. Note, however, that to address an Army man or a Marine as "soldier," or to use the word in reference to him, is a term of approval.

solo
To fly or operate an aircraft with sole and complete responsibility for it.

soluble washer
Device used to delay the arming of a mine after planting.

sonar
Sound navigation and ranging. Underwater sound equipment for submarine detection and navigation.

sonic depth finder
Device measuring time for a sound signal to reach bottom and return, giving reading in terms of depth. See *fathometer*.

sonobuoy
A small sound receiver-transmitter normally dropped from aircraft to detect submarine noises and transmit them to the plane.

son of a gun
Technically, a child born on board ship alongside one of her broadside cannons. The spaces between guns on the broadside were regular berthing spaces, and the term recalls the old days when sailors were sometimes permitted to have their wives live on board. The result of the custom, of course, was an occasional birth—and, circumstances being as they must have been, the term implied questionable paternity. An old saying was that a true *"man-o'-war's man was begotten in the galley and born under a gun."* Because of the romantic nautical toughness ascribed by the title, to be a *son of a gun* quickly lost its opprobrious connotation.

soogey moogey
Solution of strong soap, lye, etc., for cleaning paintwork. Rarely used now.

soot blower
Soot removal device using a stream jet to clean the firesides of a boiler while in use.

SOP
Standard operating procedure; senior officer present.

SOPA
See *senior officer present afloat.*

sortie
To depart; the act of departing. A naval force *sorties* from a port.

sound
To measure depth of water at sea or the depth of a liquid in a ship's tanks. Result is a *sounding.* A whale *sounds* when it dives. Also to blow, as a bugle. A long wide body of water connected to the sea, larger than a *strait* or *channel.* The air bladder of a fish, with which it controls its buoyancy.

sound absorption
The change of sound into some other form of energy, usually heat, as it passes through a medium or strikes a surface.

sound channel
A nautical phenomenon at mid-depth which forms a wave guide permitting the transmission of sound over great distances through the sea.

soundhead
The container for a transmitting projector and listening hydrophones.

sounding fixing and ranging (SOFAR)
An underwater distress signal whose location is determined by measuring its different times of reception at several stations where, by triangulations and time differential calculation, a position can be established.

sounding lead
Same as leadline.

sounding machine
An obsolete system of a heavy weight, a long wire and a reel for measuring depth of water in deep water. Called "deep sea" ("dipsy") lead. Replaced by echo sounder or fathometer.

sounding patrol
Duty men who periodically sound the ship's tanks and report the results to the OOD.

soundings
Reference to a ship's being able to reach bottom with a deep-sea (dipsy) lead. She is said to be *off soundings* or *on soundings.* Nowadays, reference is to being within the 100 fathom curve.

sound-powered telephones
Telephones that generate their own power by the sound vibrations of the voice moving in the field of a magnet.

spademan
Man who operates the rammer on a five-inch gun.

span
Line made fast at both ends with a tackle, line, or fitting made fast to its bight. Wire rope stretched between davit heads to which lifelines are secured.

span wire
Steel cable between ships during underway replenishment that supports the fuel hose, or by which cargo is transferred. See *replenishment at sea.*

spanker
See *sail nomenclature.*

spanner
Wrench with fixed jaws designed for coupling hoses.

spar
Long, round stick of wood or steel, frequently tapered at one or both ends, generally associated with masts or rigging.

spar buoy
Type of buoy which looks like a large spar floating upright, or nearly so.

spar deck
The topmost or weather deck of a wooden sailing ship, from which the sails, rigging, and spars were handled, and where spare spars were stowed, as well as boats, anchors, and other topside gear requiring quick access. Originally, ships had raised forecastles and aftercastles, and between them was the waist. As the heights of the two "castles" decreased, the after one became known as the poop, and its upper deck as the poopdeck or quarterdeck. It became customary to bridge the waist with gangways on either side of the ship, building up the ship's sides accordingly, and the gangways gradually became heavier and larger until the appearance was that of a single deck from bow to stern with a large hatch amidships. The forecastle retained its distinctive name, but when the poopdeck was no longer elevated above the regular level it became simply the quarterdeck. Interestingly, John Barry, while supervising the construction and fitting out of USS *United States*, insisted on adding a raised poop, which can be seen in early drawings of the ship. She differed from her sisters, the *Constitution* and the *President*, in this particular (although the *President*, being the last completed, had some much admired design refinements). See *double-banked frigate.*

spares, equipment
Spare parts to be retained with equipment to which they pertain.

spares, tender
Spare parts placed on tenders or at advanced bases.

speak
To communicate with a vessel that is in sight.

special devices
Term covering synthetic training aids, teaching aids, research in human engineering, tactical evaluation, and training methods.

special duty officer
An officer who specializes, for example in public information, but usually does not command.

special money
Pay drawn other than on pay day.

special sea detail(s)
Persons assigned duties in connection with getting underway, mooring, and anchoring. They relieve or are relieved by the regular sea detail.

special services
Activities involving the welfare and recreation of personnel.

special services officer
One who is responsible for recreational activities.

specialty mark
The design or insignia, part of a petty officer's rating badge, that indicates his rating.

special weapons
Those involving nuclear or atomic energy.

specified command
A command that has a broad continuing mission and is established and so designated by the President through the Secretary of Defense with the advice and assistance of the Joint Chiefs of Staff. Normally composed of forces from one Service. See *joint command.*

speed
Speeds ordered are commonly one-third, two-thirds, standard, full, and flank. One-third and two-thirds are fractions of *standard speed; full speed* is a designated speed slightly—usually about one-eighth—more than standard; *flank speed* is as fast as the ship can go. For going astern, the common speeds are one-third, two-thirds, full, and emergency. In the merchant service, *half-speed* is used instead of one-third and two-thirds, and a similar system is followed by the British navy. See *standard speed.*

speed cones
Yellow conical shapes, hoisted at the port and starboard yardarms to indicate engine speed to ships astern. No longer used in U.S. Navy.

speed key
Special telegraph key for sending code at high rate. Also called a bug.

speed letter
Priority form of abbreviated correspondence sent by mail.

speed light
Red or white, steady or flashing light on the mainmast that indicates the speed the ship is making to other ships in company. No longer used in the U.S. Navy.

speed, normal
Speed at which ships are to proceed if a signaled speed has not been ordered. A reference speed used by U.S. Navy which corresponds to standard speed.

speed, operational
The highest speed at which ships will be required to proceed during a particular period or operation.

speed, signaled
The speed at which the guide of a group of ships has been ordered to proceed.

speed, standard
Speed prescribed as standard for that type of ship, commonly 15 knots.

speed, stationing
Speed slower than highest operational speed, used for economy reasons when maneuvering or changing station.

spider
Portable magnifying glass on a compass.

spike a gun
To choke up the vent of a muzzle-loading cannon, usually by hammering a large spike into it, so that the gun is unserviceable until the spike can be drilled out. See *vent*.

spin stabilize
To stabilize a missile in flight by having it rotate around its long axis.

spinnaker
A large, lightweight triangular sail, like a large jib, set out on a boom by a yacht when sailing before the wind.

spit
Small point of land or a long, narrow shoal, usually sand, extending outward from shore.

spit kit
Spittoon; ashtray. Also derisive term for small, unseaworthy vessel.

splash boards
Boards rigged on stern of small craft to keep water out of cockpit.

splash line
In night underwater demolition unit operations, the point off the enemy beach at which swimmers enter the water from rubber boats.

Splashnik
Buoy for wave measurement by telemetry. Information on its vertical motion is sent to ship or shore.

splice
To join two lines or two parts of a line by unlaying them and intertwining their strands.

splice the main brace
To have a drink. See *main brace*. Usually used in the sense of all hands having an authorized drink.

splinter deck
One fitted with armor. See *deck, protective deck*.

splinter screen (shield)
Light metal armor around bridge and gun stations in a ship. Designed for moderate protection only against bomb and shell fragments.

split plant operation
Subdivision of engineering plant of a ship into two or more independent units for purposes of damage control. Usually each main engine or turbine is driven by the steam from one fireroom.

spoiler board
Boards lashed across the leading edges of aircraft wings to destroy lift when aircraft are secured in windy weather.

sponson
Projecting structure, platform, or short wing on hull of ship or aircraft.

sponsor
The woman who christens a ship at its launching.

spot
To observe the fall of shot. A gunnery correction to range, deflection, or fuze range. To station aircraft on a carrier's decks. The location of aircraft on deck, e.g., a *flight deck spot*. To move cargo or cargo handling gear.

spotting board
Miniature flight and hangar decks with aircraft models used to plan aircraft carrier spotting of aircraft. Also, a synthetic fall of shot trainer used to instruct gunnery spotters.

spread
Multiple salvo of torpedoes fired to insure a hit.

spring
A mooring line that makes an acute angle with the ship and the pier to which moored, as opposed to a breast line, which is perpendicular, or nearly so, to the pier face. To spring a mast or yard is to crack it so that it is unsafe to carry the usual sail thereon; the spar is then said to be *sprung*. A hawser laid out to an anchor or to some fixed object so that a ship may be turned or slewed at her berth. To turn a ship with such lines or

hawsers. In 1814 Thomas MacDonough anchored his squadron in Lake Champlain with springs out to extra anchors. He was thus enabled to wind ship, when his engaged battery was disabled, continued the battle with the previously unengaged gun battery, and won a victory of incalculable importance. In this context, wind is pronounced "wined" See *after bow (quarter) spring.*

spring range
The average semi-diurnal range of tides at *syzygy.*

spring rise
The mean height of high water above chart datum at *syzygy.*

spring stay
See *triatic stay.*

spring tidal currents
Tidal currents of increased velocity during *syzygy.*

spring tides
The increased range of tides occuring when the moon and the sun are in phase. Caused by *syzygy.* Opposite condition from neap tides.

sprinkling system
Emergency water system for putting out fires and keeping boundaries cool in all types of magazines containing explosives or pyrotechnics.

spud
A post or pile used to secure a dredge or scow.

spud locker
Slang for topside shipboard potato storage.

spur shore
Short wooden spar used to hold a vessel clear of a pier.

squadron
Administrative or tactical organization consisting of two or more divisions of ships. Also, administrative unit of aircraft, for tactical purposes divided into divisions and sections.

squall
Short but intense windstorm.

square
To straighten, as *square your hat.*

square away
To straighten, make shipshape, or to get settled in a new job or home. Also, to inform or admonish someone in an abrupt or curt manner.

square knotting
Hobby of making belts, watch bands, etc., out of knotted cord. See *sennet, coxcombing.*

square-rigger
A sailing ship the majority of whose sails are square sails. Distinguish from such ships as schooner, sloop, lateen-rigged.

square sail
A sail cut into an approximate square or rectangular shape and mounted on yards which extend equally on both sides of a mast. The standard sail of a square-rigger. Distinguish from a fore-and-aft sail.

squatting
The change of trim and overall lowering of a ship's stern in the water at high speed.

squawk-box
Inner-office or inter-station voice communication unit; intercom.

squealer rings
The rings in the glands of a turbine that have the smallest clearance. Their rubbing is an audible alarm signal for stopping the turbine.

squib
Miniature, electrically fired explosive, used in rockets as an igniter or on a sand table to represent bomb and shell bursts.

Squid
Forward-launched ASW weapon developed by the British navy.

squilgee
Wooden, rubber-shod deck dryer. Pronounced "squeegee." Also *squillagee*.

stability
Ability of a ship to right itself after being heeled over. See *metacenter, metacentric height*.

stability board
Visual representation, used by damage-control personnel, of liquid loading, location of flooding, effect on list and trim, etc.

stabilize
Maintain on horizontal plane by means of a gyro mechanism.

stable element
Gyro mechanism that stabilizes an instrument, such as a gun sight, against the roll and pitch of a ship.

stack
A large pipe extending above the main deck to exhaust smoke and gas from the furnaces or fireboxes under the boilers. Also the assembled electronic components of sonar gear are referred to as the "sonar stack."

stack cover
Canvas cover for stack when not in use. Also called a watch cap.

stack wash
Air turbulence astern of a ship due to stack gases.

stadimeter
Instrument for measuring distance to objects of known height by mechanical solution of a right triangle. Commonly used to measure distance to other ships in formation.

staff
Personnel without command function who assist a commander in administration and operation.

staff officers
Those who perform staff functions, such as doctors, chaplains, dentists, civil engineers, supply officers, and medical service officers, as distinct from line officers.

stage
Platform hung over the side from which men can work, paint, etc.

staging
Processing, in a specific area, of troops in transit from one area to another.

staging area
Place where an amphibious expedition has final training.

stanchion
Vertical metal post aboard ship.

stand
Brief period of no change in water level at high or low tide.

standard commands
Official phrases used in such activities as gunfiring, shiphandling, etc.

standard compass
The magnetic compass used by the navigator as a standard; psc means "per standard compass." A direction, or course, by the standard compass (psc) differs from the true direction by the amount of the compass error. See *gyro compass, per standard compass.*

standard rudder
That amount (number of degrees) required to cause a ship to turn with standard tactical diameter. Full rudder is usually maximum rudder less a few degrees to avoid possibility of jamming the rudder.

standard speed
Usually, 15 knots. See *speed.*

standard stock
Material listed in the *Catalog of Navy Material*—general stores section.

standard terminology
Words, terms, and phrases used in official directives. Those in naval warfare publications (NWP) are considered the standard for all other publications.

standard written agreement (SWAG)
Contract signed by reserve officers going on voluntary active duty.

stand by
To wait. To subsitute for someone who has the day's duty. A subsitute. A preparatory expression, e.g., *stand by: commence firing.*

stand from under
Literally, to get out and away from danger. Also to avoid wrath of a superior.

standing lights
Dim red lights throughout interior of ship.

standing order
A semi-permanent order or directive.

standing part
That part of a tackle that is made fast. The part on which power is applied is the hauling part. See *purchase.*

standing rigging
Heavy ropes, usually made of wire or rod nowadays, that support spars or masts and are permanently secured.

stand out
To depart from port or harbor and take a course to seaward.

starboard
Directional term for right, as opposed to port, which means left.

star finder
Mechanical or graphic device for identifying celestial bodies.

star gauge
Device for measuring accurately the bore diameter of a gun.

star shell
Projectile that detonates in the air and releases an illuminating parachute flare.

star tracker
A light-sensing device properly gimballed and electronically controlled to detect and maintain the line of sight to a star. When mounted on a stable platform, it becomes an automatic sextant.

stateroom
An officer's living space aboard ship.

station
To assign. A post of duty, as a battle station. A position in formation of ships. A naval activity. In ship's plans a "section" perpendicular to the keel is sometimes called a *station*.

station bill
Listing of crew's drill stations.

station keeping
The art of keeping a ship in its proper position in a formation of ships.

stay
Wire supporting a mast fore-and-aft.

steady
An order to the helmsman, following that to put the rudder amidships, meaning to steady the ship on whatever heading she comes to. Useful in evasive maneuvers by a submarine during depth charging to minimize rudder action, Also sometimes used when conning by seaman's eye.

steady as you go or **steady as she goes**
An order to the helmsman to steer the course upon which the ship's head lay at the moment the order was given, even though she might be swinging through that particular heading. The helmsman should respond with (for example) "Mark! Two five seven !" to indicate the reading of his lubber's line at the instant designated by the order, and his understanding that this is the ordered course to which he will return the ship's head.

steam drum
See *drum, steam.*

steam fog
Fog formed when water vapor is added to air that is much colder than the vapor's source; most commonly, when very cold air drifts across relatively warm water.

steam generator
Takes the place of the boiler in a nuclear-powered ship. An ordinary boiler has fire outside of the boiler tubes and feed water, to be converted into steam, inside. The steam generator has pressurized water in the primary loop on what corresponds to the fire side. Heat is transferred from the primary loop to the boiler feed water to generate steam.

steam lance
Device for using low-pressure steam on deck to remove ice.

steep to
Said of a coast or shore that rises abruptly from the water.

steerageway
The lowest speed at which a ship can be steered.

steering engine
The machine that turns the rudder. Usually a steam engine. Newer ships now use hydraulically operated rams instead of a steering engine. See *ram, rudder.*

steersman
The man who steers the ship, same as a helmsman.

Steinke hood
Bonnet placed over an individual's head enclosing an air pocket and permitting him to escape from a submarine sunk at moderate depth. Fitted with a transparent plastic visor for vision.

stem
The principal timber at the bow of a wooden ship, to which the bow planks are rabbeted. Its lower end is scarfed to the keel, and the bowsprit rests on the upper end. The cutwater, or false stem (analogous to *false keel*), is attached to the fore part of the stem and may be carved or otherwise embellished, especially in the vicinity of the figurehead, which usually rests upon it. In steel ships, the stem is the foremost vertical or near-vertical strength member, around which or to which the plating of the bow is welded or riveted. Compare *stern-post.*

sterilizer
Device for making a mine harmless after a certain period. Required by International Law.

stern
The aftermost section of a ship.

stern anchor
Any anchor carried aft. May be used for a stream anchor or, as in certain amphibious ships of WWII whose special configuration made them ride better stern-to than bow-to, it may be the ship's principal anchor. Ships designed to beach themselves to land troops and equipment (e.g., the WWII LST) needed stern anchors to hold themselves in position and to withdraw off the beach when their missions were completed, in a manner similar to kedging. See *kedge anchor.*

sternboard
The commencement of motion astern. See *sternway.*

stern fast
Stern line used to secure a boat.

stern hook
Member of a boat's crew who stands aft and makes the stern of the boat secure. See *bow hook.*

sternpost
The principal timber in a wooden ship's stern frame, to which the rudder is hung and the transoms bolted. In a steel ship, the casting that forms the aftermost member of the ship's frames. Opposite of stem. The stem and sternpost are the two extremes of the ship's framing.

stern tube
Circular bearing for the propeller shaft when it emerges from the ship. Also, a stern torpedo tube.

sternway
Progress astern. Opposite of headway. See *sternboard*.

stevedore
A man who loads and unloads ships' cargo. Generally, same as longshoreman.

steward elbow
Special fitting used at the end of a hose where it enters fuel trunk during underway fueling.

stock
The cross bar of an old-fashioned anchor.

stockage objective
Maximum quantities of material maintained to sustain current operations.

stockless anchor
An anchor without a stock, so that it can be housed right up into its own hawse and secured merely by putting a stopper on the chain. The old-fashioned anchor was very difficult to secure for sea because of the stock. When larger ships required much heavier anchors, the old-fashioned anchor became impractical. The stockless anchor was a natural development. Also called patent anchor. See *anchor* (n).

stopper
Short length of line wrapped around a line in order to stop it from running, e.g., *boat-fall stoppers*. A *chain stopper* is a short length of chain with one end secured firmly to the deck and the other end fitted with a heavy pelican hook or clamp. When a ship is anchored, the strain is taken by the stopper so that the capstan and anchor engine can be used for other purposes or secured.

stops
Short pieces of line used to secure a sail or clothing that is rolled up. See *clothes stop*.

storekeeper (SK)
Petty officer who performs clerical and manual duties in the supply department.

stores
Supplies.

storm
Meterological disturbance; literally, a wind of 56 to 65 knots. See *breeze, gale, hurricane*.

stove
Broken in; smashed. Generally used with the word "in," as *"the sea stove in the bulkhead"*

stow
To put away; to store.

stowage factor
Number of cubic feet that cargo will occupy in a vessel.

stowage plan
Paper showing location of all cargo on board.

straddle
A salvo in which some of the shots are seen to fall beyond the target and some short of it, or some right and others left. The mean point of impact is thus on or near the target. Splashes beyond the target are known as "overs," and those short of it are "shorts." Minimum dispersion is of course desired, and thus a *straddle* generally insures that at least some of the projectiles are hitting.

straggler
See *unauthorized absentee.*

strakes
Continuous lines of fore-and-aft planking or plating in a boat or ship.

strand
Part of a line or rope made up of yarn. To go aground.

strap
A ring of wire or line, made by splicing the ends together, used for handling weight, etc. Also, a metal band such as those used to secure lead ballast in the bottoms of ships.

strategic minefields
Calculated to reduce and impede the enemy's war-making ability by destruction of his seaborne communications.

strategy
The basic overall plan by which a naval commander intends to accomplish his mission. Not to be confused with national strategy, with which it must of course be compatible.

stream
Bay, river, or fairway, e.g., anchored in the stream. To extend a flag or line out to its length, in air or water as appropriate.

stream anchor
A small anchor dropped off the stern or quarter to prevent a ship from swinging to a current. Now rare.

strike
A combat flight against ground or ship targets. To work for an improvement or promotion in one's job, as in *he is striking for chief.* Also to learn the trade of, as a person may *strike for* yeoman. See *striker, Appendix B.*

strike below
Take below decks, as stores are *struck below* after being brought aboard.

striker
An apprentice or learner. See *Appendix B.*

strip ship
Process of removing inflammable and superfluous material from a ship when war or emergency is imminent. See *clear ship.*

strongback
Padded spar between the davits against which a boat is griped in. A damage-control bar or beam, shorter than a shore. Also, a supporting girder for a hatch cover.

strut
The bracket supporting a ship's propeller shaft outside of the hull.

studding sails
Extra sails rigged alongside a square-rigger's regular sails, on light yards called *studding booms.* Suitable only for light winds. With all studding sails set, a ship would add at least half again to her sail area. Many of the paintings of the *Constitution* show her with studding sails.

stuffing box
Device to prevent leakage between a moving and a fixed part in a ship, particularly where a moving part comes out through the hull.

stuffing tube
Packed tube making a watertight fitting through a bulkhead for a cable or small pipe.

subcaliber
Pertaining to a much smaller-caliber gun mounted on or in a larger gun for practice purposes.

sublittoral zone
Subdivision of the littoral system of the benthic division including waters 50 to 200 meters in depth.

submarine (SS)
Warship designed for under-the-surface operations. Attack submarines have the primary mission of locating and destroying ships, including other submarines. Missile submarines have primarily the mission of attacking land targets. See *Appendix A.*

submarine chaser (PC) (SC)
Small (100- to 200-foot) patrol vessel. See *Appendix A.*

submarine combat air patrol (SUBCAP)
One of the variations of rescue combat air patrol, over a submarine.

submarine emergency buoyancy system (SEBS)
Gas generator emergency deballasting system to permit rapid surfacing of a submarine

submarine emergency identification signals
Black or green smoke—torpedo has been fired. Yellow—sub is coming up. Red—sub is in danger.

submarine escape lung
See *Steinke hood.*

submarine haven
Ocean area for submarines only. See *haven, submarine* and *moving havens.*

submarine marker buoy
Buoy released from a sunken submarine that floats to the surface and marks the spot for salvage and rescue.

submarine patrol areas
Stretch of water with specific geographic limits, assigned to a submarine as her area of action. Essentially the same as submarine patrol zones except more permanent in nautre and associated with probable focal points of enemy traffic.

submarine patrol zones
Restricted sea areas established for the purpose of permitting submarine operations unhampered by the operation of or possible attack by friendly forces. Differ from *havens,* which are established for training or transit.

submariner
Officer or man assigned to duty in submarines. U.S. Navy pronunciation is "submarine-er." Royal Navy says "sub-mariner," as though "mariner" were a separate word.

submarine radio rescue buoy
Device released from a sunken submarine that can rise to the surface and broadcast an emergency signal.

submarine rescue chamber
Device similar to a diving bell, which can be lowered to a disabled submarine and fitted over an escape hatch in which a few men may be brought to the surface at a time. See *deep submergence rescue vehicle.*

submarine rocket (SUBROC)
Model designation: UUM-44. Submarine-launched rocket-powered depth bomb. Can be fired from a submerged torpedo tube.

submarine sanctuaries
Restricted areas established for the conduct of noncombat submarine or antisubmarine exercises. They may be either stationary or moving and are normally designated only in rear areas. See *haven, submarine.*

submarine striking force
A group of submarines formed for a specific offensive action against the enemy. In modern context they would probably have missile-launching capabilities. U.S. SSBNs could be considered such a striking force today, or could be formed into several different submarine striking forces for different specific objectives.

submerged ordnance recovery device (SORD)
Surface-manipulated, closed-circuit-television-guided snare for recovery of sunken ordnance.

submersible pump (portable)
Watertight electric pump that can be lowered into a flooded compartment in order to pump it out.

subsistence (allowance)
Money paid in lieu of food furnished. For officers only, unless there is no general mess. See *commuted rations.*

substitute
Flag used to repeat another flag in the signal hoist, formerly called repeater.

subsurface currents
Currents flowing below the surface. Normally they have different speed and set from surface currents.

Suitcase
Portable command center for use on the bridge of a surfaced submarine, about the size of a portable typewriter; designed to replace several bridge instruments. It is taken below prior to diving.

sundowner
An extremely strict officer. The term nowadays carries a connotation of sadism in the application of the rules. See *martinet* for the same meaning without the sadistic implication. Derived from the ancient regulation that officers and men of a ship in commission must spend the night on board and must in fact be back aboard by sundown. A captain who insisted on observance of this regulation after it had outlived its purpose was called a *sundowner.*

sun over the yardarm or sun over the foreyard
An expression meaning that it is about time for the first drink.

superheaters
Heating units to raise the temperature of saturated steam to gain greater efficiency. Result is superheated steam.

super high frequencies (SHF)
3,000-30,000 megacycles or megahertz (mHz).

superstructure
All structure above the main deck of a ship. May be split or all in one group.

superstructure deck
A partial deck above the main deck. See *deck*.

Supply Systems Command
Functional command created in 1966 Navy Department reorganization, replacing Bureau of Supplies and Accounts (BUSANDA). Component of the Naval Material Command.

surf forecasting
Technique of predicting size and nature of surf. Important for amphibious operations.

surface effect ship (SES)
New name for *ground effects machine*. A vehicle designated to move across water or flat earth supported by a downward blast of air.

surface reverberation
A form of sound scattering, generally called reverberation.

surge
To hold a line taut on a winch drum without hauling in. To slack off a line or let it slip slowly around a fitting. Also, the horizontal water motion accompaning a *seiche*.

surging
Motion of a ship in which it is displaced alternately forward and aft, usually when moored. See *heaving, pitch, roll, sway, yaw*.

survey
Official procedure in expending accountable material from books or records. May be a special, formal, or informal survey. To *survey* an area is to explore and chart it. To *survey* a useless thing is to throw it away.

surveying ship (AGS)
Ship that conducts surveys and makes charts on board.

suspect nonmilitary vessel category
Vessel of doubtful classification whose movements are controlled or believed to be controlled by a hostile nation, or within the past six months has touched a port in such nation.

swab
Mop.

swallow
The larger opening in a block between the sides, through which the fall leads or the line reeves.

swamp
To fill with water, as a boat may do in heavy seas. The boat might or might not sink as a result.

swash
The rush of water up onto the beach following the breaking of a wave. See *backrush, uprush*.

swash plates
Metal plates in steam drums, oil tanks, etc. to prevent the surging of liquid with motion of the ship.

sway
Motion of a ship in which it is displaced laterally as distinct from rolling. See *heaving, pitch, roll, surge, yaw.*

sweep
Minesweeping operation. May be either a clearance or exploratory sweep. A rotating radar antenna is also said to sweep.

sweepers
Those who sweep down: *"sweepers, start your brooms; clean sweep down fore-and-aft."*

swell
Wind-generated waves which have advanced into a calmer area and are decreasing in height and gaining a more rounded form. The heave of the sea. See *roller.*

swept channel
Area that is kept clear of mines.

swing ship
To steam on various courses to determine a curve of compass error (deviation).

swivel
Removable anchor chain link fitted to revolve freely and thus keep turns out of a chain. See *mooring swivel.*

sword arm
The device, somewhat resembling a sword blade and containing a pitot tube, that is lowered beneath the hull when the ship is clear of port or anchorage. See *pitometer log.*

syzygy
The two opposite points in the orbit of the moon when it is in conjunction with or in opposition to the sun. Points of the new and full moon. Cause of *spring tides.*

T

tab
Part of an operation order (OPORD) or operation plan (OPPLAN). So named because of the standard *tabs* put on the edges of the pages for quicker location.

tablemount
See *seamount.*

table of organization (TO)
In the Marine Corps, a list of numbers, ranks, and duties of personnel.

tack
Lower forward corner of a fore-and-aft sail. The direction relative to the wind in which a sailing vessel goes, either on the port or starboard *tack* depending on the direction from which the wind strikes the sails, port or starboard. *To tack* is to come about or change tacks, thus a sailing boat *tacks* or zigzags upwind. Distance a boat sails on a port or starboard *tack* is called a tack. To come about by turning the bow through the wind; opposite of *wear.*

tackle
Any arrangement of line and blocks to gain a mechanical advantage. Pronounced "Tay-kul."

tackline
Short length of line used in a flaghoist to increase the normal distance between flags. Separates two signals on the same hoist, or may have a special meaning. Derogatory term when applied to a person, meaning "six feet of nothing."

tactical air control
The direction of aircraft in close support of amphibious troops, exercised from aboard ship or from the beach. Personnel are organized into tactical air control squadrons (TACRONs) and tactical air groups (TACGRUs).

tactical air control group (TACGRU)
An administrative and tactical component of a force that provides aircraft control and warning facilities.

tactical air navigation (TACAN)
A form of secondary radar used in air navigation.

tactical command ship (CC)
One designed to serve as a command ship for fleet/force commander. It is equipped with extensive communication equipment. Now in reserve fleet.

tactical diameter
Perpendicular distance between path of a ship on the original course and the path of the ship when steadied on new course after having turned through 180 degrees with a constant rudder angle. Standard tactical diameter is that prescribed by competent authority.

tactical range recorder
Equipment used in evaluation of visual presentation of ranging echoes from an underwater target.

tactics
The employment of units in battle. Distinguish from strategy.

TAD
See *temporary additional duty.*

TADIL
Tactical digital information link.

taffrail
A rail at the stern of a ship.

taffrail log
Old device that indicated the speed of a ship through the water. It was trailed on a line from the taffrail and consisted of a propeller-like rotator and a recording instrument.

tag, identification
Metal tag worn by all personnel when directed, recording their name, file or service number, blood type, and religious affiliation (optional). Slang: dog tag.

tag line
Line used to steady a load being swung in or out.

tail block
A block with a tail of rope instead of a hook.

tailhook
The hook lowered from the after part of the carrier aircraft which engages the arresting gear upon landing. Slang: a"tailhooker" is a naval aviator qualified in carrier operations.

tail on
Order to lay hold of a line and haul away.

tailor-mades
Slang for non-regulation enlisted men's uniforms.

take a strain
To apply tension on a line, wire, or chain. *Take an even strain:* relax.

take a turn
To pass a line around a cleat or bitts. Usually followed by order to hold it, check it, or ease it.

take charge
 To assume command or direction of. To become uncontrollable, as a vehicle might take charge on the deck of a rolling ship if not secured.

take in
 Command to take aboard a designated mooring line or lines. See *cast off*, the term used when the other ship (or the dock or pier) will retain the lines.

talker
 Usually telephone talker. A person assigned to pass orders and information to and from his station, usually by telephone.

tally-ho
 Sight contact with his target by a fighter pilot.

Tango
 Phonetic word for the letter *T*.

tanker
 A ship that transports fuel to a base or service squadron. An oiler fuels other ships at sea or at an anchorage.

tank top
 Top side of tank section or double bottom of a ship.

taps
 Bugle call sounded as last call at night for all hands to turn in.

TAR
 Designates a naval reserve officer or enlisted man on active duty in the training and administration of the naval reserve.

tar
 General name for a sailor of the old school. Derived from the old custom of a sailor *tarring* his trousers as well as other wearing apparel in order to make them waterproof.

tar down
 To coat standing rigging with tar.

tare
 An allowance for the weight of a container.

target angle
 Relative bearing of the firing ship from the target measured from the bow of the target to the right through 360 degrees. See *angle on the bow*.

target bearing
 True compass direction of a target from the firing ship.

target-grid method
 Standard shore bombardment procedure.

target indication
Information on targets available.

tarpaulin (tarp)
Any flat piece of canvas used for a cover.

tarpaulin muster
Collection of funds aboard ship for some common purpose such as to assist a shipmate's widow. Now rare.

task element (TE)
Component of a task group organized for specific tasks. Assigned a four-digit number, such as TE 58.1.1, making it subordinate to CTG 58.1.

task fleet
Mobile command of ships and aircraft necessary for a specific, major, continuing task.

task force (TF)
Major component of a task organization capable of large-scale combat or support operations. Usually assigned a two-digit number, such as 58, making it TF 58.

task group (TG)
Component of a task force organized for specific tasks. Assigned a 3-digit number such as TG 58.1, by CTF 58.

task organization
Fleet, Force, Group, Element, Unit: Standard operation organization format for U.S. Navy. Example: for Fifth Fleet, Task Fleet is 5th Fleet.

Task Force	—a major component of	5th Fleet	—TF 58
Task Group	—component of	TF 58	—TG 58.1
Task Element	—component of	TG 58.1	—TE 58.1.3
Task Unit	—component of	TE 58.1.3	—TU 58.1.3.3

Commanders are designated CTF 58, CTG 58.1, CTE 58.1.3, CTU 58.1.3.3.

tattoo
Bugle call sounded just before taps as signal to prepare to turn in.

taut
Tight, without slack. Well-disciplined, as a taut ship.

taximen
Plane handlers who assist in the taxiing of aircraft.

TDY
See *temporary additional duty (TAD)*.

telemetering system
Measuring, receiving, and transmitting instruments carried by a test missile together with receiving and recording instruments at a control system

telemetry
Science involving the taking of measurements and their transmission to detached stations where they can be displayed, interpreted, or recorded.

telephone talker
Person who handles a telephone during general evolutions such as general quarters. See *talker*.

telescope, ship's
Mounted scope of up to 32 power carried by ships for spotting flaghoists and other signals.

temporary additional duty (TAD)
A short assignment in addition to regular duties. Pronounced "tee-ay-dee." Navy and Marine Corps only. Other services use TDY for "temporary duty."

tend
To attend, as to *tend the side*. To take care of, as to *tend* a diver's air line. To extend, as an anchor chain *tends* forward. To act as a *tender* for; to service.

tender
Logistic support and repair ship such as a destroyer tender (AD).

tend the side
See *attend the side*.

that's high
Order to cease hauling or hoisting on a line.

thermocline
An ocean layer of rapidly changing temperature in comparatively small change of depth. Layer refracts sound waves causing a serious submarine detection problem.

thief sample
Sample of oil or water taken from a ship's tank for analysis.

thieving paste
A chemical coating on a sounding rod which reveals the level of the oil or water.

thimble
Metal ring grooved to fit inside a grommet or eye splice.

thole pin
Pin fitting into gunwale of a boat, carrying a rope grommet for use as a rowlock.

three sheets in the wind or three sheets to the wind
Well under the influence of liquor. Metaphoric reference is to a sailing ship in disarray, with sheets (lines) flying in the breeze.

throttleman
Person in the engine room who handles the throttles and thus controls the speed of the ship.

thrums, thrumming
Short yarns sewed to canvas to improve performance of collision mat, or make chafing gear called thrum mat.

thwarts
The cross seats or planks in a boat just below the gunwales.

tidal bore
Wave created when tidal pressure overcomes river current in a restricted area. The bore moves upstream against the current as the tide comes in.

tidal current
Current caused by rise and fall of tides.

tidal day
Period of a complete tidal cycle, as determined by lunar day.

tidal prism
Total amount of water that flows in and out of a harbor as a result of tide.

tidal range
Total rise (or fall) from low water to high water or vice versa.

tidal wave
A tremendous wave, an abberation of nature, that sweeps across an area and generally does great damage. The correct term for such waves is *tsunami*. They are considered to result from submerged earthquakes or volcanic action and have no relation to tidal action.

tide
The vertical rise and fall of the ocean level caused by the gravitational forces of the moon and the sun. Rising tide is a flood tide; a falling tide is an ebb tide.

tide race
A very rapid tidal current in a narrow channel or passage.

tide rips
Turbulent water produced by opposition to tidal currents.

tide tables
Publications giving data, including time and height, on tides at various locations. Published by National Ocean Survey (formerly Coast and Geodetic Survey). See *Current Tables*.

tie downs
Fittings to secure aircraft on deck.

tier
A layer of anchor chain in a chain locker.

tie-tie
Cloth straps or strings that tie together, as on a kapok life jacket.

tiller
Casting or forging attached to rudder stock. Lever that turns the rudder on a boat. In line with rudder and extension forward of rudder post. Same as helm in a large vessel. See *yoke*.

time charter
Lease of a vessel in which the owner operates, equips, and maintains the ship. Distinguish from *bare boat charter*.

Time, Greenwich Mean (civil)
Mean or civil time at the meridian of Greenwich and universally used in almanacs as well as in worldwide communications.

time, mean or civil
Time measured by the average rate of the sun's apparent movement.

time, Navy
Expressed in four digits, 0000-2400, based on 24-hour day. 1430 ("fourteen thirty") is 2:30 p.m. 0230 ("oh two thirty") is 2:30 a.m.

time orderly
Messenger whose duty it is to strike the hour and half hour on the ship's bell.

time, sidereal
Time measured by the rotation of the earth with respect to the stars. Useful mainly in locating stars for navigational use.

time, standard or zone
Mean or civil time fixed for zones, generally 15 degrees in width for both land and ocean areas with some arbitary redesignation for convenience.

tincan (can)
Slang for a destroyer.

tin fish (fish)
Slang for a torpedo.

toggle
Pin fitted into an eye or ring used to secure gear and to permit quick release.

Tom Cat
Special picket destroyer that operates with a fast carrier task force.

tomming
To brace from above, as shores may be used in a cargo hold.

tompion
A plug that fits into the bore of a gun at the muzzle to keep out dirt and spray. Pronounced "tom-kin."

ton
   A unit of measurement or weight. Units of weight: *Short ton* = 2000 lb; *long ton* = 2240 lb; *metric ton* = 2205 lb (1000 kilograms). Units of volume: *measurement ton* (ship ton) = 40 cubic ft; *register ton* = 100 cubic ft.

Tongue of the Ocean
   Deep natural basin in the Bahamas running more than 100 miles along the eastern shore of Andros Island. Site of the Atlantic Undersea Test and Evaluation Center (AUTEC).

tonnage
   Gross register = entire cubic capacity of a ship expressed in register tons. Net register = cubic capacity, less certain non-cargo spaces, expressed in register tons. Displacement = weight of a ship in long tons either with cargo, fuel, water, etc. (loaded), or without (light). Deadweight cargo = difference between displacement loaded and displacement light.

tons per inch immersion
   The number of tons necessary to increase a vessel's mean draft one inch.

top
   A platform on a mast, now obsolete. In sailing ships this was usually located at the juncture of the lower mast and the topmast (i.e., about one-third of the height of the entire mast, which was usually made of three sticks attached together in such a way that the upper two could be lowered down to the deck upon necessity). Sharpshooters were detailed to the tops (often called *fighting tops*) during battle. Such a sharpshooter killed Horatio Nelson at Trafalgar in 1805, and James Lawrence of the USS. *Chesapeake* in the battle with HMS *Shannon* in 1813. A modern warship has only one fighting top, a bulky structure called the foretop, which contains fire-control equipment and is built integrally into the highest point of an extremely strong, usually a tripod, foremast. Tops in other masts, if any, are of secondary importance and are rarely at the highest points of their masts. The top of a mast is called the cap. See *foretop, maintop, mizzentop, masthead.*

topgallant
   See *sail nomenclature.*

top hamper
   General item for superstructure and rigging. Masts, spars, antennas, etc., are known collectively as a ship's *top hamper.*

top off
   To fill up, as a ship *tops off* in fuel oil before leaving port.

topping lift
   Tackle made up of one or more blocks around which run one or more parts of fiber or wire rope connecting the end of a boom to its mast or post. Thus a boom may be used as a derrick, being raised or lowered to a suitable position

topsail

One of the principal sails of a square-rigger. The lowest sail on a mast that can be spread between an upper and a lower yard. The large, fast clippers of the mid-19th century carried crews insufficiently large to handle the huge topsails their size required, and the sails were therefore split horizontally into upper and lower topsails, causing them to resemble narrow horizontal rectangles instead of the approximate square of earlier ships. Except for the spanker, the lowest sail of any mast, with clews led down to the deck, or rail, instead of to a lower yard, is known as a course, or simply by the name of the mast. Thus the fore course is also the foresail, the main course the mainsail. See *sail nomenclature.*

topsail schooner

Two-masted sailing vessel with essentially a schooner rig except that the fore-and-aft sail on the foremast is not quite so high, leaving room on the mast for two or three yards from which one or two topsails can be carried.

top secret

Refers to national security information or material that requires the highest degree of protection. The test for assigning such a classification is whether unauthorized disclosure of the information could reasonably be expected to cause *exceptionally grave damage* to the national security. See *classified matter, confidential, secret.*

topside

Above, in a ship, referring to the deck above, as distinguished from overhead, which refers to the ceiling of a compartment. The topside (or topsides) means the upper deck (or decks); any deck or area which is exposed to the weather is considered topside.

top up

To raise a boom with its topping lift.

torch pot

The chamber or pot in a steam torpedo where air, fuel, and water are mixed together and ignited to produce steam to drive the torpedo engine. See *combustion chamber.*

torpedo

Self-propelled underwater explosive weapon designed to be aimed or to seek a target, and detonated by contact, sound, or magnetic force. Various types identified by mark and modification numbers. Slang is fish or tin fish.

torpedo range

Distance torpedo can run with its available fuel supply.

torpedo retriever

Fast boat for recovering practice torpedoes.

torpedo run

Actual distance torpedo travels to target.

torpedo tube
Movable fairings on outboard end of submarine torpedo tubes whose closure preserves the streamlined form of a hull.

torpedo tube shutters
Movable fairings on outboard end of submarine torpedo tubes whose closure preserves the streamlined form of the hull.

torpedoman's mate (TM)
Petty officer who performs upkeep and repair of torpedoes and ASW ordnance.

torsionmeter
Device for measuring the twist in the propeller shaft from which the horsepower developed by the turbine is calculated.

toss oars
An order to raise oars from the rowlocks to a vertical position, blades fore and aft, with handles resting on the bottom of the boat.

touch and go
A near thing. Reference is to a ship barely touching ground, but coming loose immediately and not damaged. In such a case, reporting the incident becomes a matter of ethics and honor. In any situation, to be touch and go is to have a close call.

tow
The vessel being towed. To pull along through the water.

tow glider
Antiaircraft gunnery target.

towing bridle
See *bridle.*

towing light
Two or three vertical white lights required of a vessel towing by the *Rules of the Road.*

towing spar
Wooden device towed astern by ships in formation in low visibility to assist in station keeping. Also called fog buoy and position buoy.

towing winch
Special winch, used by large tugs in towing, which compensates for variation in the tension on the towline.

tracer
A message sent to ascertain reason for nondelivery of a prior message. Also, a projectile trailing smoke or showing a light for correction in aim; most usually employed in machine-gun ammunition.

track
To mark the course of a target on a radar scope or plotting board. To follow a target, noting course and speed, as a patrol aircraft tracks a convoy. Also, the course made good over the ground.

track angle
Angle between the target course and the reciprocal of the torpedo course measured from the bow of the target to the right, through 360 degrees, or to port or starboard through 180 degrees. See *angle on the bow, target angle.*

tracking
Observation of a mobile object to report its composition, location, course, and speed.

track spacing
The distance between tracks of successive searches or the distance between adjacent sweeping units in a simultaneous search.

tractor
Term referring to landing ships and craft; as the *tractor group* of a task force moving to the objective area. Also an aircraft that tows target for antiaircraft practice.

trade or trade winds
Those generally steady winds from the northeast in the northern hemisphere and southeast in the southern hemisphere in the lower latitudes so important for commerce in the days of sail. They are caused by the normal flow of air from the poles towards the sun-heated equator, deflected by the rotation of the earth.

train
Service or logistic support ships attached to a fleet.

trainer
Man who controls gun or mount in horizontal movement (deflection or train). See *pointer.*

train in and secure
Put away equipment and cease present exercise.

training aid
Material (audio or visual) to facilitate the learning process.

training bill
Schedule and outline of training for a particular unit of men.

training cycle
Period between successive ship overhauls, theoretically. Because of constant personnel changes, few ships are able to complete their training cycle, and instead start over every year.

train out (in)
To move a gun or missile mount from the rest position, usually fore-and-aft and horizontal, to a ready position (or vice versa).

trajectory
The path of a projectile, missile, or bomb in flight.

transducer
Device for conversion of energy from one form to another, e.g. electrical to mechanical or acoustic.

transfer
Distance gained by a ship at right angles to original course when turning. The movement of enlisted men from one duty assignment to another.

transit navigation satellite
A development to provide an all-weather global system by which the positions of surface craft, submarines, and aircraft can be accurately fixed.

transom
Planking or steel plates across the stern of a boat or a ship. A settee or sofa aboard a ship.

transponder
An atomic transmitter that emits a signal when interrogated by another signal.

transport area
Station area for the transports that disembark troops during an amphibious assault.

transport division (squadron)
The attack transport and cargo ships that carry and land a regimental combat team. Several divisions organized to carry a reinforced infantry division comprise a transport squadron.

transport group
Subdivision of an amphibious attack force comprising the assault transports and cargo ships.

trapping
Atmospheric distortion of radar signals

trials, machinery
Tests of main propulsion machinery of a ship. May be builders, acceptance, post repair, standardization, or tactical.

triatic stay
Wire from foremast to after stack or mast of a ship. Also spring stay.

trice
To haul up, as to *trice up* all bunks, which means to push up all bunks and secure them.

trick
Steersman's watch is known as a *trick* at the wheel.

trick wheel
Steering wheel in the steering engine room or emergency steering station of a ship.

Trident

Model designation: UGM-96A. New sea-based strategic system consisting of three-stage, solid propellant, multi-warhead missiles with inertial guidance, a quieter submarine, and a CONUS support complex. Initial operational capability 1982 with Trident submarines operating from Bangor, Washington. Eventual replacement for Polaris/Poseidon. Originally designated ULMS (undersea long-range missile system).

trim

The fore-and-aft inclination of a ship—down by the head or down by the stern. Sometimes used to include list. To *trim* a submarine is to adjust water in the variable ballast tanks, or *trim* tanks, to establish neutral buoyancy. Also means shipshape; neat. See *even keel.*

trimming system

The entire system of pipes, valves, pumps, and tanks by which a submarine compensates for expenditure of variable weights so as to maintain neutral buoyancy and stability when submerged. The compensation is done before diving whenever possible, by careful calculation, and when the requisite amounts of water are in the variable ballast tanks the submarine is said to be in *diving trim.* A *trim dive* is a dive made for the purpose of checking and correcting the compensation.

trim tanks

Forward and after variable ballast tanks of a submarine. Known as *forward trim* and *after trim.* Amidships auxiliary tanks are also part of the *trimming system.*

trip

To let go, as to *trip* a pelican hook.

triplane target

Towed sonar target used in training of ASW ships.

tropic range

Same as great tropic range.

trough

The hollow between two waves.

truck

The highest part of a ship's tallest mast, known as *fore truck* or *main truck,* as appropriate. Highest parts of other masts are caps. See *cap.*

true airspeed

Rate of motion of aircraft relative to the air.

true bearing

Direction of an object relative to true instead of magnetic north.

true heading

Horizontal direction in which an aircraft or ship is heading, relative to true north.

trunk
Space aboard ship used for ventilation, access, etc.

trunnions
The major supports of a gun that provide the axis about which the gun rotates in elevation. Tilt of trunnions introduces range and deflection errors. In days of sail, trunnions were cast integrally with the gun. Nowadays they are part of the gun mount instead of the gun itself.

try cocks
Small faucets on the steam drum used to verify the water level if the gauge glass fails.

tsunami
See *tidal wave*.

tumble
To lose stability, as a gyroscope *tumbles*.

tumble home
Upward curve of a ship's side above the waterline, generally convex but may be a compound of convex and concave, such that the width of the main deck is narrower than the ship's beam at the waterline. Opposite of flare, which was frequently designed into bow and stern to reduce pitching. Sailing men-of-war were designed with *tumble home* to permit serving the broadside guns while grappled alongside an enemy, and to make boarding more difficult. See *flare*.

turbine
Multi-bladed rotor, driven by steam or hot air, which, in turn, drives a propeller or a compressor.

turbo blower
Also called low-pressure blower. A blower used to complete evacuating water from submarine ballast tanks after the submarine has been brought to the surface by compressed air, and opened to the atmosphere. A far more economical way of completing the surfacing procedure than by using the precious high-pressure air.

turbo-jet
Type of engine which uses a turbine-driven compresser.

turbo-prop
Aircraft engine in which a gas turbine drives a propeller and also provides thrust with tail pipe exhaust.

Turk's head
An ornamental collar on an oar, rail, spar, etc., braided from small line.

turnbuckle
Metal appliance consisting of a threaded link with a pair of opposite-threaded screws with eyes, capable of being set taut or slacked and used for setting up standing rigging or other gear.

turn count masking
Practice of changing propeller revolutions at random to prevent a submarine from estimating speed of attacking ship.

turn in
Go to bed. To *turn in all standing* is to do so fully clothed.

turning circle (of a ship)
Path followed by a ship with constant rudder angle when turning.

turn out
To awake and get up.

turn to
Go to work.

turn (together)
A maneuver in which all ships turn simultaneously to a new course. A tactical maneuver for a group of ships. Now obsolete, because of demise of the battle line.

turret
The armored enclosure for the heavy guns of a man-of-war. Invented approximately simultaneously by John Ericsson, a Swedish-born American engineer, and Captain Cowper Coles, Royal Navy, in the mid-19th century. There were, of course, engineering differences between the two designs, and for a time naval officers spoke of "Coles turrets" and "Ericsson turrets." As it evolved, turret became the name for the entire huge rotating mechanism inside the armored barbette that supported it, extending far down into the lower levels of the ship where ammunition was supplied from the magazines. Nowadays the protective shield around smaller guns, such as the five-inch antiaircraft gun of destroyers, is loosely called a turret, but technical purists insist this is incorrect. As with many such arguments, the distinction is of little importance today. See *barbette, gun house.*

turret guns
Those guns, six-inch or larger, mounted in a turret.

Tuscarora, **USS**
A mythical ship, claimed to have had 17 decks and a straw bottom.

'tween deck
Any deck in a ship below the main deck. Generally used in the plural: *'tween decks,* to mean inside the ship, between decks.

twilight
The period before sunrise and after sunset during which light is reflected from the sun. The four kinds, depending on angular distance of the sun below the horizon, are: civil at 6 degrees; observational at 10 degrees; nautical at 12 degrees; astronomical at 18 degrees.

two-blocked
Hoisted all the way up. Same as close up.

two-fold purchase
A tackle, both blocks of which contain two sheaves. See *purchase*.

typhoon
See *hurricane*.

U

UA
Unauthorized absence.

UCMJ
Uniform Code of Military Justice.

ultra high frequencies (UHF)
300-3,000 megacycles. See *hertz*.

ULMS
Undersea long-range missile system. The acronym ULMS may still be encountered, but it is now called Trident.

unauthorized absence, unauthorized absentee (UA)
The proper all inclusive term for a man absent from his command without authority. Replaces old terms *straggler, absentee,* and *absent without leave (AWOL)*.

unbend
To untie, loosen, cast adrift.

Uncle
Previous phonetic word for the letter *U*; now *Uniform*.

uncover
To remove the hat.

undercarriage
Landing gear of an airplane.

underfoot
Said of an anchor when it is directly under ship's forefoot.

under hack
Restriction to specified limits; a nonjudicial punishment of an officer awarded by his commanding officer (slang).

undertow
The brief downward and seaward thrust of a collapsing wave top as the wave breaks on a beach. Results from the essentially circular motion of water within a wave. It can drive a swimmer under for a few seconds only. See *rip current* for description of current that may carry him offshore, often incorrectly called "the undertow."

underwater demolition team (UDT) unit
Team of specially trained men who do reconnaissance and demolition work along the beaches just prior to an amphibious assault.

underway
Said of a vessel when she is not made fast to the ground in any manner. She may or may not have way on (i.e., she may be hove to), but she is free floating in the sea, subject to wind, currents, and of course her own propulsion system.

underway replenishment (UNREP)
See *replenishment at sea.*

underway replenishment group
A task group organized to provide logistic replenishment of ships underway by transfer-at-sea methods.

Uniform
Phonetic word for the letter *U*; formerly *Uncle.*

Uniform Code of Military Justice (UCMJ)
Enacted by Congress for all armed services. For the Navy it replaces the Articles for the Government of the Navy (AGN). See *rocks and shoals.*

uniform of the day
Prescribed by the commanding officer or by the senior officer present afloat (SOPA). To be worn at all times except when working uniform is authorized.

union
The inner, upper corner of a flag if it has a distinctive design. The union of the flag of the United States, for example, is the blue field with 50 white stars on it. It signifies the union of the states into a single country. See *jack* or *union jack*

union jack
Flag flown at the bow of a ship moored or anchored, consisting of the union of the national flag. Also flown in the boat of a high civil official, and at yardarm during a general court-martial or court of inquiry.

unit
Refers to a command unit. May be a single ship or aircraft, or a group of ships or planes under a single commander. The important point is that the unit behaves like one. If split into two or more component parts, each becomes a unit in its own right, until the irreducible individual man, aircraft, or ship is reached.

United States Armed Forces
A collective term for the regular components of the Army, Navy, Air Force, and Coast Guard in time of war. See *Armed Forces.*

United States Naval Ship (USNS)
A ship owned by the U.S. Navy, but not commissioned as part of the Navy. Normally manned with civilian crews and operated by the Military Sea Lift Command.

United States Navy Regulations
Principles for guiding of the naval establishment, particularly the duties, responsibilities, and authority of all offices and individuals, issued by the Secretary of the Navy and approved by the President.

unit of fire
A unit of measure for ammunition supply, representing a specified number of rounds per weapon.

universal time
Greenwich Mean Time, as measured for Greenwich, England.

unlay
To untwist and separate a rope's strands.

unload through the muzzle
To fire in a safe direction in order to empty a gun of its charge.

unship
To remove from place, in the sense of taking a smaller thing, such as a boat, gun, spare tire, etc. out of the larger one in which it has been secured: the ship, or something which a sailor might consider comparable under the circumstances, such as a building, aircraft, automobile, even his own person (he might "unship" his wristwatch, or a ring).

up anchor
The order to weigh anchor and get underway.

up and down
Said of an anchor chain when the anchor is under the forefoot during the process of weighing anchor. See *short stay, underfoot.* As anchor comes up it is reported as: *"Anchor in sight! Clear (foul) anchor!"*

up behind
An order to cease hauling and to slack a line quickly.

uprush
The rush of water onto the foreshore after the breaking of a wave. See *backrush.*

uptakes (exhaust trunks)
Large enclosed passages for exhaust gases from boilers to the stacks.

upwelling
A mass of cold, dense sea water that rises up from the depths of the ocean to the surface.

V

van
The forward part or group of a formation of ships, opposite of rear.

vang
Line used to steady or support a boom or spar. Also called a *guy.*

variable tanks
Also called *variable ballast tanks* or *trimming tanks.* Specific application is to a submarine. See *trim tanks, ballast tanks, trimming system.*

variable time (VT) fuze
Fuze that is actuated by the reflection of self-generated radar emissions from the target as the projectile passes near it. Also called proximity fuze. See *fuze.*

variation
Magnetic compass error caused by the difference between the geographic and magnetic poles. Expressed in degrees east or west. Also known as "magnetic declination" by earth scientists. Daily fluctuation in variation is called diurnal change, which is too small to be significant to navigators except in polar regions.

vector
An aircraft's course or heading. To direct; to give a course to.

veer
To let out or pay out a chain or line. Also, when the wind changes direction clockwise or to the right, it is said to *veer.* See *haul.*

vent
Valve in a tank or compartment to permit escape of air when filling it, or when pressure builds up for other reasons. The large valve at the top of a submarine's main ballast tank(s) by which trapped air is released to permit diving. The touch hole or aperture through which fire was communicated to the powder charge of a muzzle-loading gun.

ventilation system
Series of air supply and exhaust lines to all parts of a ship.

vertical envelopment
A tactical maneuver in which troops, either air-dropped or air-landed, attack the rear and flanks of an enemy force, in effect cutting off or encircling it.

vertical replenishment (VERTREP)
Replenishment in which helicopters are used in connection with supply ships to resupply the fleet while underway. See *replenishment at sea*

VERTOL
Vertical takeoff and landing.

very good; very well
Response by a senior to a report by a junior.

very high frequencies (VHF)
30-300 megacycles. See *hertz.*

very high frequency omnidirectional range (VOR)
VHF omnidirectional range used principally in air navigation. It provides a magnetic bearing from ground stations. When combined with distance-measuring equipment, DME, this system produces bearing and distance establishing a fix.

**very high frequency omnidirectional range
and tactical air navigation (VORTAC)**
A military designation for an omnidirectional range station including tactical air navigation (TACAN), a distance-measuring system.

very low frequencies (VLF)
10-30 kilocycles. See *hertz.*

Very's pistol
Device for firing small pyrotechnics into the air as signals. Commonly called Very pistol.

vessel
By U.S. statutes, includes every description of craft, ship or other contrivance used as a means of transportation on water.
"Any vehicle in which man or goods are carried on water."
—Dr. Samuel Johnson.
At one time *vessel* differed from *ship* in that a ship was defined as a square-rigged vessel with three masts, distinguished from a brig, bark, schooner, snow, etc. This distinction for ship no longer holds, although those for the others still do. Thus, the traditional three-masted square rigger is the only one that does not possess its own specific, exclusive, semantic identification. See *ship.*

vice admiral
The rank between admiral and rear admiral. See *admiral.*

vice commodore
Second in command of a convoy. See *commodore.*

Victor
Phonetic word for the letter *V.*

virtual PPI reflectoscope (VPR)
A navigational chart fitted to the PPI of a radar for comparing the PPI picture with a chart of the area.

visible
Capable of being seen on a dark, clear night at sea. Legal definition of navigational light, generally combined with the distance at which it is visible.

visit and search
A visit to a private vessel to determine its nationality, character of cargo, nature of employment, etc.

visiting
Routine visiting is for friends and relatives of the crew at specified times. General visiting is for the general public on holidays, etc.

visit, official
See *official visit.*

voice tube
Tube for voice communication within the ship. Now generally replaced by telephones.

void
Empty compartment below decks.

volume reverberation
Type of sound scattering; general term is reverberation.

VOR
Very high frequency omnidirectional range.

VORTAC
Very high frequency omnidirectional range and tactical air navigation.

voyage repairs
Emergency work needed by a ship which will not affect its operating schedule.

W

waist
Amidships portion of ship; the part of the deck between forecastle and poop. Rarely used now.

wake
The disturbed water astern of a moving ship.

wake light
Dim light at stern directed down on wake to assist following ships to keep station.

wale shore
Long spar, or shore, used to brace a ship upright in a drydock. Longer and heavier (larger cross-section) than a regular shore.

walk back
An order to keep a line in hand or on the capstan, ready to hold it or resume hoisting, but to *walk it back*, i.e., ease it backward. *Walk back handsomely* means to walk back slowly and carefully, ready for instant emergency. Usually used in connection with hoisting a boat by hand.

walkback
Improper functioning of carrier arresting gear which causes the airplane to be pulled backward along the flight deck after its forward motion is stopped.

walk back the cat
Expression meaning to start all over again or to retire to a previously held position and start a process or procedure again.

walkways
Space adjacent to a flight deck aboard an aircraft carrier.

wall knot
Knot formed at the end of a line by looping each strand around the one behind it and passing its end through the loop of the strand in front.

wardroom
The compartment in which officers gather to eat and to lounge aboard ship.

warhead
Forward section of a torpedo missile that carries the explosive. For training shots, an exercise head is fitted.

warp
To haul a ship ahead or astern, or to change the heading of a ship by pulling on lines and/or chain to a pier, dock or outlying anchor. See *spring*.

warping head
Revolving vertical cylinder for hauling in on lines, part of a windlass.

warping tug
A special tug made up from pontoon sections and used by an amphibious construction battalion during an amphibious assault. See *pontoon barge*.

warrant officer
An officer, senior to all chief petty officers and junior to all commissioned officers, who derives his authority from a warrant issued by the Secretary of the Navy. A *commissioned warrant* officer is the highest grade of warrant officer, who actually holds a commission under authority of the President and confirmed by Congress.

wash-deck hose
Special hose connected to a fireplug, used for washing down the decks.

watch
Duty period, normally four hours long. A day's *watches* are: *evening* or *first watch* 2000-2400, *mid watch* 0000-04000, *morning watch* 0400-0800, *forenoon watch* 0800-1200, *afternoon watch* 1200-1600, *first dog watch* 1600-1800, *second dog watch* 1800-2000. A buoy is said to *watch* when it is floating in its proper position and attitude.

watch and watch
See *heel* and *toe*.

watch cap
Stack cover, usually of canvas. Also, an enlisted man's blue knitted cap.

Watch Dog
Special picket destroyer with a carrier task force.

watch officer
An officer regularly assigned to duty in charge of a watch or a portion of it. For example, the officer of the deck, OOD, or the engineering officer of the watch, EOOW (or sometimes simply OOW). A qualified watch officer is one to whom his commanding officer entrusts the ship without reservation.

watch, quarter and station bill
List showing the duties and billet assignments of all enlisted men. Opposite the men's names are listed their battle, cleaning, and emergency stations, etc.

water breaker
Container for fresh water.

water drum
See *drum, water.*

waterline
Point to which ship sinks in water; line painted on hull showing point to which ship sinks when properly trimmed. Also, more loosely, the top of the boot-topping, since this highly visible line can be seen from a greater distance. See *Plimsoll mark.*

waterlogged
Filled or soaked with water but still floats; or, a thing that normally floats, now so soaked with water that it does not; e.g., a waterlogged timber might or might not float. A waterlogged boat, or ship, is scarcely afloat, but a sunken ship would never be described as merely "waterlogged." General reference is to absorption of water by the material itself.

water sky
Dark streak on sky caused by reflection of leads, polynyas, and open water.

waterspout
A tornado-like phenomenon occurring over water in which very low pressure in center sucks up water.

water taxi
Shore boat, available for hire like a taxi.

watertender
Person in charge of a fireroom, responsible to keep the level of water in the boilers at the right height, and to supervise the entire watch to the end that the boilers remain at maximum efficiency. The watertender was in his heyday during days of the coal-fired boilers, when his function was an art.

watertight closure log
Log recording the special openings made of the watertight closures by permission of the officer of the deck (OOD).

watertight door
A door that is strongly made and fitted with special closure equipment, gasket and dogs, so that when it is closed water cannot pass through it in either direction even if accompanied by considerable pressure.

waterway
The gutter under the lifelines to carry off deck water through the scuppers.

waterway bar
Sometimes used in place of the footline. See *lifelines.*

wave height
Vertical distance between the wave trough and the wave crest. "Significant height" is the average of the highest third of all waves. Such measurements do not take account of the rare, but still occasionally encountered, "super wave" which is much higher than any average and causes the greatest danger and damage. Such freak waves are the result of occasional harmonic reinforcement of two or more different wave systems moving in different directions. Since their frequency of occurrence is statistically predictable, prudent seamen can take precautions.

wave off
Signal from landing signal officer (LSO) of a carrier to "pull up and try again."

wave period
Time interval between passage of two consecutive, identical wave segments. Normally expressed in seconds.

wave refraction
Tendency of a wave to swing so that its crest parallels the shore. Caused by lower portions of the wave slowing as they "feel" bottom.

WAVES
Women Accepted for Voluntary Emergency Service.

waves, internal
See *internal waves.*

way
A ship's movement through the water, as *the ship has way on."* See *underway.*

way enough
In a pulling boat, an order to complete the stroke, then hold the oars in mid-stroke position (see *oars*), awaiting the next command. As the order indicates, there appears to be sufficient way to complete the maneuver intended. The next order may be to back water, or boat the oars, or any of a number of combinations possible depending on the circumstances. See *in bows.*

ways, building
Inclined slides leading into the water upon which a ship is built. When it is time to launch her, the regular supports under the hull are replaced with skids designed to slide down the inclination and support the hull upright until it enters the water. The ways are carefully greased, and at the last moment, just after the christening ceremony, the final holding devices are removed or cut and down she goes.

wear
For a sailing vessel to change tacks (to bring the wind on her other side and thus change direction of her motion) she may either pass her bow through the wind, known as tacking, or pass her stern through it, called *wearing.* Fore-and-afters almost always tack, while square-riggers

usually wear, in both cases to avoid stress on rigging from the shock of having sails suddenly catch the wind on the other side. An accidental wear by a fore-and-after is called a jibe. A square-rigger thrown up into the wind will be taken flat aback.

weather
Toward the wind, opposite of lee. To survive, as to *weather* a storm. To pass an obstacle successfully, despite wind and sea setting one down on it, as to *weather* a cape. To have been exposed to the elements, as a *weathered* timber. Exposed, or topmost, as the *weather* deck. See *windward*.

weathercocks
Said of a ship that comes up into the wind readily, or must carry *weather helm* to stay on course. Such a ship is also said to be *ardent*. *See lee helm*.

weather deck
Top-most deck of a ship, or any exposed deck. See *deck*.

weather eye
To keep a weather eye is to be on the alert. Also: to keep a weather eye out.

weather helm
A sailing vessel which *weathercocks*, or is ardent, requires a bit of *weather helm* (helm up, toward the wind, rudder down, away from the wind) to stay on course. See *lee helm*.

weaving
A form of zigzag steered by ships. Also, sinuous course steered by aircraft in which two or more aircraft turn toward each other for mutual support.

web belt
Broad, woven, cotton belt, fitted with eyelets for carrying canteen, pistol, etc. Part of landing party uniform and worn as badge of office by enlisted sentries, messengers, orderlies, and others. Sometimes called a duty belt.

wedge cleat
See *cleat*.

weekend warrior
Slang for a member of the Naval Reserve.

weigh
To lift the anchor off the bottom in getting underway.

well deck
Part of the weather deck having some sort of superstructure both forward and aft of it.

wet down
Slang meaning to celebrate. A newly promoted person *wets down* his new stripe

whaleboat
Small double-ended boat. Good in a seaway because it is high at both ends. Favored for lifeboat use.

wharf
Structure parallel to the shore line to which ships moor for loading, unloading, or repairs. Sometimes called a quay, which is usually a solid masonry structure.

wharfage
Charge for use of berthing space.

wheel
To alter a course in such a manner that all ships of a convoy remain in the same relative position. The steering wheel of a ship is known as the *wheel.*

wheelhouse
Pilothouse. The location of the steering wheel in normal cruising. The covered, enclosed portion of the bridge of a ship. The wings of the bridge are the uncovered portions on either side of the wheelhouse. The topside compartment where, in most ships, the OOD, helmsman, quartermaster of the watch, etc. stand their watches.

whelps
Projections on the periphery of the wildcat drum that fit the anchor chain and pull it by a sort of gear-tooth action.

where away?
Answering call acknowledging a lookout's report of a sighting and requesting its direction.

wherry
Light, handy pulling boat with a transom stern.

whip
To wrap, as the end of a line is *whipped* with small stuff. Also, a tackle used to lift minor weights.

Whiskey
Phonetic word for the letter *W.*

whistle, ship's
A noisemaker, normally using steam or air, usually attached to the forward stack of a ship.

white hat
Slang for an enlisted man.

whiteout
Optical phenomenon occuring at northern latitudes in which no shadows are discernible; sense of depth and orientation is lost, and only very dark, nearby objects can be seen.

wide berth
At a considerable distance, as "we gave him (the other ship) a wide berth."

wilco
Term indicating receipt and understanding of a voice radio message. Means *will comply*. Not to be confused with Roger, which means only *message received*.

wildcat
That part (drum) of an anchor windlass that engages and moves the anchor chain. Also called a chain grab. See *whelps*.

Williamson turn
Maneuver used to recover a man lost overboard. Put rudder over toward man, shift rudder at 70 degrees from original heading, steady on reciprocal of original heading, and ship should return to place where man went overboard.

williwaw
Violent squall characteristic of mountainous coasts, particularly the Aleutian Islands.

winch
An electric, hydraulic, or steam machine aboard ship used for hauling in lines, as in boat and cargo lifting. Fitted with a horizontal gipsy or a vertical warping head.

winch-head
A gipsy. See *winch*.

wind bird
An anemometer.

windlass
Machine primarily used for handling an anchor chain with a drum called a wildcat or chain grab fitted with whelps that engage the links. Also fitted with a warping head, a revolving concave vertical cylinder similar to a gypsy and used for hauling in lines.

windsail
Canvas wind catchers fitted with canvas tubes to lead fresh air below decks.

wind scoop
Metal scoop fitted into a port to direct air into the ship for ventilation.

wind ship
To turn a ship end for end, usually with lines at a pier, although it may also be done with prepared anchors and cables. Thomas MacDonough did this with conspicuous success at the Battle of Lake Champlain, thereby achieving victory at a crucial point in the War of 1812. Pronounced to rhyme with "mind." See *spring, warp*.

windward
Toward the wind. Similar to weather but not used interchangeably.

wing
Two or more squadrons (groups) of aircraft or airships. Also, the part of a hold to either side of the square of the hatch, or the uncovered ends of the bridge on either side of the wheelhouse or pilothouse.

wingman
A pilot who flies formation on another, on his wing.

wire drag
To explore for uncharted shoals or pinnacles with a weighted wire dragged at a fixed depth.

wiredrawn steam
Steam that has lost pressure because of friction of ports, passages, etc.

wire rope
Rope made of wire strands twisted together, as distinguished from the more common and weaker fiber rope. Sometimes called a cable, or wire cable.

wishbone
Supporting rods for the upper accommodation ladder platform

wolf pack
Coordinated submarine attack group of two or more submarines.

wooden
Slang for stupid; slow.

word, the
News; information. Slang: the dope.

work a ship
To handle ship by means of engines and other gear; for example, to *work* a ship into a slip using engines, rudder, and lines to docks.

working party
Group of men assigned to a specific job.

work request
The formal application, with detailed information, from a ship to a repair activity asking that specific work be done. Not a job order.

world grid
A grid dividing the world into 1,000-meter (yard) squares. Used to designate targets.

worm
To fill the lays of line or wire before parcelling. "Worm and parcel with the lay. Turn and serve the other way." See *serve, parcel.*

X

X-ray
Phonetic word for the leter *X*.

XO
Executive officer, exec. Slang.

Y

yacht ensign
A modified ensign, flown by yachts, whose dip is answered by men-of-war. May be saluted upon arrival aboard or upon departure from the yacht.

Yankee
Phonetic word for the letter Y.

yard
Spar attached at the middle of a mast and running athwarships, used as a support for square sails. A shipbuilding and repair facility as Boston Naval Shipyard, called colloquially a "Navy yard" or simply the "yard."

yardarm
Either end of a yard, referring to the spar.

yardarm blinker
White, all-around, signal lights at the ends of a small yard near top of a mast.

yarn
Twisted fibers used for rough seizings, which may be twisted into strands; also, a story, as to *spin a yarn*, meaning to tell a story not necessarily true. In the old days one could refer to *yarning* with this meaning.

yaw
Rotary oscillation about a ship's vertical axis in a seaway. Sheering off alternately to port and starboard while at anchor is also called yawing. An aircraft yaws like a ship. See *roll, pitch, heaving, sway, surge.*

yawl
A small sailing craft, generally a yacht, fitted with a single tall mast, generally called the main, and with a much shorter one abaft of the rudder post, called the jigger. Sails are fore-and-aft rigged and may be with or without a gaff boom. In appearance very similar to a ketch, except that the aftermost mast of a ketch is forward of the rudder and most often is larger than that of the yawl.

yeoman (YN)
Petty officer who preforms clerical and secretarial duties. See *Appendix B.*

Y-gun
Depth charge launching device used to propel depth charge laterally away from the side of a ship, thus enlarging the size and effectiveness of the pattern. The Y-gun is shaped like the letter Y and can fire depth charges in two directions (either side of the ship) at once. The K-gun can shoot only one depth charge at a time, in a single direction.

yielding elements
Spring-loaded mechanisms to support the arresting gear.

yoke
The piece fitting across the head of a rudder, to which the ends of the steering lines or rudder rams are attached. The yoke usually has two arms of equal length across the rudder head, or the vertical rudder shaft, and is almost always at right angles to the line of the rudder, though in modern design it need not be. The helm, or tiller, are of older derivation and are always in line with the rudder, with a single arm. See *ram, rudder*.

Z

zenith
That point of the celestial sphere vertically overhead. See *nadir*.

zenith distance
Angular distance from the zenith to a position on the celestial sphere measured on a vertical circle.

zerk fitting
Small plug to which a grease gun can be applied to force lubricating grease into important parts of machinery.

zigzag
Series of relatively short, straight-line variations from the base course. See *evasive steering*.

zinc
Metal secured to underwater body of a ship to counter electrolysis.

ZIPPERS
Dawn and dusk combat air patrols.

zone inspection
In times past, active commanding officers prided themselves on personally inspecting all spaces of their ships at regular intervals, followed by the inspecting party that made notes of discrepancies found. In large, modern ships this is no longer practicable, and it has been replaced with the *zone inspection*, in which a designated officer is responsible for each zone, with his own inspection party. Frequently, the captain will join one of the zone inspection parties.

zooplankton
Animal plankton as distinct from plant plankton.

Zulu
Phonetic word for the letter Z.

Appendix A

SHIP AND SERVICE CRAFT DESIGNATIONS

Every U.S. Navy ship and service craft is given a letter designation which broadly classifies it as to function, major capability, or specific use. In general, the letter designation for ships is followed by a hull number which precisely identifies the ship from among those bearing similar designations, and thus the combination is the equivalent of a name itself. For example, the USS *Enterprise* is designated CVN 65 (formerly CVAN 65). In addition to her name in appropriate places, she carries her number on her bows, and on the flight deck in huge numerals where it may easily be read by approaching aircraft. For service craft this rule is followed in part only. Sometimes, instead of a hull number, a model designation takes its place.

Clearly, the designations are not as systematic as they might be. They are further complicated by frequent changes to satisfy bureaucratic fluctuations, and by the occasional conversion of a ship to a different type from that originally designed. In such cases the original hull number is sometimes retained and sometimes not.

The letter *N*, when used as the last letter of a ship classification symbol, denotes nuclear propulsion. When used as the last letter or sometimes the next-to-last letter of a service craft classification, it indicates a non-self-propelled version of a similar craft that does have its own propulsion.

In the lists following, the letters *OBS* are used to indicate obsolescence of the designation. Many of the ships involved are still in existence, in the reserve fleet, and might be restored to service with the original, or a different designation. In other cases, designations have been switched, or disestablished.

Combatant Ship Classifications

1. Warships:

   Battleships ....OBS.... **BB**

   Cruisers:

   Heavy Cruiser ....OBS.... **CA**
   Battle Cruiser ("Large Cruiser")..........OBS.... **CB**
   Guided Missile Cruiser.......................... **CG**
   Guided Missile Cruiser (nuclear propulsion) .... **CGN**
   Light Cruiser ....OBS... **CL**
   Guided Missile Light Cruiser ....OBS... **CLG**
   Command Ship ....OBS... **CC**

   Aircraft Carriers:

   Aircraft Carrier (Multipurpose) .... **CV**
   Aircraft Carrier (Multipurpose)
       (nuclear propulsion) .... **CVN**
   Attack Aircraft Carrier ....OBS... **CVA**
   Attack Aircraft Carrier (nuclear propulsion) .OBS... **CVAN**

ASW Aircraft Carrier............................... CVS

Destroyers:

Destroyer .... DD
Guided Missile Destroyer .... DDG
Frigate ....OBS... DL
Guided Missile Frigate ....OBS... DLG
Guided Missile Frigate (nuclear propulsion).OBS... DLGN

Frigates:

Frigate .... FF
Guided Missile Frigate .... FFG
Radar Picket Frigate ....OBS... FFR

Submarines:

Submarine .... SS
Submarine (nuclear propulsion) .... SSN
Ballistic Missile Submarine (nuclear propulsion).... SSBN
Guided Missile Submarine...................OBS. SSG
Radar Picket Submarine (nuclear propulsion) .OBS. SSRN

Patrol Combatants:

Patrol Escort .... PCE
Patrol Combatant .... PG
Patrol Combatant Missile (Hydrofoil).............. PHM

2. Amphibious Warfare Ships:

Amphibious Command Ship LCC
Inshore Fire Support Ship........................ LFR
Amphibious Fire Support Ship ....OBS ... LFS
Amphibious Assault Ship (general purpose)........ LHA
Amphibious Cargo Ship .... LKA
Amphibious Transport........................... LPA
Amphibious Transport Dock .... LPD
Amphibious Assault Ship .... LPH
Amphibious Transport (small).................... LPR
Amphibious Transport Submarine .... LPSS
Dock Landing Ship............................. LSD
Tank Landing Ship .... LST

3. Mine Warfare Ships:

Mine Countermeasures Ship .... MCS
Minesweeper, Coastal (nonmagnetic) .... MSC
Minesweeper, Fleet (steel hull) ....OBS... MSF
Minesweeper, Ocean (nonmagnetic) .... MSO
Minesweeper, Special (device) ....OBS... MSS

Combatant Craft Classifications

1. Patrol Craft:

Coastal Patrol Boat	CPC
Coastal Patrol and Interdiction Craft	CPIC
Patrol Boat	PB
Patrol Craft (Fast) .. (sic)	PCF
Patrol Craft (Hydrofoil)	PCH
Patrol Gunboat (Hydrofoil)	PGH
Fast Patrol Craft.. (sic)	PTF

2. Landing Craft:

Amphibious Assault Landing Craft	AALC
Landing Craft, Mechanized	LCM
Landing Craft, Personnel, Large	LCPL
Landing Craft, Personnel, Ramped	LCPR
Landing Craft, Utility	LCU
Landing Craft, Vehicle, Personnel	LCVP
Amphibious Warping Tug	LWT

3. Mine Countermeasures Craft:

Minesweeping Boat	MSB
Minesweeper, Drone	MSD
Minesweeper, Inshore	MSI
Minesweeper, River (Converted LCM-6)	MSM
Minesweeper, Patrol	MSR

4. Riverine Warfare Craft:

Assault Support Boat	ASB
Mini-Armored Troop Carrier	ATC
River Boat Patrol	PBR
Shallow Water Attack Craft, Medium	SWAM
Shallow Water Attack Craft, Light	SWAL

5. SEAL Support Craft:

Landing Craft Swimmer Reconnaissance	LCSR
Light SEAL Support Craft	LSSC
Medium SEAL Support Craft	MSSC
Swimmer Delivery Vehicle	SDV

6. Mobile Inshore Underseas Warfare (MIUW) Craft:

MIUW Attack Craft	MAC

Auxiliary Ship Classifications

Destroyer Tender	AD
Degaussing Ship	ADG
Ammunition Ship	AE
Store Ship	AF
Combat Store Ship	AFS
Miscellaneous	AG

Auxiliary Deep Submergence Support Ship .... AGDS
Frigate Research Ship .... AGFF
Hydrofoil Research Ship .... AGEH
Environmental Research Ship..................... AGER
Miscellaneous Command Ship .... AGF
Patrol Combatant Support Ship .... AGHS
Missile Range Instrumentation Ship............... AGM
Major Communications Relay Ship .... AGMR
Oceanographic Research Ship .... AGOR
Patrol Craft Tender .... AGP
Surveying Ship................................. AGS
Auxiliary Submarine............................ AGSS
Hospital Ship .... AH
Cargo Ship .... AK
Light Cargo Ship.............................. AKL
Vehicle Cargo Ship .... AKR
Net Laying Ship .... ANL
Oiler .... AO
Fast Combat Support Ship .... AOE
Gasoline Tanker .... AOG
Replenishment Oiler........................... AOR
Transport .... AP
Self-propelled Barracks Ship .... APB
Repair Ship................................... AR
Battle Damage Repair Ship..................... ARB
Cable Repairing Ship .... ARC
Internal Combustion Engine Repair Ship .... ARG
Landing Craft Repair Ship .... ARL
Salvage Ship .... ARS
Submarine Tender .... AS
Submarine Rescue Ship .... ASR
Auxiliary Ocean Tug .... ATA
Fleet Ocean Tug .... ATF
Salvage and Rescue Ship .... ATS
Guided Missile Ship .... AVM
Training Aircraft Carrier .... CVT
Surface Effects Ship.......................... SES

Service Craft Classifications

Large Auxiliary Floating Dry Dock
 (non-self-propelled) .... AFDB
Small Auxiliary Floating Dry Dock
 (non-self-propelled) .... AFDL
Medium Auxiliary Floating Dry Dock
 (non-self-propelled)......................... AFDM
Barracks Craft (non-self-propelled) .... APL
Auxiliary Repair Dry Dock (non-self-propelled)..... ARD

Medium Auxiliary Repair Dry Dock
(non-self-propelled) .... ARDM
Deep Submergence Rescue Vehicle .... DSRV
Deep Submergence Vehicle .... DSV
Unclassified Miscellaneous IX
Submersible Research Vehicle (nuclear propulsion) . NR
Miscellaneous Auxiliary (self-propelled)........... YAG
Open Lighter (non-self-propelled)................. YC
Car Float (non-self-propelled).................... YCF
Aircraft Transportation Lighter
(non-self-propelled) .... YCV
Floating Crane (non-self-propelled)............... YD
Diving Tender (non-self-propelled) .... YDT
Covered Lighter (self-propelled).................. YF
Ferryboat or Launch (self-propelled) .... YFB
Yard Floating Dry Dock (non-self-propelled) ...... YFD
Covered Lighter (non-self-propelled) .... YFN
Large Covered Lighter (non-self-propelled)........ YFNB
Dry Dock Companion Craft (non-self-propelled).... YFND
Lighter (Special Purpose) (non-self-propelled)...... YFNX
Floating Power Barge (non-self-propelled) .... YFP
Refrigerated Covered Lighter (self-propelled) ...... YFR
Refrigerated Covered Lighter (non-self-propelled)... YFRN
Covered Lighter (Range Tender) (self-propelled) .... YFRT
Harbor Utility Craft (self-propelled) .... YFU
Garbage Lighter (self-propelled) .... YG
Garbage Lighter (non-self-propelled) .... YGN
Salvage Lift Craft, Heavy (non-self-propelled) ...... YHLC
Dredge (self-propelled) .... YM
Salvage Lift Craft, Medium (non-self-propelled) .... YMLC
Gate Craft (non-self-propelled)................... YNG
Fuel Oil Barge (self-propelled) .... YO
Gasoline Barge (self-propelled).................... YOG
Gasoline Barge (non-self-propelled) .... YOGN
Fuel Oil Barge (non-self-propelled)................ YON
Oil Storage Barge (non-self-propelled) .... YOS
Patrol Craft (self-propelled)...................... YP
Floating Pile Driver (non-self-propelled) .... YPD
Floating Workshop (non-self-propelled)............ YR
Repair and Berthing Barge (non-self-propelled)..... YRB
Repair, Berthing and Messing Barge
(non-self-propelled) .... YRBM
Floating Dry Dock Workshop (Hull)
(non-self-propelled) .... YRDH
Floating Dry Dock Workshop (Machine)
(non-self-propelled) .... YRDM
Radiological Repair Barge (non-self-propelled) ..... YRR
Salvage Craft Tender (non-self-propelled) .... YRST

Seaplane Wrecking Derrick (self-propelled) .... YSD
Sludge Removal Barge (non-self-propelled)......... YSR
Large Harbor Tug (self-propelled) .... YTB
Small Harbor Tug (self-propelled) .... YTL
Medium Harbor Tug (self-propelled) .... YTM
Water Barge (self-propelled) .... YW
Water Barge (non-self-propelled) .... YWN

Appendix B

ENLISTED RATING STRUCTURE

Two basic systems are used to designate the U.S. Navy's enlisted people. The simpler and newer is the paygrade system, in which the lowest ranking are at the E-1 paygrade and the highest at the E-9 level. If a person advances beyond E-9, he or she either becomes a *warrant officer* or is given a commission, usually as a *limited duty officer (LDO)*. The older system combines the designation of a specialty with the individual's level within the specialty, e.g., Boatswain's Mate Second Class, who is at the paygrade E-5 level.

There are various paths of advancement within each primary rating. For example, a seaman might want to advance through the Gunner's Mate rating, further specializing later in guns, missiles, or as a technician; or he might choose one less complex, such as the Quartermaster rating. A person interested in engineering might begin as a Fireman Recruit (the E-1 paygrade) and advance through either the Engineman, Electrician's Mate, or Machinist's Mate ratings.

A paygrade (E-4, E-5, E-6, etc.) within a rating is called a rate and reflects a level of achievement within that rating.

Paygrade

E-1 Airman recruit, construction recruit, dental recruit, fireman recruit, hospital recruit, seaman recruit

E-2 Airman apprentice, construction apprentice, dental apprentice, fireman apprentice, hospital apprentice, seaman apprentice

E-3 Airman, constructionman, dentalman, fireman, hospitalman, seaman

E-4 Petty officer, third class (PO3)

E-5 Petty officer, second class (PO2)

E-6 Petty officer, first class (PO1)

E-7 Chief petty officer (CPO)

E-8 Senior chief petty officer (SCPO)

E-9 Master chief petty officer (MCPO)

A *rating* is defined as an occupation in the Navy made up of duties calling for closely related kinds of skills, abilities, and aptitudes. Each rating has its own specialty mark which is worn on the left sleeve by all properly qualified men. The Navy rating structure is divided into three classifications: *general, service,* and *emergency.*

General ratings: Broad occupational fields, encompassing similar duties and functions, which require related patterns of aptitudes and qualifications and which provide paths of advancement for career development.

Service ratings: Subdivisions of certain general ratings which provide for required specialization in training and utilization of personnel.

Emergency ratings: Additional specialized ratings required in time of war or national emergency.

When asked his rate, a person will sometimes simply answer *Boatswain's Mate*, as an example, merely to indicate his or her specialty. Or the person might say *Third Class*, meaning that he or she is a Third Class Petty Officer, in the E-4 paygrade, without specifying the branch or specialty concerned. *Boatswain's Mate Third* would be a specific and complete answer. In recent years, use of the paygrade designation alone has become more common, and it is not unusual for such a question to be answered simply by stating the paygrade, in this instance, E-4.

For illustration, following are the advancement steps for the Quartermaster rating:

Title	Symbol or abbreviation		Paygrade
Seaman Recruit	SR	⎫	E-1
Seaman Apprentice	SA	Nonidentified	E-2
Seaman	SN	⎬ Strikers	E-3
Quartermaster Third Class	QM3	⎭	E-4
Quartermaster Second Class	QM2	⎫	E-5
Quartermaster First Class	QM1		E-6
Chief Quartermaster	QMC	⎬ Petty Officers	E-7
Senior Chief Quartermaster	QMCS		E-8
Master Chief Quartermaster	QMCM	⎭	E-9

The people in grades E-1 through E-3 are collectively known as nonidentified *strikers*, signifying that they have yet to select their specializations. In the example given, the recruit chose the seaman branch. He could have chosen any of the six named, each with a different path of specialization. Procedures exist for changing branches, particularly at this early stage, should another prove more attractive. After recruit training, a person is designated an *apprentice*, and after further training and qualification is advanced to paygrade E-3. At this point, he or she takes on, as his or her *rate*, the basic title of the branch selected: airman, fireman, seaman, constructionman, hospitalman, dentalman.

GENERAL RATINGS
(Grades E-4 through E-9)

Having reached paygrade E-3, personnel begin their training for the lowest of the petty officer ranks, which simultaneously begins their specialization. For paygrades E-4 through E-9 there are many general ratings, each tied to one of the basic branches. An airman might aspire to become an Aviation Boatswain's Mate, or an Air Controlman, or any other of the ratings associated with the airman branch. Our seaman example *strikes* for Quartermaster and our fireman, having selected the engineering branch, might strike for Machinist's Mate. The following is the current list of general ratings:

AB   Aviation Boatswain's Mate
AC   Air Controlman
AD   Aviation Machinist's Mate
AE   Aviation Electrician's Mate

AFCM	Master Chief Aircraft Maintenanceman (E-9 only)
AG	Aerographer's Mate
AK	Aviation Storekeeper
AM	Aviation Structural Mechanic
AO	Aviation Ordnanceman
AQ	Aviation Fire Control Technician
AS	Aviation Support Equipment Technician
AT	Aviation Electronics Technician
AVCM	Master Chief Avionics Technician (E-9 only)
AW	Aviation Antisubmarine Warfare Operator
AX	Aviation Antisubmarine Warfare Technician
AZ	Aviation Maintenance Administrationman
BM	Boatswain's Mate
BT	Boiler Technician
BR	Boiler Repairman
BU	Builder
CE	Construction Electrician
CM	Construction Mechanic
CT	Cryptologic Technician
CUCM	Master Chief Constructionman (E-9 only; *Constructionman* is also the title of the E-3 rate and is not used in intervening grades.)
DK	Disbursing Clerk
DM	Illustrator Draftsman
DP	Data Processing Technician
DS	Data Systems Technician
DT	Dental Technician
EA	Engineering Aid
EM	Electrician's Mate
EN	Engineman
EO	Equipment Operator
EQCM	Master Chief Equipmentman (E-9 only)
ET	Electronics Technician
EW	Electronics Warfare Technician
FT	Fire Control Technician
GM	Gunner's Mate
HM	Hospital Corpsman
HT	Hull Maintenance Technician
IC	Interior Communications Electrician
IM	Instrumentman
IS	Intelligence Specialist
JO	Journalist
LI	Lithographer
LN	Legalman
MA	Master-at-Arms
ML	Molder
MM	Machinist's Mate

MN	Mineman
MR	Machinery Repairman
MS	Mess Management Specialist
MT	Missile Technician
MU	Musician
NC	Navy Counselor
OM	Opticalman
OT	Ocean Systems Technician
PC	Postal Clerk
PH	Photographer's Mate
PICM	Master Chief Precision Instrumentman (E-9 only)
PM	Patternmaker
PN	Personnelman
PR	Aircrew Survival Equipmentman
QM	Quartermaster
RM	Radioman
SH	Ship's Serviceman
SK	Storekeeper
SM	Signalman
ST	Sonar Technician
SW	Steelworker
TD	Tradevman (i.e., Training Devices Man)
TM	Torpedoman's Mate
UT	Utilitiesman
YN	Yeoman

SERVICE RATINGS

These are subdivisions of some of the previously listed general ratings and are subject to change from year to year, as techniques, requirements and perceptions change.

ABE	Aviation Boatswain's Mate Launching and Recovery Equipment
ABF	Aviation Boatswain's Mate Fuels
ABH	Aviation Boatswain's Mate Aircraft Handling
ADR	Aviation Machinist's Mate Reciprocating Engine Mechanic
AME	Aviation Structural Mechanic Safety Equipment
AMH	Aviation Structural Mechanic Hydraulic Mechanic
AMS	Aviation Structural Mechanic Structures
ASE	Aviation Support Equipment Technician Electrical
ASH	Aviation Support Equipment Technician Hydraulics and Structures
ASM	Aviation Support Equipment Technician Mechanical
ETN	Electronics Technician Communications
ETR	Electronics Technician Radar
FTB	Fire Control Technician Ballistic Missile
FTG	Fire Control Technician Gun Fire Control

FTM   Fire Control Technician Missile Fire Control
GMG   Gunner's Mate Guns
GMM   Gunner's Mate Missiles
GMT   Gunner's Mate Technician
STS   Sonar Technician Submarine
STG   Sonar Technician Surface

ALPHABETICAL INDEX

DATA PROCESSING TECHNICIAN	DP
DATA SYSTEMS TECHNICIAN	DS
DENTALMAN	DN
DENTAL TECHNICIAN	DT
DISBURSING CLERK	DK
ELECTRICIAN'S MATE	EM
ELECTRONICS TECHNICIAN	ET
Electronics Technician (Communications)	ETN
Electronics Technician (Radar)	ETR
ELECTRONICS WARFARE TECHNICIAN	EW
ENGINEERING AID	EA
ENGINEMAN	EN
EQUIPMENT OPERATOR	EO
FIRE CONTROL TECHNICIAN	FT
Fire Control Technician (Ballistic Missile Fire Control)	FTB
Fire Control Technician (Gun Fire Control)	FTG
Fire Control Technician (Surface Missile Fire Control)	FTM
FIREMAN	FN
GUNNER'S MATE	GM
Gunner's Mate (Guns)	GMG
Gunner's Mate (Missiles)	GMM
Gunner's Mate (Technician)	GMT
HOSPITAL CORPSMAN	HM
HOSPITALMAN	HN
HULL MAINTENANCE TECHNICIAN	HT
ILLUSTRATOR DRAFTSMAN	DM
INSTRUMENTMAN	IM
INTELLIGENCE SPECIALIST	IS
INTERIOR COMMUNICATIONS ELECTRICIAN	IC
JOURNALIST	JO
LEGALMAN	LN
LITHOGRAPHER	LI
MACHINERY REPAIRMAN	MR
MACHINIST'S MATE	MM
MASTER-AT-ARMS	MA
MESS MANAGEMENT SPECIALIST	MS
MINEMAN	MN
MISSILE TECHNICIAN	MT
MOLDER	ML
MUSICIAN	MU
NAVY COUNSELOR	NC
OCEAN SYSTEMS TECHNICIAN	OT
OPERATIONS SPECIALIST	OS
OPTICALMAN	OM
PATTERNMAKER	PM
PERSONNELMAN	PN
PHOTOGRAPHER'S MATE	PH

POSTAL CLERK..................................... PC
QUARTERMASTER .... QM
RADIOMAN .... RM
SEAMAN .... SN
SHIP'S SERVICEMAN.............................. SH
SIGNALMAN .... SM
SONAR TECHNICIAN .... ST
   Sonar Technician (Surface) .... STG
   Sonar Technician (Submarine) .... STS
STEELWORKER..................................... SW
STOREKEEPER .... SK
TORPEDOMAN'S MATE............................ TM
TRADEVMAN .... TD
UTILITIESMAN .... UT
YEOMAN.. YN

EMERGENCY RATINGS

None exist at this time. Required ratings may be created in time of war or national emergency, according to the needs of the service and availability of qualified persons.

Appendix C

AIRCRAFT DESIGNATION SYSTEM

This system, applicable to all the services, is complicated and difficult to follow. It consists of the following in the order given: status or classification prefix symbol, modified mission symbol, basic mission symbol, type symbol, a hyphen, design number, and series letter. As a basic aircraft is designed and built, it will first be given its basic designation, e.g., A-7. As service indicates modifications, improvements and adaptations, a later model might be the XEA-7A. For a full explanation of symbols, caveats and exceptions, refer to DOD 4120.15-L, *Model Designation of Military Aircraft, Rockets and Guided Missiles,* published annually by Wright Patterson Air Force Base, Ohio 45433.

Each aircraft, missile, or rocket also has a popular name, in addition to the official designation. All current popular names are indexed in this volume, with a brief of characteristics and the model basic designation. In building up the designation of a later modification or adaptation, not all letters in the system need be used; for example, the PHANTOM II, the famous F-4, has a photo reconnaissance version, the RF-4B. The prototype of the plane would have been the YRF-4B, the "Y" later being lifted.

The following tables explain the meaning of the symbols.

STATUS PREFIX SYMBOL or CLASSIFICATION LETTER

When applicable, status prefix symbols, also called classification letters, indicate that the aircraft are being used for experiments or testing. If employed, the status symbol is the first of the designation symbols for that aircraft. The letters used for this purpose are not repeated elsewhere in the designation system:

Letter	Title	Description
G	Permanently Grounded	An aircraft permanently grounded, utilized for ground instruction and training.
J	Special Test, Temporary	Aircraft on special test programs by authorized organizations or on bailment contract having a special test configuration or whose installed equipment has been temporarily removed to accommodate the test. At completion of the test, the vehicle will be returned either to its original configuration or to standard operational configuration.
N	Special Test, Permanent	Aircraft on special test programs by authorized activities or on bailment contract, whose configuration is so drastically changed that return of aircraft to its original configuration, or conversion to standard operational configuration, exceeds practicable or economical limits.

Letter	Title	Description
X	Experimental	Aircraft in a developmental, experimental stage where basic mission and design number have been designated, but the aircraft is not established as a standard vehicle for service use.
Y	Prototype	Aircraft procured in limited quantities to develop the potentialities of the design.
Z	Planning	Designations used for identification purpose during the planning or predevelopment stage.

MODIFIED MISSION SYMBOLS

Modified mission symbols, or prefix letters, are assigned to an aircraft or airship when required by the individual services. This letter appears to the immediate left of the basic mission or type letter in the designation.

Letter	Title	Description
A	Attack	Aircraft modified to search out, attack, and destroy enemy land or sea targets, using conventional or special weapons. Also used for interdiction and close air support missions.
C	Cargo/ Transport	Aircraft modified for carrying cargo and/or passengers.
D	Director	Aircraft capable of controlling a drone aircraft or a missile.
E	Special Electronic Installation	Aircraft modified with electronic devices for employment in one or more of the following roles: a. Electronic countermeasures. b. Airborne early warning radar. c. Airborne command and control including communications relay. d. Tactical data communications link for all nonautonomous modes of flight.
H	Search/Rescue	Aircraft having special equipment for performance of search and rescue missions.
K	Tanker	Aircraft having special equipment to provide inflight refueling of other aircraft.
L	Cold Weather	Aircraft modified for operation in the arctic and antarctic regions: includes skis, special insulation, and other ancillary equipment required for extremely cold weather operations.
M	Missile Carrier	Aircraft modified for carrying and launching guided and nonguided missiles as part of the weapon system.

Letter	Title	Description
Q	Drone	Aircraft capable of being controlled from a point outside the aircraft.
R	Recon-naissance	Aircraft having equipment permanently installed for photographic and/or electronic reconnaissance missions.
S	Anti-submarine	Aircraft modified so that it can function to search, identify, attack, and destroy submarines.
T	Trainer	Aircraft specially equipped or modified for training purposes.
U	Utility	Aircraft having small payload, utilized or modified to perform miscellaneous missions such as carrying cargo or passengers, towing targets, etc.
V	Staff	Aircraft having accommodations such as chairs, tables, lounge, berths, etc., for the transportation of staff personnel.
W	Weather	Aircraft having meteorological equipment permanently installed.

BASIC MISSION/TYPE SYMBOLS

The basic mission or type letters appear in each designation. They will always be to the immediate left of the hyphen in the designation. Only two "type" designations are used; they are marked by asterisks (*) in the listing which follows. A plane assigned the "H" type designation will carry either a modified or a basic mission letter only in addition to the type letter. The only exception to this rule is the use of the combination "R/S" symbol to indicate aircraft designed for integrated reconnaissance strike use.

Letter	Title	Description
A	Attack	Aircraft designed to search out, attack, and destroy enemy land or sea targets, using conventional or special weapons. Also used for interdiction and close air support missions.
B	Bomber	Aircraft designed for bombing enemy targets.
C	Cargo/ Transport	Aircraft designed for carrying cargo and/or passengers.
E	Special Electronic Installation	Aircraft equipped with electronic devices permitting employment in the following roles: a. Electronic countermeasures. b. Airborne early warning radar. c. Airborne command and control including communications relay aircraft.

Letter	Title	Description
		d. Tactical data communications link for all nonautonomous modes of flight.
F	Fighter	Aircraft designed to intercept and destroy other aircraft and/or missiles.
*H	Helicopter	A rotary-wing aircraft.
K	Tanker	Aircraft designed for in-flight refueling of other aircraft.
O	Observation	Aircraft designed to observe (through visual or other means) and report tactical information.
P	Patrol	Long range, all-weather, multi-engine aircraft operating from land and/or water bases, designed for independent accomplishment of antisubmarine warfare, maritime reconnaissance, and mining.
R	Reconnaissance	Aircraft designed to perform reconnaissance missions.
S	Antisubmarine	Aircraft designed to search out, detect, identify, attack, and destroy enemy submarines.
T	Trainer	Aircraft designed for training personnel in the operation of aircraft and/or related equipment, and having provisions for instructor personnel.
U	Utility	Aircraft used for miscellaneous missions such as carrying cargo and/or passengers, towing targets, etc. These aircraft include those having a small payload.
*V	VTOL, V/STOL and STOL	Aircraft designed for vertical take-off or landing (VTOL), or an aircraft capable of short take-off and landing rolls (STOL). Nearly all VTOL aircraft are also STOL-capable, hence they are usually designated V/STOL.
X	Research	Aircraft designed for testing configurations of a radical nature. These aircraft are not normally intended for use as tactical aircraft.

DESIGN NUMBER

The design number will always appear in any designation to the immediate right of the hyphen in the designation. This number is assigned sequentially to all new aircraft in each basic mission group or when an existing aircraft in a basic group is modified to the extent that it no longer reflects the original configuration or capability—e.g., redesign from a straight to a delta-wing configuration or changing the number of engines

SERIES LETTER

Each basic series of aircraft begins with the letter "A" immediately following the design number—e.g., the Corsair II is now designated the A-7A. If it is adapted in the future to uses other than attack missions without major configuration changes, these modifications will be indicated by new designations such as the A-7B, etc. Frequently, use of the "A" is deferred until a new configuration requires the letter "B"—thus establishing the need to distinguish between the two.

POPULAR NAMES OF AIRCRAFT

Popular Name	Model Designation	Cognizant Service
ACADEME	TC-4C	Navy
AERO COMMANDER	U-4/U-9	Air Force/Navy
AZTEC	U-11	Navy
BEAVER	U-6	Air Force/Army/ Navy
BRONCO	OV-10	Navy/Air Force
BUCKEYE	T-2	Navy
CORSAIR II	A-7	Navy/Air Force
CRUSADER	F-8	Navy
GREYHOUND	C-2	Navy
HARRIER	AV-8A	Navy
HAWKEYE	E-2	Navy
HERCULES	C-130	Air Force/Navy
HUEYCOBRA	AH-1G	Army/Navy
INTRUDER	A-6	Navy
IROQUOIS	UH-1	Army/Navy
JET STAR	C-140	Air Force/Navy
LIFTMASTER	C-118	Air Force/Navy
MENTOR	T-34	Air Force/Navy
NEPTUNE	P-2	Navy
ORION	P-3	Navy
OTTER	U-1	Air Force/Navy
PHANTOM II	F-4	Navy/Air Force
SABRELINER	T-39	Air Force/Navy
SAMARITAN	C-131	Air Force/Navy
SEA KING	H-3	Navy
SEA KNIGHT	H-46	Navy
SEA RANGER	TH-57	Navy
SEASPRITE	H-2	Navy
SEA STALLION	CH-53	Navy
SHOOTING STAR	T-33	Air Force/Navy
SKYHAWK	A-4	Navy
SKYTRAIN	C-47	Air Force/Navy/ Army
SKYTRAIN II	C-9	Navy
SKYWARRIOR	A-3	Navy/Air Force

Popular Name	Model Designation	Cognizant Service
SUPER CONSTELLATION	C-121	Navy
TALON	T-38	Air Force/Navy
TOMCAT	F-14A	Navy
TRACER	E-1	Navy
TRACKER	S-2	Navy
TRADER	C-1	Navy
TROJAN	T-28	Air Force/Navy
VIGILANTE	A-5	Navy
VIKING	S-3A	Navy
WARNING STAR	C-121	Navy

Appendix D

MISSILE DESIGNATION SYSTEM

Missiles, guided missiles and rockets are designed in a single system similar to the *aircraft designation system*. All have popular names and are indexed herein in accordance with such names, as for aircraft. For fuller explanation, see DOD 4120.15-L, *Model Designation of Military Aircraft, Rockets and Guided Missiles,* published annually by Wright Patterson Air Force Base, Ohio 45433. By reference to the tables of symbol meanings which follow, the AIM-9E, for example, is an *Air-launched, Intercept, Guided Missile, Model 9-E. Sidewinder,* the popular name for the AIM-9 series missiles, cannot be derived from the tables, but will be found indexed under "S" in the *Popular Names* section of this appendix.

STATUS PREFIX SYMBOLS
(Classification Letters)

Letter	Title	Description
J	Special Test, Temporary	Vehicles on special test programs by authorized organizations and vehicles on bailment contract having a special configuration to accommodate the test. At completion of the test the vehicles will be either returned to their original configuration or returned to standard configuration.
N	Special Test, Permanent	Vehicles on special test programs by authorized activities and vehicles on bailment contract, whose configurations are so drastically changed that return of the vehicles to their original configurations is beyond practicable or economical limits.
X	Experimental	Vehicles in the departmental or experimental stage, but not established as standard vehicles for service use.
Y	Prototype	Preproduction vehicles procured for evaluation and test of a specific design.
Z	Planning	Vehicles in the planning or predevelopment stage.

LAUNCH ENVIRONMENT SYSTEM

Letter	Title	Description
A	Air	Air launched.
B	Multiple	Capable of being launched from more than one environment.

Letter	Title	Description
C	Coffin	Stored horizontally or at less than a 45 degree angle in a protective enclosure (regardless of structural strength) and launched from the ground.
F	Individual	Carried and launched by one man.
M	Mobile	Launched from a ground vehicle or movable platform.
P	Soft Pad	Partially or entirely unprotected in storage and launched from the ground.
R	Ship	Launched from a surface vessel such as a ship, barge, etc.
U	Underwater	Launched from a submarine or other underwater device.

MISSION SYMBOLS

Letter	Title	Description
D	Decoy	Vehicles designed or modified to confuse, deceive, or divert enemy defenses by simulating an attack vehicle.
E	Special Electronics	Vehicles designed or modified with electronic equipment for communications, countermeasures, electronic radiation sounding, or other electronic recording or relay missions.
G	Surface Attack	Vehicles designed to destroy enemy land or sea targets.
I	Intercept-Aerial	Vehicles designed to intercept aerial targets in defensive or offensive roles.
Q	Drone	Vehicles designed for target, reconnaissance, or surveillance purposes.
T	Training	Vehicles designed or permanently modified for training purposes.
U	Underwater Attack	Vehicles designed to destroy enemy submarines or other underwater targets or to detonate underwater.
W	Weather	Vehicles designed to observe, record, or relay data pertaining to meteorological phenomena.

VEHICLE TYPE SYMBOLS

Letter	Title	Description
M	Guided Missile	Unmanned, self-propelled vehicles designed to move in a trajectory or flight path all or partially above the earth's surface and whose trajectory or course while the vehicle is in motion is capable of being controlled remotely or by homing systems, or by intertial and/or programmed guidance from within. This term does not include space vehicles, space boosters or naval torpedoes, but does include target and reconnaissance drones.
N	Probe	Non-orbital instrumented vehicles not involved in space missions that are used to penetrate the aerospace environment and transmit or report back information.
R	Rocket	Self-propelled vehicles without installed or remote control guidance mechanisms, whose trajectory or flight path cannot be altered after launch. Rocket systems designed for line-of-sight fire are not included.

POPULAR NAMES OF ROCKETS, MISSILES, AND PROBES

Popular Name	Model Designation	Cognizant Service
ASROC	RUR-5	Navy
BULLPUP	AGM-12	Air Force/Navy
CONDOR	AGM-53	Navy
FIREBEE	BQM-34	Air Force/Army/ Navy
FOCUS I	AGM-87	Navy
HARM	AGM-88A	Navy
HARPOON	AGM-84A	Navy
HAWK	MIM-23	Marine Corps/Navy
HONEST JOHN	MGR-1	Army/Navy/ Marine Corps
LITTLE JOHN	MGR-3A	Army/Marines
PETREL	AQM-41	Navy
PHOENIX	AIM-54	Navy
POLARIS	UGM-27	Navy
POSEIDON	UGM-73	Navy
REDEYE	MIM-43	Army/Navy/ Marine Corps
REGULUS	RGM-6/15	Navy
SEA MAULER	RIM-46	Navy
SHRIKE	AGM-45	Navy/Air Force
SIDEWINDER	AIM-9	Navy/Air Force
SPARROW	AIM-7	Navy/Air Force
STANDARD	RIM-66/67	Navy

STANDARD ARM	AGM-78	Navy
SUBROC	UUM-44A	Navy
TALOS	RIM-8	Navy
TARTAR	RIM-24	Navy
TERRIER	RIM-2	Navy
TRIDENT	UGM-96A	Navy
TYPHON	RIM-50/55	Navy
WALLEYE	AGM-62	Navy
WEAPON ALPHA	RUR-4	Navy

Appendix E

ELECTRONICS NOMENCLATURE (AN) SYSTEM

Most electronic equipment has no popular name. These short titles are unclassified, whereas the actual name of the equipment may be classified. All begin with AN/, and the system is often called the AN system. Three indicator letters follow, signifying the kind of installation, type of equipment, and purpose. Thus, AN/APB-2D: AN/=listed in the Joint Electronics Type Designation System; A=aircraft; P=radar; B=bombing; 2=model number; D=modification D of model 2.

EQUIPMENT INDICATOR LETTERS

Installation (1st letter)	Type of Equipment (2nd letter)	Purpose (3rd letter)
A-Piloted aircraft	A-Invisible, heat radiation	B-Bombing
B-Underwater, mobile submarine	C-Carrier	C-Communications (receiving and transmitting)
D-Pilotless carrier	D-Radiac	D-Direction finder reconnaissance and/or surveillance
F-Fixed ground	G-Telegraph or Teletype	
G-General ground use		E-Ejection and/or release
K-Amphibious	I-Interphone and public address	G-Fire control, or searchlight directing
M-Ground, mobile	J-Electromechanical or Inertial wire covered	H-Recording and/or reproducing (graphic meteorological and sound)
P-Portable		
S-Water	K-Telemetering	
T-Ground transportable	L-Countermeasures	K-Computing
	M-Meteorological	M-Maintenance and/or test assemblies (including tools)
U-General utility	N-Sound in air	
V-Ground, vehicular	P-Radar	N-Navigational aids (including altimeters, beacons, compasses, racons, depth sounding, approach and landing)
W-Water surface and underwater combination	Q-Sonar and underwater sound	
	R-Radio	
Z-Piloted and pilotless airborne vehicle combination	S-Special types, magnetic, etc. or combination of types	Q-Special, or combination of purposes
	T-Telephone (wire)	R-Receiving, passive detecting
	V-Visual and visible light	S-Detecting and/or range and bearing, search
	W-Armament (peculiar to armament, not otherwise covered)	T-Transmitting
		W-Automatic flight or remote control
	X-Facsimile or television	X-Identification and recognition
	Y-Data processing	

Installation (1st letter)	Type of Equipment (2nd letter)	Purpose (3rd letter)
		Y-Surveillance (search, detect, and multiple target tracking) and control (both fire control and air control)